DESERT CAPITALISM

DESERT CAPITALISM

Maquiladoras in North America's

Western Industrial Corridor

Kathryn Kopinak

The University of Arizona Press: Tucson

HD
9734
.M42
K67
1996

The University of Arizona Press
© 1996
The Arizona Board of Regents
All Rights Reserved
♾ This book is printed on acid-free, archival-quality paper.
Manufactured in the United States of America
01 00 99 98 97 96   6 5 4 3 2 1
Library of Congress Cataloging-in-Publication Data
Kopinak, Kathryn.
    Desert capitalism : maquiladoras in North America's western
industrial corridor / Kathryn Kopinak.
        p.   cm.
    Includes bibliographical references and index.
    ISBN 0-8165-1598-0 (cloth : acid-free paper)
    1. Offshore assembly industry—Mexico.   2. Offshore assembly
industry—Employees—Mexico.   3. Mexico—Social conditions—1970– .
I. Title.
HD9734.M42K67   1996   95-32506
338.4'7'0009721—dc20   CIP
British Cataloguing-in-Publication Data
A catalogue record for this book is available from the British Library.

This book is dedicated to my father.

CONTENTS

ILLUSTRATIONS

Map

Figures

TABLES

ACRONYMS

BIP	Border Industrialization Program
CANAMEX Corridor	Canada-America-Mexico Corridor
COLEF	El Colegio de la Frontera Norte
CTM	Confederación de Trabajadores de México
ESAF	Encuesta Socioeconomica Anual de La Frontera
GSP	General System of Preferences
GATT	General Agreement on Tariffs and Trade
IMF	International Monetary Fund
IMSS	Instituto Mexicano del Seguro Social
INA	Industria Nacional de Auto-partes
INEGI	Instituto Nacional de Estadistica Geografía e Información
NAFTA	North American Free Trade Agreement
NAO	National Administrative Office
NIDL	New International Division of Labor
SECOFI	Secretaría de Comercio y Fomento Industrial
SPC	Statistical Process Control
TELMEX	Teléfonos de México

ACKNOWLEDGMENTS

Several institutions and individuals were essential in helping to complete the research on which this book is based. I gratefully acknowledge the support of King's College, at the University of Western Ontario, for sabbatical leave in 1990–91 to collect the data, and for annual research grants between 1990–1996. The study would not have been possible, however, without the bulk of the funding coming from the Social Sciences and Humanities Research Council of Canada (Grant number 410-90-0941) in 1990. The Center for U.S.-Mexican Studies at the University of California, San Diego (UCSD), supported me through a Visiting Research Fellowship and with the research assistance of Liliana Ferrer. Liliana worked with me for seven months while a master's student and was especially helpful in administering workers' interviews, getting the data on which the third chapter is based out of the field, and translating workers' questionnaire responses. I translated the quotations from the academic literature and newspaper articles. Several other individuals at the Center for U.S.-Mexican Studies made this an effective research base, especially Wayne Cornelius, Patricia Rosas, Jim Beaudry, and Jeff Weldon. Harley Shaiken of the Communications Department at UCSD and John Saunders of the Washington office of the *Globe and Mail* gave important advice on fieldwork. Daniel Paight of the Sociology Department at UCSD provided data-analysis services for almost two years on a part-time basis, and methodological advice at every step of the process after the data were collected. He also redrew figures and tables for this book. Roberto Torres of International Relations and Pacific Studies at UCSD helped with data analysis in the area of wages.

While I collected data in Mexico in 1991, my research base was *El Colegio de la Frontera Norte* (COLEF) in Nogales, Sonora. I gratefully acknowledge the assistance of Francisco Lara Valencia, who acted as a consultant for the project and was an invaluable colleague. Dolores Esquer helped supervise interviewers, collected archival data, and provided support in many other areas. Martín Pérez gathered publicly available statistical data and advised on the scheduling of interviews. Martha Payán and Oscar Reyes carried out excellent interviews with workers. Jorge Carrillo and Jorge San-tibañez at COLEF in Tijuana were also very supportive in the area of data analysis. I am most grateful to all of the workers and managers in Nogales, Sonora, who cooperated in the study, and *La Voz del Norte* for allowing access to the newspaper's archives.

Several colleagues and friends nelped once the data were analyzed and being written up, especially Lawrence Fric, David MacGregor, Bill Renner, and Jim Rinehart. Judith A. Hellman, Harvey Brown, and John Clouston were also invaluable advisers at different points in the research and publi-cation process. Julienne Patterson drew the map of the western industrial corridor. Editorial assistance was provided by Valerie Alia, Margaret Elgie, and Vic Granholm. Valerie's support and friendship during the writing of the final draft made the hard work much easier. It is impossible to thank everyone who helped with this research along the way. Numerous conver-sations with colleagues at professional meetings helped me to develop the analysis, express my ideas more clearly, and access other literature.

I would like to acknowledge the helpful comments of three anonymous reviewers who read earlier drafts of this manuscript. Thanks are also ex-tended to Christine Szuter and Alexis Noebels of the University of Arizona Press for facilitating the publication process. Only the author is responsible for the contents of this book and any errors that might be contained.

DESERT CAPITALISM

INTRODUCTION

During the decades when great deserts effectively prevented close contact between people of the two countries, bilateral relations were generally marked by fears of imperial dominance. . . . From the outset of the twentieth century, citizens of northern Mexico had begun to establish commercial and cultural links with residents of the U.S. Southwest. Business and personal ties eventually undermined the barriers of mutual distrust. It is not surprising . . . that the current struggle for democracy developed in the northern part of the country, where the public was most directly affected by U.S. lifestyles and where maquiladora plants sprang up two decades before NAFTA was conceived. . . . NAFTA has extended the investment and trade benefits previously reserved for the maquiladora industry to the rest of the country. (Sarmiento, 1994: 6)

Sarmiento's words link many of the themes examined in this book: maquiladoras—companies at Mexico's northern border that import materials in order to transform and re-export them—and the diffusion through maquilas of new ways of doing things to other locations and economic sectors of the country. Lazaroff, who coined the phrase "desert capitalism," has said that the "trend to locate away from the congested U.S.-Mexico border, and into cities to the south, is accelerating in the border states" (1992: 24).

Deserts are not the only geographic containers of this phenomenon. The same kind of industry has also characterized the Gulf of Mexico region of the border. In place of the mutual distrust between Mexico and the United States, against which the desert served as a buffer, the era of free trade has brought greater economic cooperation. Under the North American Free Trade Agreement (NAFTA), maquilas have become the engine of industrial development throughout Mexico.

The capitalism of the 1990s had the potential to reverse many of the negative meanings associated with the idea of desert. In our cultural history, the desert is often depicted as a "barren wasteland" or "badlands." The people who first chose the word "desert" to refer to arid territory obviously thought such places should be abandoned, or literally deserted.[1] Sarmiento suggests above that the desert no longer separates Mexicans from other North Americans, nor is the idea of desert an adequate metaphor for the buffer between the two wary states. Instead, the desert is becoming the meeting place for highly profitable enterprises that comprise a model for the development of the rest of Mexico.

Industrial capitalism arose in the last thirty years in the Sonoran and Chihuahuan Deserts as well as in the Gulf region. It began with the importation of materials, tools, and machinery from outside Mexico to maquila centers such as Tijuana, Nogales, and Ciudad Juárez. There, workers assemble and manufacture new products, and in the process they increase the value of the materials and machinery with which they began. The desert has become increasingly capitalized because of maquila investment, and it seems likely that the economic integration promoted by NAFTA will encourage the spread of industrial capitalism in maquila form.

In the past, the law governing maquiladora production did not allow the products to be sold in Mexico. Although Mexico has not been a consumer market for maquila products, it has been an important labor market generating the goods. Mexican labor has attracted industrial capitalists because of its low wages and the lax enforcement which makes Mexican labor law much more flexible than elsewhere on the continent. Beginning in 1983, maquilas were allowed to sell 20 percent of what they made within Mexico, as long as they used a certain amount of Mexican goods in their production. Within eight years of NAFTA's implementation in 1994, more maquiladora goods will be available for sale inside Mexico, allowing Mexicans to become part of the consumer market.

The rise of a maquiladora-based economy along the U.S.-Mexico border is quite different from earlier forms of capitalism that thrived in this region's deserts. For example, the desert capitalism which is the subject of this book is unlike that previously established in Las Vegas, in the Mojave Desert. People voluntarily come to Las Vegas to spend money for tourist services. It is an entertainment center that draws people into a market to buy the various indulgences provided there. Nothing new is really produced, but a profit is made by circulating capital and expropriating some of it as it changes hands.

As Mexico's economy has opened and has begun to integrate with other larger economies through NAFTA, the maquila has been the first major connecting point. However, with the treaty implemented only recently—on January 1, 1994—it is too soon to be certain whether, or how, the expectations raised by the treaty will be met. No one wants to wait until the next millennium to evaluate possible outcomes, and there is no need to wait that long. Along Mexico's northern border, where most maquiladoras are still located, we are presented with an example of industrial integration that has been proceeding for thirty years.[2] Many companies with head offices in the United States produce both in Canada and in Mexican maquiladoras, so that the industrial structure of the three nations is tied through the transnational corporation. Possibilities for the future direction of continental economic integration can be predicted by studying the maquilas. They have in many ways acted as a pilot project for free trade, an economic enclave in which practices associated with it could be tested and pioneered.[3]

The goal of this study is to contribute to the understanding of continental economic reorganization through an in-depth investigation of transport-equipment maquilas in the area around Nogales, Sonora. Lazaroff (1992: 24) says that "in Sonora—where maquiladoras pumped US $300 million into the economy in 1991—the importance of the maquiladoras cannot be overstated." Maquila industries have become the chief form of integrating Mexico's economy with the world economy in an era when industrial organization has undergone great transformation globally. This study examines whether Mexican transport-equipment maquiladoras in the Nogales area have changed in ways that parallel world trends.

Some observers suggest that two or three types of maquiladoras have arisen—the early labor-intensive type and one or two more automated varieties, which incorporate more advanced technology and organizational forms learned from the Japanese. In this study we look for analogous distinctions in the transport-equipment sector, which has been observed to be one of the most dynamic. Several conceptual models predict different types of maquilas in Mexico and how they might best be characterized. Questions derived from these broad notions are posed to explore the extent to which Nogales-area transport-equipment maquilas correspond to alternative forms of maquiladora development.

Chapter 2 details the motivation for this study; chapter 3 focuses on the construction of the labor market; chapter 4 looks at the composition of the labor force; chapter 5 explores levels of technology, skill, and organization of work; and chapter 6 examines wages and workers' reactions. The data collected for this study originated from many sources: maquila job advertisements throughout the eighties, the annual socioeconomic survey of the border carried out in Nogales in 1988, surveys of both workers and managers in all transport-equipment plants in Nogales and Imuris in 1991, interviews with a longtime leader of the maquiladora association in 1991, government records on the growth of Nogales-area auto-parts maquilas throughout the eighties, and secondary sources. The interpretation of the findings will help predict whether increased investment under NAFTA will transform this area from the third world to the first, or reinforce its specialized role as a supplier of low-waged labor. Comparisons with findings from maquilas in other locations will help develop a regional characterization of maquiladoras.

THIRTY YEARS OF MEXICAN MAQUILADORAS

The word "maquiladora," often shortened to "maquila," is one of the most recent examples of the wholesale adoption of Spanish words into English without being translated. Linguists call these loan-words (Strang, 1970: 25), words borrowed from other languages when they cannot be translated adequately. Angulo P. (1990: 139) says that the modern meaning of the word "maquiladora" evolved "in practice from its use to designate any partial activity in an industrial process, such as assembly or packaging effected by a party other than the original manufacturer." While this new English word comes from Mexico, the industry of which maquiladoras are a part originated in the United States. Most Mexican maquiladoras have head offices in the United States, although Japanese- and European-based companies have increased in the eighties and nineties.

The word "maquiladora" cannot yet be found in most English-language dictionaries. Its definition is complicated by the fact that the phenomenon it represents has changed since it first appeared. Since it is this change that the book investigates, some attention is devoted here to the transitions observed in maquiladoras.

Mexican legislation permitted factories called maquiladoras at the northern border for the first time in 1965. With the elaboration one year later of a set of rules organized under the Border Industrialization Program (BIP), the Mexican government took advantage of U.S. tariff schedules 806 and 807, which allowed U.S. components to be assembled in other countries and then re-exported back to the United States without being taxed on re-entry. Machinery, vehicles, parts, and anything else needed for processing were imported into Mexico duty free for transformation, assembly, or other processing. Then the product returned to the United States with Mexico taxing only the value added.[1] The program was limited to the northern border region at first, where the Mexican government had experimented with free trade zones years before, but was expanded to non-border areas as early as 1971.

The Mexican government stated that these legislative changes were intended to provide jobs lost through the U.S. cancellation of the *Bracero* Program, which since 1942 had permitted Mexican males to migrate to the United States to work temporarily in agriculture. But as Sklair (1989: 27) points out, the broader goal of the BIP was to change the isolated northern border of Mexico into a dynamic growth pole for the whole northern border, and possibly the whole country. For U.S. capitalists, on the other hand, it was a way of using cheap Mexican labor without having to negotiate with U.S. unions, the main group lobbying for an end to the Bracero Program. The timing of the BIP also dovetailed perfectly with private enterprise's efforts to restructure and cope with falling profits. This unanticipated last factor has been responsible for the rapid growth of maquiladora industries in Mexico.

At first maquiladoras were often known as the "in-bond" industry because materials could only be imported to Mexico temporarily for processing. After 1982, maquilas no longer had to put up a bond to insure that materials were re-exported, but could simply make a verbal promise. Maquiladoras were also called twin plants, which referred to the proposal that companies would set up plants on either side of the U.S.-Mexico border, with the one on the U.S. side doing capital-intensive production, and the one on the Mexican side providing cheap labor. However, the U.S. twin rarely materialized, and when it did, it was more likely to be a warehouse or office than a high-technology facility providing good jobs for U.S. workers (Sklair, 1989: 48). Nevertheless, the term is still used popularly, as in the periodical titled *Twin Plant News,* published in El Paso, Texas.

In order to evaluate Nogales transport-equipment maquilas, it is important to set some benchmarks to indicate what the early maquilas were like, and the direction in which they appear to be moving. George (1990: 221–22) says:

> In the late sixties all maquila plants were engaged in routine assembly operations of mature products. The labor-intensive operations of the maquilas were rudimentary, using unsophisticated, outdated, and almost

obsolete capital equipment. Up to 98 percent of the maquilas' work force were *obreros* or direct labor; the rest were receptionists and secretaries. All managers, engineers, and trouble-shooting technicians were Americans sent from the parent companies in the United States to run the plants on the border. About 90 to 95 percent of direct labor were single females with very low educational backgrounds.

In a 1988 study of maquilas in Juárez and Chihuahua, the same researcher noted many differences. The labor force had changed; more workers were older, married, male, hired through advertisements, and lured by fringe benefits than in the late sixties. He found almost all technicians and engineers to be Mexican, along with an increasing number of managers. He also identified what he called second-generation maquilas, which "extended the old dimension of routine assembly of mature products to attempting state-of-the art production. Traditional horizontal expansion is being gradually replaced by vertical integration" (George, 1990: 224).

These changes are not unique to Ciudad Juárez or the state of Chihuahua. In the thirty years since maquiladoras were established in Mexico, there has been a tremendous increase in the numbers of plants and workers, and important shifts in their location, ownership, products, and markets served. By July 1994 there were 2,065 factories operating under maquiladora legislation in Mexico, employing 579,519 people. In the same year, maquiladoras were predicted to become the main source of foreign investment in Mexico, surpassing the amount of foreign currency brought into the country by petroleum or tourism (González Pérez, 1994). Along with increasing numbers, they had also changed qualitatively, with manufacturing gaining ground over simple assembly. The products they processed were more likely to be finished than in earlier years, and a maquiladora auto industry emerged, with textile maquilas a smaller proportion of all maquilas (Scheinman, 1990a: 27). While most maquilas are still owned or subcontracted by U.S.-based firms, Japanese electronics firms have expanded significantly in recent years.

Maquiladora history has been divided into four stages (Carrillo, 1989a); we are actually in a fifth period, which the published research has only begun to document. This periodization is defined by the policies of the Mexican government, which are contained in executive decrees shaping the character of maquilas. The strong direction by the executive branch of the government is indicative of the fundamental role the state has played in the opening of the economy. Changes in maquiladora legislation have been undertaken by the state, however, on behalf of the maquila industry. Schoepfle (1990: 6) indicates that "Looking back at the evolution of the BIP, a pattern emerges of informal concessions initially given to specific firms (exceptions) that over time became more formal and widely given in practice and eventually became law by presidential decrees."

The first period—between 1965 and 1974—is seen as one of installation and consolidation. The new industries did not hire braceros, as had been hoped, but preferred young women who had not previously worked outside the home. Although this met with some disapproval, it is not surprising, since young women have been preferred by export processors in other parts of the world as well. By 1974, there were 455 maquiladoras employing 75,974 people in Mexico (Carrillo, 1989b: 40).

Several restrictions were relaxed during this first period. After 1972 maquiladoras were allowed to locate in most of the interior, except those areas already highly industrialized. In 1973, they were exempted from the law limiting foreigners to a maximum of 49 percent ownership of Mexican firms, allowing 100 percent foreign ownership of maquiladoras except for some minor restrictions in textiles and apparel.

The steady growth of the first period was halted in 1974 by a recession in the United States that caused a crisis in maquiladora industries. During this second period, lasting two years, it is estimated that 32,000 workers lost their jobs in ten months (Carrillo, 1989b: 39). Labor militancy in Mexico also discouraged U.S. investors. The loss of more than a third of all jobs was followed by the Mexican government's exemption of maquiladoras from some federal labor-law requirements.

Probation periods for workers were lengthened from 30 to 90 days. A worker on probation does not have to be paid the minimum wage and does not receive the package of benefits legally due full-time employees, which includes health care, pay for maternity leave, and one day's paid holiday per week. Companies were also allowed to dismiss workers they judged inefficient without the severance pay required by federal labor law.[2] They were permitted to adjust the size of their workforce or length of their workday according to their needs (Tiano, 1987: 21; Gambrill, 1981: 50). After the crisis of the mid-seventies, there was an increase in *cláusulas leoninas* (one-sided clauses) in collective agreements that explicitly established conditions below the standards of federal labor law (Gambrill, 1989: 199). Although one-sided clauses were contrary to the law, this type of deregulation was not disputed in practice. These agreements tended to eliminate that which was originally guaranteed under federal labor law; that is, job security for an indeterminate time that could not be violated without sufficient cause or compensation. Thus, temporary or permanent suspensions could more frequently be carried out without compensation, and temporary workers could be used in an unlimited way.

Despite its brevity, this second period from 1974 to 1976 is important because it shows how maquiladoras operated outside federal labor law early in their history. The Mexican government has responded to charges that NAFTA will harmonize continental labor standards downward to the level pioneered in the maquilas by demonstrating that in some ways, its federal labor law is more progressive than that of Canada and the United States. Critics of this position counter that if industry is structured so that unions systematically bargain for conditions of work below the legal standard, labor law cannot protect workers.[3]

As the U.S. economy revived, a third period characterized by expansion occurred, but 1974 to 1976 was remembered critically as evidence of the inability of maquiladoras to form a stable economic base. In fact, there was widespread disappointment with the results of the maquila program in these years on the part of Mexican officialdom. This was due to maquilas' dependence on the U.S. economy, their lack of fixed capital, and their tendency to close quickly if dissatisfied with local conditions. Because of northern Mexico's historic lack of integration with the rest of the Mexican economy, it has always been especially vulnerable during its northern neighbor's economic difficulties. Maquiladoras follow this pattern even more strongly, since they were created as an export platform to the United States, which is still their market in most cases.

The third period—from 1977 to 1982—was marked by higher rates of growth and the beginning of the move away from the economic strategy of import substitution to that of export-led development. While the government encouraged the growth of maquiladoras as a source of employment and foreign currency, it still considered them too transitory to totally sustain economic development at the border or nationally (Carrillo, 1989a: 42). Nevertheless, increased facilities and the devalued peso led to 13.8 percent annual growth in maquilas between 1977 and 1980.

The most powerful forces shaping maquilas during the fourth period—
between 1983 and 1989—came from outside Mexico in the form of pressure from the International Monetary Fund (IMF) for economic liberaliza-
tion. This occurred as Mexico was thrown into a debt crisis, to which the
government responded by attempting to turn maquiladoras into permanent
industries that could consolidate border development. While providing
more jobs was still an important objective, the government was beginning
to support more capital-intensive maquiladoras with fewer workers. State
planners specified that maquilas making machinery, electric and electronic
supplies, and automotive equipment had top priority, and they tried to encourage more local sourcing. Devaluation of the peso also continued, so
that by 1986, Mexican labor was cheaper than in South Korea, Taiwan,
Hong Kong, Singapore, and Brazil (González-Aréchiga and Ramírez, 1989:
878). Thus, when new jobs were added to the maquila labor force, they
tended to cost foreign investors fewer dollars, and pay workers lower
wages in real terms.

The increase in people employed in maquiladoras tripled in response to
these policies. Whereas 12,032 jobs had been created between 1978 and
1983, almost three times as many (34,658) new maquila jobs were added
between 1984 and 1986 (Carrillo, 1989b: 44). Between 1982 and 1986, a
new maquiladora opened in Mexico every five days, on average (Ramírez,
1988: 63). Concurrent with this increase in maquila employment was a
drop in the proportion of women in the maquiladora labor force. The decrease in women workers was not the same across all subsectors of maquiladora industries, however, and in some important areas—automotive, for
example—the proportion of women increased.

In fact, a process of feminization took place nationally in auto-parts maquilas, with more women incorporated in this traditionally male-dominated
industry in labor- as well as capital-intensive plants (Carrillo, 1992: 21).
Women first entered auto-parts maquilas as direct workers in 1975, when
they were set up at the northern border. Their numbers grew slowly for five
years and then increased, so that by 1987, they made up 51 percent of direct
workers in auto parts in border municipalities, and 72 percent in non-border
municipalities. This occurred at the same time as a decrease of women
workers in non-auto maquiladoras, even though women still made up 73
percent of direct workers in 1987 in border municipalities, and 78 percent
in non-border municipalities.[4]

"New investment" during this period was also used to transform already-existing foreign-owned plants that had not been installed under maquila legislation, into plants that functioned much like maquiladoras. Occurring in electronics, auto, and auto-parts production, these changes did not necessarily represent net additions to the wealth of the country, but instead a qualitative change in the production process. A growing number of transnational non-maquiladora plants—which had been introduced in Mexico in the sixties and seventies to serve the domestic market—changed their internal organization, redefined their market focus as external, adapted their productive capital, and thereby converted themselves into *de facto* if not *de jure* maquiladora plants (González Aréchiga and Ramírez, 1989: 876). This shift was linked to the collapse in demand for goods within Mexico due to the economic crisis.

This conversion process was especially visible in multinational automotive companies in the mid-eighties. They had originally set up operations in Mexico that sent products back to the United States with a greatly reduced tariff under the General System of Preferences (GSP), rather than under maquiladora legislation. The United States stimulates exports from less-developed countries with the GSP by reducing tariffs on a certain quota of goods. Companies using this entrance into the U.S. market were referred to in Mexico as "new" maquilas (Gambrill, 1991: 37), even though they are not legally maquiladoras. The name seemed quite suitable because, even though they incorporated more value added than the early maquilas, the form in which production and labor was organized was greatly influenced by the early maquiladoras.

Maquilización (Carrillo, 1990a: 110), *maquiladorización* (Pradilla Cobos, 1993: 143), and *maquilación* (Domínguez Y., 1994: 203) were new Spanish words invented to name this change. English uses similar words or cognates, such as "maquilazation" (Schoepfle, 1990), "maquilization" (Sklair, 1989), and "maquiladorization" (Kopinak, 1993). Carrillo (1990a: 110) defined the process of maquilization on the basis of the social type of industry maquilas have been, not on the customs rules under which they operate. He specified four dimensions of maquilization, which he derived from observing the restructuring of the auto industry: 1) feminizing the labor force; 2) highly segmenting the skill categories (with the majority of workers in unskilled jobs); 3) lowering real wages; and 4) introducing a non-union orientation.

Before the 1980s, the so-called traditional auto industry in Mexico—which had been established after the Second World War in the center of the country to serve the domestic market—did not employ women as production workers, and had a ladder of job descriptions with more variations by skill. With the growth of relatively strong unions, workers' wages and working conditions improved, giving them some of the best jobs in Mexican manufacturing. Real wages paid in maquiladoras were about half of those paid in the non-maquiladora manufacturing sector in Mexico from 1975 to 1992 (Gambrill, 1994a). Restructuring took place when traditional auto plants in central Mexico closed and moved to the northern industrial belt, to reopen with technological innovations and transformations along the four dimensions indicated.[5] Flexible union contracts were negotiated before the northern plants even opened, with much lower wages than in the center of the country.

Many new auto plants relocating production from the United States were also built in northern Mexico as legally recognized maquiladoras. The term "maquilization" has also been used to refer to the increase in legally constituted maquilas, since their increase represents a greater proportion of the Mexican economy involved in maquila-type activities. As maquilas boomed in the eighties, Mexican-owned non-maquila industries were finding it difficult to survive the opening of the economy, and companies were failing in record numbers. The growth of the maquila sector with the simultaneous shrinkage in the domestic sector reached a turning point when in the first three months of 1993, maquila products outnumbered domestic products among Mexico's exports (Domínguez Y., 1994: 203). Neither did Mexican industry benefit as suppliers, since maquiladoras import 98 percent or more of their materials from outside the country.

Husson (1991: 10) argues that maquiladoras and other factories producing for export paid lower wages than industry serving the domestic market because they were using cheap labor to capture foreign markets. Lower wages were necessary in Mexican factories serving export markets in order to compensate for lower productivity in Mexico, Husson says, and he shows how wages increased in maquiladorized auto plants and the legal maquiladora sector at the same rate as productivity from 1983 to 1989. Wage inequalities between legal maquilas and maquilized auto plants, on the one hand, and traditional Mexican industry on the other, can be traced back to the high proportion of women in the legal maquilas and maquilized auto plants. Men probably would not have accepted such low wages in the beginning, when the norms for industrial pay were higher, even though the companies saw the low wage level as a necessary comparative advantage. Thus, Husson shows that there is a relationship between two of the maquilization dimensions outlined by Carrillo, feminization and low wages, which he refers to as part of the logic of maquilization. It is not difficult to imagine how the other two maquilization dimensions, classifying more workers as unskilled and a non-union orientation, might also be related to lower wages.

Maquilization forces were so strongly felt that Mexico began to be characterized as a maquiladora country, with the phrase having several shades of meaning depending on the type of maquila being studied. Domínguez Y. (1994: 220) says that being a maquiladora country implies that investment does not promote integration with national production, but that the vast majority of components and costs are introduced from the most diverse parts of the world. Another usage of this idea is that Mexico will be turned into a maquiladora by having its economy converted into an assembly plant for the United States and other foreign countries (Hanson, 1992: 309). Taking into account advanced manufacturing more than assembly, Carrillo (1992: 79–80) concludes that the question of the maquilization of the country in industrial terms is no longer hypothetical but is being realized.

A diffused process of industrial restructuration exists in the automotive sector which includes both traditional companies as well as exporters. Export assembly plants and the auto parts maquiladoras of the same company have come to appear more alike with regard to the use of technology, the quality standards required, policies of work, wages, and skill. Generally speaking, it could be said that the automobile company studied was continuously becoming more like a maquiladora in the social sense, at the same time as it was restructuring, automating, and flexibilizing. That is, the most advanced part of the traditional sector is maquilizing. Here, it is concluded that the discussion of whether or not the country might be maquilized does not now seem so speculative in industrial terms. . . . It will be necessary to continue investigations which specifically address the evaluative question.

This brief historical sketch has shown how between the mid-sixties and late eighties, maquiladoras changed from being the industrial exception to being the rule. Restrictions that had been removed in the maquila sector in its early period were repealed in the larger economy at the end of the eighties as well—for example, the regulation that foreigners could own only 49 percent of an enterprise, which had been revoked for maquilas in 1973, was abolished in 1989 in all economic sectors except mining, petrochemicals, auto parts, and communications (Teichman, 1995).

When Mexico requested that the United States consider the possibility of free trade in 1990, it also brought its policies on maquilas into line with the *de facto* maquilization that had occurred in the previous decade. Maquilas were so essential to Salinas's plans that the 1989 decree expressly recognized them for the first time as "an instrument necessary to help increase the international competitiveness of Mexican industry." Foreign investment was seen as "the principal means of inserting the Mexican economy into the global world economy," and the connection between the two was to be made through the maquiladora, which the Mexican government believed to be "the most agile vehicle for the integration of Mexican industry with foreign markets" (Angulo P., 1990: 140, 143).

NAFTA's formalization and extension of what had already been occurring in the maquilas has been widely acknowledged. Before NAFTA was passed, Gambrill (1992: 46) said that "The impact of free trade on the maquila industry is being shown before and independently of the signing of NAFTA as a product of the progressive globalization of the industry and the commercial opening of Mexico since 1985." "Silent integration" is a common phrase used to describe maquiladora development before NAFTA (Martínez Morales, 1993: 67), and it was expected to continue even if NAFTA had not been signed.

With the 1989 decree governing maquilas, the Mexican government was preparing for the free-trade environment which it was to later negotiate, creating in this economic enclave a microcosm functioning with rules compatible with free trade, and not necessarily requiring further modifications through the treaty itself. The decree provided for the creation of maquiladoras through idle capacity. Industries that were not legally maquiladoras were allowed to switch to production for export and act as if they were under maquila legislation when they were producing less than capacity for the Mexican market. This has led to more companies being part-time maquiladoras, or doing both maquiladora and non-maquiladora production.

In addition, the decree broadened maquiladora legislation to include agro-industry—companies exploiting mineral resources, fishing, forestry—and firms undertaking shelter programs. As a corollary of this blurring of distinctions between the maquiladora and non-maquiladora sectors, bureaucratic regulation of the maquila industry was simplified along with customs inspections at border crossings, and the possibility of maquiladoras selling more in the domestic Mexican market increased.

NAFTA extended the maquila's ability to produce "in bond" (i.e., import materials to Mexico from foreign countries and re-export them after transformation duty free) to all of Mexican industry. Countries other than NAFTA members (for example, Germany and Japan) that had been allowed under maquila legislation to process their goods in Mexico with tax on only the value added will lose this right on January 1, 2001, and will be subject to tariffs unless they use a certain quota of North American content.[6] NAFTA will also eliminate tariffs between its signatories altogether, so that after January 1, 2001, tax will no longer have to be paid by Mexican-, U.S.-, or Canadian-owned maquilas on even the value added. It also allows maquilas to sell progressively more in Mexico for seven years after the implementation of the treaty, when they will be allowed to sell all of their products within Mexico. This means that products made by Mexican-owned businesses that were not established under maquila rules, which would have never been able to compete with maquilas, will have no protection against maquila products after this date.

Mexico's strategy for modernizing its industry with NAFTA was to reconvert it through the maquiladora program.[7] Gambrill (1994a: 16, 17) predicts that Mexican business will "have to completely reconvert traditional production adopting the maquila formula consisting of U.S. technology, capital and components and administration, Mexican labor and overhead, and huge economies of scale. Without an equally swift and comprehensive conversion of all sectors of the economy during the short transition period established by NAFTA . . . the balance could be unfavorable for business and workers."

Although the legal regulations established by the maquiladora program will continue indefinitely under NAFTA with modifications such as those indicated above, the word "maquiladora" will not be maintained. As Lazaroff (1993) has said, "Say good-bye to maquiladora, in-bond assembly—but not before 2001. . . . Eventually, though, the name of the maquiladora program will be changed to the Export Manufacturing Industry, and maquiladoras officially will be a part of Mexico's domestic manufacturing industry." By 2001, the Japanese and Europeans who import their materials from outside of North America will find duties to the United States cheaper than the ones they will have to pay to enter Mexico for their (ex-)maquilas. They may move to the United States in response (Fernandez, 1993), but it is more likely that Mexico will lower its duties to keep them.

Dualism or Heterogeneity in Maquiladoras

It is often assumed that the changes maquiladoras underwent meant a clear break with the past. González-Aréchiga and Ramírez (1989: 874) start from the premise that the maquiladora industry is at a turning point that will greatly influence what they are like at the end of the century. Carrillo (1991b: 57) describes the sharpness of the turn as 180 degrees in some areas of government policy. Wilson (1990: 136) said that the maquila industry was "at a historic crossroad with respect to its role in global corporate strategy. Will it continue to provide mainly a cost-saving respite for U.S. manufacturers faced with stiff international competition? Or will it find a role in the new corporate strategies of flexible production that permit a longer-term competitive advantage in the global economy?"

The alternatives available at the maquila "crossroad" are often conceptualized by the dual-technology thesis, which is a central premise of modernization theory. This theory sees developing societies at the stage of early industrialization containing a small modern sector with high productivity and high wages, which encroaches on a traditional agricultural sector with low productivity and low wages. As industry develops, more of the labor force shifts from the older, less-productive sectors to the newer ones where wages are higher. This process is accompanied by high inequality when industry is first introduced, but low inequality at the end point when industry predominates (Nielsen, 1994: 656). The evidence that supports the hypothesis that recent industrialization has increased inequality in Mexico shows that between 1983 and 1989, wages in maquila and non-maquila industries stayed relatively level, while incomes in the nonindustrial sector and the minimum-wage jobs dropped (Husson, 1991: 11).

Although maquila research does not focus on agriculture, the word "traditional" is often applied to the early maquilas, as well as the non-maquila industrial sector, that was established to serve the domestic market. The same argument that modernization theory makes about the traditional agricultural sector is applied to traditional industries; that is, they will be displaced by the new maquilas. With regard to industrial restructuring in Latin America, Fajnzylber (1990: 55, 177) also argues that countries develop when their industrial sectors become internationally competitive through systematic incorporation of advanced technology and increased productivity, not when industrial growth is based on low real wages.

The dual-technology thesis suggests a bifurcation between new and old maquilas. The path to a modern Mexico was identified by the Mexican government as the "second-wave" maquilas, which used more automated technology and hired more unionized men. Workers were paid better wages and benefits than in the early maquilas, but less than was customary in industries that had served the domestic market. The second wave was first detected in the auto and advanced-electronics subsectors, but its characteristics were expected to become the norm as old maquilas left for the Caribbean and Central America (Gereffi, 1992: 148). The labor-intensive maquilas that hired mostly women at low wages to do simple assembly were seen as a historic first step, but a thing of the past. The dual-technology thesis predicted that the proportion of women in the maquila labor force would continue to drop, and cheap female labor would become less relevant in understanding Mexican maquila development.

Although modernization theory, from which the dual-technology thesis originates, implies that the old maquilas will become extinct, there is some debate. Griffith (1991: 6–7), for example, has said that with NAFTA, "Mexico will out-compete the Caribbean not only for unskilled assembly jobs, but also for high-tech skilled jobs." Carrillo (1990b: 160) argues that there had been a double strategy for the reorganization of work in all maquiladora industries, including auto, during the eighties. He sees a consolidation as opposed to a disappearance of the old maquilas. On one hand, the capital-intensive, high-tech maquilas developed new forms of organization like workers' teams and quality circles, which involve multiskilled workers. In the more labor-intensive sector with less advanced technology, long assembly lines with unskilled workers performing repetitive tasks remain, and are intensified with an increase in the hours worked, quotas, increased rates of production, and weak or nonexistent unions.

Other researchers believe that the old maquila will predominate (Velasco, 1993). They say technological intensification is too expensive to be continued by either the public or private sector. The new Mexican financial oligarchy may be unwilling or unable to invest in the massive resources necessary to acquire more technology, or training and education.[8] Such investment would also be difficult to make if Mexico continues repaying its debts. Thus, technological innovation is not expected to continue to make Mexican industry in general more competitive, even though high-technology enclaves like the automotive industry have arisen. Many researchers believe that Mexican government policies of fiscal austerity, in conjunction with its commitment to repay debts, impose limits on state spending that will prevent any transition to a higher-paid, more-skilled labor force in a modernized industrial plant.

It has also been suggested that the crossroads that the maquila industry has just passed had three directions from which to choose, rather than two (Wilson, 1992). Assemblers make up the first category in the old maquilas, but manufacturers incorporate more technology and actually fabricate as opposed to simply putting together prefabricated parts. In the third category are plants using more-advanced forms of technology, and organizing workers as the Japanese have. The number of options goes back to two, however, if assemblers leave Mexico. Even if they remain, assemblers and manufacturers are often considered to be on the same side of the second industrial divide, which sought to automate work through computerized machines (Piore and Sabel, 1984). This last distinction is seen as most important conceptually, since "there is increasingly widespread belief that the groundrules of industrial competitiveness have altered since the 'golden age' of the postwar boom. A wide set of literature addresses these issues and contrasts the old paradigm with the new" (Kaplinsky, 1994: 337). Some of the key differences between these two paradigms are listed in table 1.1.

Production facilities in the new system incorporate microelectronic technology which can be programmed to switch quickly from one production process to another. The more specialized technology of the old system took more time to alter, while the production process came to a wasteful standstill. This difference led to the tendency under the old system for large runs of standardized products, whereas under the new system, smaller batches of more differentiated products could be produced in response to demand. If products under the old system were not immediately sold, they had to be stored as inventory. In the new system, inventory was eliminated by having manufacturing supplies delivered as needed, and producing only what was

Table 1.1   Key Dimensions in Comparison of Paradigms of Industrial
Competitiveness

Dimensions	New System	Old System
Production Facilities		
Technology	Reprogrammable	Specialized
Models and parts	Differentiated	Standardized
Size of run	Batch	Long series
Markets for products	Niches	Mass
Competitive base	Variety and quality	Cost efficiency and economies of scale
Inventory	Just in time	Stockpiled
Production Location		
Organizational form	Industrial district	Globalization through Fordist organizations
Suppliers	Networked close by	Determined by comparative advantage
Work Organization		
Concept execution	Together	Separate
Social structure	Team, circle	Hierarchy
Social relations	Cooperation	Conflict
Labor Process		
Job descriptions	Few, adaptable	Many, detailed
Qualifications	Multiskilled	Unskilled
Hours of work	Variable	Fixed
Tasks assigned	Changeable	Rigid
Place of work	Several	One
Wages	Flexible	Fixed
Number of workers	As needed	Negotiated
Administration	Minimal	Broad
Supervision of workers	Light	Heavy

ordered—a set of practices called "just in time." The new system could respond to smaller niches in the market when they proved to be more profitable than production for mass markets. While competition under the old system was based on economies of scale and cost efficiency, the main selling points under the new system were the high quality and variety of products.

The location of different parts of the production process might be quite distant from each other under the old paradigm, since it was considered most efficient if each area took advantage of its strong points (known as comparative advantages). Under this assumption, less-developed countries increased their share of industrial production by providing cheap labor and unprocessed natural resources, while more-advanced countries carried out more capital-intensive parts of the industrial process. Advances in communication and transportation make links over long distances possible. The new paradigm pointed instead to how small firms of suppliers were best located close by their larger clients so that delivery could be quick and responsive to changes brought about by fragmented markets. The relocation of small supplier firms to the same geographical area as the larger client they served created industrial districts, which Howes and Markusen (1993, 16) have defined as "groups of firms performing complementary tasks in the production of the same or similar products."

The organization of work under the old system tended to separate the conception of different parts of the production process from their actual execution. In the late nineteenth century, F. W. Taylor advised managers to collect the traditional skills of workers and codify them into rules. Rather than thinking through problems as they arose in the process of their jobs, workers were to simply obey the rules given to them by management. Managers divided the work up into as many categories as possible so that each job description contained only the most unskilled, detailed tasks. Jobs were classified as either "direct work," where there was involvement in immediate production, or "indirect work," such as machine set-up, preparation, and repair. In this model, the secrets of production, embodied in machines and the way work was organized, are carefully guarded by managers so that work can be speeded up and production increased.

In response to such hierarchical social relations and the refusal of managers to share power voluntarily, workers formed unions to defend themselves and represent their interests. Conflict was a frequent method of resolving problems and disagreements in the workplace. Workers' pay was increased in this paradigm when their unions successfully negotiated contracts that held the promise of coping with the inherent alienation of this system in return for higher monetary rewards and job security.

Microelectronic technology is often associated under the new paradigm with the adoption of new forms of work organization and more highly skilled workers, whose productivity is enhanced when they are organized consensually through work teams and quality circles.[9] The labor process proposed by the new paradigm includes flexibility in work patterns, with a decreasing division of labor. Some of the operators not only oversee machines but also change settings and do maintenance and repair, and their job descriptions would merge several of the more-specialized jobs under the old paradigm. This represents a blurring of the distinction between direct and indirect labor that Taylor implemented in Fordism. This system requires that workers be multitasked or multiskilled, and it requires flexibility in terms of hours worked. Enhanced quality-control procedures are important in reaching the goal of zero defects, with every operator being his or her own quality-control inspector. All of this implies giving some measure of control back to the worker in the form of quality circles, work teams, other exhortatory activities, a positive work environment, and welcoming suggestions from workers.

It is hypothesized that workers are less alienated and more satisfied under the new paradigm. They are more involved in their work and more likely to be paid according to productivity. It is predicted that their multiple skills will bring higher wages. Under the new model, unions that defend workers' rights through conflict are thought to be unnecessary and a vestige of the past. Contracts between companies and workers, when they do exist, are flexible, since the two are thought to share many of the same interests.

The old system is most often referred to as Fordism. The theory known as the New International Division of Labor (NIDL) (Fröbel, Heinrichs, and Kreye, 1980) explains how the labor process of the old system was extended globally beginning in the 1960s. Instead of having specialization take place only within one plant or area, different jobs could be located anywhere in the world depending on where they were performed most efficiently. The least-skilled parts of production were relocated to developing countries, where the cheapest and most compliant labor was found among women. The traditional maquilas doing assembly, and also those doing manufacturing, are examples of production transferred to Mexico through the NIDL. Using the principles of Taylorism, both manufacturers and assemblers organize workers with specialized jobs along assembly lines. The number of traditional maquilas exploded in the eighties because of the fall in Mexican wages, and they have been a transmission belt for the arrival of global standards and practices. Sklair (1993: 248) predicts that under NAFTA this will probably continue. "However, if NAFTA were to lead to an intensification rather than a solution of Mexico's problems, the status of the maquila industry and its leading personnel would suffer."

While the way work is organized by the assemblers and manufacturers in Mexico may be similar to Fordism, wages are much lower, and the tendency for plants to close quickly in difficult periods did not provide job security to workers. Thus, they are referred to as neo-Fordist or peripheral Fordist. Neo-Fordism shared Fordism's ability to alienate workers through the separation of conceptualization and execution, and through hierarchical management, but it had none of Fordism's advantages (high wages and job security). Some authors see neo-Fordism as a transitory form between the old and the new paradigm. Others, who reject the bifurcation of paradigms, see it as a legitimate option for firms that do not envision themselves located on either side of the dichotomy implied by the dual-technology thesis. This latter position holds that neo-Fordism contains the seeds of a number of alternative new production paradigms within it (Wood, 1989: 27).

The new paradigm, often used to describe the new maquila, is referred to as post-Fordism, flexible specialization, or lean production. The prototype of the new paradigm is perhaps best represented by Womack, Jones, and Roos's (1990) analysis of Toyota's methods, believed to be the international "best practice" that will not be superseded. The underlying assumption is that lean production, including the "new" labor process, is the only way of producing in every manufacturing field. This claim is based on the fact that the new methods are less wasteful of material and human resources than was prevalent under the old paradigm because they require skilled workers who are involved in the labor process. If this form of production is indeed the most efficient, then presumably everyone will have to adopt it to remain competitive.

As Sklair (1993: 255) says, "the implication is not that maquilas will become more like traditional Mexican industry, but that Mexican industry will become more like the best maquilas." In this scenario, the best maquilas are those doing flexible or lean production. While they may not be representative of Mexican industry yet, they do show what is possible and expected to become the norm. They have the capacity to hire more well-paid Mexican administrative personnel and skilled workers, and to transfer technology. Because patriarchal social structures and cultures make women more flexible workers, feminist analysts of the new paradigm predict an increase in the proportion of women workers, or the feminization of the labor force.[10]

Despite the assumption by some of great difference between the old and new paradigms, others see the new paradigm as a refinement and revitalization of the old, suggesting more continuity than change (Fukuyama, 1989: 10). Even Kaplinsky (1994: 344), who argued strongly for differences between the old and the new paradigms, says that production systems have homeostatic features that make them return to a balance after an outside interruption, based on his observation that companies move from mass production to flexible specialization, and back again.

Some recent research findings indicate that the differences between the old and the new maquilas—or between the assemblers and manufacturers on one hand, and flexible producers on the other—are less than was first predicted. Instead, the second wave seems to have maintained and reproduced the social aspects of its predecessors, referred to above as the four dimensions of maquilization. Gereffi (1994: 14) has argued that "In order to successfully carry out this shift from the 'old' to the 'new' maquiladoras, Mexico needs to move from its wage-depressing export strategy to more productivity-enhancing strategies."

It was found that flexible producers have long assembly lines more characteristic of manufacturing and assembly processes. This mix of production types—at first thought to represent diametrically different paths between which Mexican maquilas would have to choose—may make them less competitive than those who adopt the most flexible techniques more consistently. Wilson (1992: 71) concludes that "the rise of flexible producers among Mexico's maquiladoras has created so far only a caricature of flexible production." Similarly, Taddei Bringas and Sandoval Godoy (1993: 134) evaluate the implementation of the new paradigm in the Japanese maquilas and Ford plant they studied as "shoddy Japanization." A recent study of Japanese-owned auto and electronics maquilas in the state of Chihuahua that failed to find a pure form of either the new or old paradigm is aptly titled *Between Two Forces of Restructuring* (Koido, 1992).

The dual-technology thesis is not unanimously accepted, and alternative conceptualizations form a null hypothesis. Carrillo (1990a: 84), for example, argues that the concept of dual technology is oversimplified. He prefers the term "technological heterogeneity"—extensive in machine technology and in the organization of the labor process of the automotive sector. "It is important to point out that the process of automation in the electronic and automotive maquiladora industry and the new forms of organization do not follow an evolutionary and linear process, but that on the contrary . . . we are witnessing technological heterogeneity" (Carrillo, 1989b: 47). Brown and Domínguez (1989) also consider maquiladoras to be technologically heterogeneous. Labor-intensive companies using rudimentary equipment coexist with others that are more technologically advanced. They observe heterogeneity within the same companies, which combine capital and labor-intensive processes. While new microelectronic technologies are quickly diffusing, many firms remain uninterested in adopting them.

Finally, some researchers do not seem to envision technological dualism and heterogeneity as mutually exclusive, but have argued for both. This idea is fairly loosely articulated, and not fully explored, in Godínez Plascencia's statement (1990: 9) that "Presently there exists a heterogeneous technological base in the maquiladora industry of Mexico, which is expressed in technological duality, both as structure and as tendential process."

The purpose of reviewing some of the key concepts in the literature on maquiladoras and industrial restructuring is to derive the questions that are addressed in this study. The focus of the book is predominantly on the workplace in transport-equipment maquilas in the Nogales, Sonora, area to show what the boom of the eighties has meant for those who work in the industry. Have maquilas doing simple assembly disappeared? Are they waning? Or will they ultimately be the most strongly represented? Are there distinctions between maquilas similar to those predicted by the dual-technology thesis? Will maquilas in the image of the new paradigm be strongly represented? Are they, in fact, the wave of the future? Have some maquilas tried aspects of the new paradigm and then returned to those predicted by the old paradigm? Or, will there be so much difference between maquilas that the concept of heterogeneity is a more accurate characterization than dualism? What are the advantages to maquilas of locating in the interior that might make them continue to move there? Are supplies coming from small local firms that might constitute an industrial district? Each of these questions has several parts that will be elaborated in the following chapters.

These questions have not been addressed by other researchers with the kinds of data collected for this study. For example, Heyman (1991) provides a very rich account of how workers in Agua Prieta make their way in labor markets outside the workplace, but does not collect data inside the factory. While there has been a great deal of discussion about the potential for skilling the maquila workforce, there has not been much focus on how labor markets are formed, who calls them into existence, how they are structured, and how workers negotiate their way through them. Wilson (1992: 3) concludes with an affirmative answer to her question, "Can assembly industry be more than just a source of low skilled low wage jobs?"—but she did not gather data from workers to show how they might access more highly skilled jobs. Tiano (1994) studied women workers and managers in electronics and apparel maquilas in Mexicali, but did not include data from male workers. This study attempts to fill some of the gaps left by previous research.

IMPLICATIONS OF ECONOMIC RESTRUCTURING FOR REGIONAL DEVELOPMENT

NAFTA's Effect on the Western Industrial Corridor

The idea that new regions will develop as maquilas—especially the second wave—increase, and proliferate in locations other than the northern border, rests on the concept of diffusion from modernization theory. Diffusionists think that an underdeveloped society's problems will be solved with the "spread of skill, technology, capital, values, institutions, and knowledge from modern countries to backward countries or from the modern sector of a given country to its backward sector" (Allahar, 1989: 75).

The northern border of Mexico is far from being uniform across its latitude. Each of the recognizably different subsectors of the border has developed in response to geography and climate, politics and society, and communities tend to gather into subregions with north-south shapes. The first basis for these longitudinal subregions was geography and climate. Most large mountain ranges of the continent tend to run in a longitudinal direction, and North American deserts are unusually mountainous. The main sources of water are often springs found in valleys. Rivers formed by these springs run through the valleys between the mountains, and people have historically settled along them, or near washes. Violent thunderstorms, or monsoons, can occur in July and August in the Sonoran Desert, dumping a large amount of rain quickly. This runs off in washes, or gullies, on hills and mountains. NAFTA, as a political treaty between nations, reinforces and encourages these north-south dynamics, although it does not erase the east-west border economically or politically.

The different subregions along the U.S.-Mexico border form industrial corridors containing one or more maquila centers in Mexico linked to industrial centers in the United States. Barajas Escamilla (1989a) has suggested that four distinct corridors can be identified:

1. Pacific corridor: Between the U.S. cities of San Francisco, Sacramento, Los Angeles, and San Diego, and the Mexican cities of Tijuana, Tecate, and Mexicali.
2. Western corridor: Between the U.S. cities of Phoenix, Albuquerque, Denver, Tempe, and Tucson, and the Mexican cities of Nogales, Agua Prieta, and Hermosillo (see map on page 30).
3. Central corridor: Between the U.S. cities of Kansas City, St. Louis, Fort Worth, Dallas, El Paso, and extending to Detroit, and the Mexican cities of Ciudad Juárez and Chihuahua.
4. Gulf of Mexico corridor: Between the U.S. cities of Houston, Fort Worth, and Austin, and extending to Dallas, Kansas City, and Chicago, and the Mexican cities of Ciudad Acuña, Piedras Negras, Nuevo Laredo, Reynosa, Matamoros, Monterrey, Saltillo, Torreón, Gómez Palacio, and Lerdo.

The process of maquilization during the eighties made Barajas Escamilla's boundaries appear too short almost as soon as they were drawn. There is evidence of a stretch northward into Canada, and to more southerly locations in Mexico. The Pacific corridor, for example, was lengthened in 1990 when logs harvested in British Columbia were shipped for processing to Ensenada in the south of Baja California Norte. Similarly, Calgary and Edmonton in Alberta appear to be a natural elongation of the western corridor northward, and the port of Guaymas on the Gulf of California is a southward extension. While the configuration of the corridors follows geographic outlines, they are not carved in stone or defined legally like national and state boundaries. Their development is more likely to be subject to the fluid economic processes affected by daily events throughout the world, such as the implementation of NAFTA and other trade agreements like the General Agreement on Tariffs and Trade (GATT), or the recovery from, or deepening of, recession.

The geographic unity of the north-south corridor shaped by the southwestern deserts was disrupted when General Antonio López de Santa Ana sold southern Arizona and New Mexico to the United States for $10 million in 1853 in order to fund his regime. Santa Ana's presidency had a very dictatorial style, and his name is invoked even today by Mexicans to symbol-

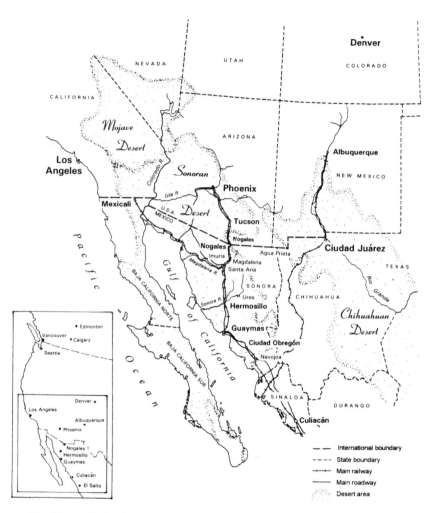

The Western Industrial Corridor on the U.S.-Mexico Border. (Map by Julienne Patterson.)

ize how some public figures have sold parts of their country to foreigners for their own personal political benefit.

Nogales was founded by President Porfirio Díaz in 1880 as a customs post between the United States and Mexico, much later than many of the Spanish colonial towns like Hermosillo, Santa Ana, Magdalena, and Tucson. As a pioneer town, it was established for the regulation of the border on behalf of the federal authorities in Mexico City. A historical plaque near the original border crossing in Nogales, Arizona, says that it was founded at this exact place, rather than a few miles in any other direction, because this is where railway lines from more interior locations in the United States and Mexico met. Nogales became a railroad station two years after it was founded, and it was only then that the city was formally laid out. In 1889 it was granted the title of "town," and in 1920, Nogales officially became a city.

Water is still a scarce resource in the region, so that its desert character prevails. Maquila industries have come to the border despite lack of infrastructure because Mexican labor itself has become an important resource for them, just as copper was in an earlier era. Sociologist S. Tiano (1987: 37) has argued that "the existence of a pool of surplus female labor has led to proliferation of maquiladoras." The maquila industry's geographical location at or near the U.S.-Mexico border constitutes its crucial comparative advantage, according to sociologist L. Sklair (1993: 243). Or, in the more colloquial words of journalist D. Wagner (1991), "Along the border, humanity is the great natural resource. People are plentiful. People are cheap. People are easy to replace."

In the U.S. debate over NAFTA, at least four different positions have been identified, with more than one having something to say about how regional economies would be affected. Marchand (1994b) identified the moderate opponents as arguing that the proposed agreement was limited because it did not provide a complete regional development strategy that would include human rights, debt, labor, environment, trade and investment, and binding enforcement mechanisms. This point of view often focused on the problems that already existed in border communities, and the fact that NAFTA might worsen rather than solve them because it contained nothing about problematic issues such as migration and smuggling of illegal goods. On the other hand, strong supporters of NAFTA, like Gambrill (1994a), argued in more narrow economic terms that the treaty would allow the maquiladora program to evolve toward regional coproduction. Similarly, Holstein (1990: 105) said that free trade would transform maquilas from "screw driver plants" that were little more than foreign enclaves on Mexican soil to "regional companies that would buy and sell on both sides of the border." The following discussion deals with how the second argument manifested itself in the area under study, and then examines how the first point of view was articulated.

Many predicted that NAFTA would turn the western corridor from an economic laggard into a leader. Those living at the border hope they will be gatekeepers at the crossroads of international trade. Proponents of NAFTA foresee Arizona serving

> as a hub for transportation and distribution of products not only from Mexico, but from the Pacific Rim. The key to the distribution network would be the development of a deep-water port in Guaymas, Mexico. . . . Japan and other Asian countries would ship increasing amounts of products past the port in Los Angeles-Long Beach to Guaymas. . . . But even aside from Guaymas, the future is bright for Arizona with the development of trade with Mexico. Thousands of jobs may be created in Arizona as U.S. firms set up factories along the border in Mexico under the maquiladora, or "twin plant," program. (Western: 1991)

Many Japanese firms came to Arizona because of expanding U.S.-Mexico trade and the mere probability of NAFTA's passage; their hope was to become established in the marketplace before the new trade block was closed to them. In 1992, Japanese firms bought record amounts from the state's copper mines and high-technology companies (Herr, 1992).

Community leaders like Nogales, Arizona, alderman Marco Rivera say, "Nogales is going to be the key factor in terms of the state taking advantage of the free trade agreement. If we don't have the facilities for these companies, they'll go elsewhere. . . . The advent of free trade is causing Phoenix and Tucson to pay attention to the border. . . . I don't think people up north are aware of what we do here and the potential that we have here" (Pérez, 1991). Silvers has suggested that the Nogales-Tucson area could become a major transshipment point—a place where goods are unloaded from one carrier, such as a train, and loaded onto another, such as a truck (Edwards, 1991).

Rural industrialization is stimulating much of the corridor. Ures, a small community of 12,000 in the center of Sonora, began dreaming of industrialization when ACME Headwear opened a maquiladora there in 1992. The mayor welcomed the industry to his community, saying, "We want Ures to become an alternative development pole to Hermosillo and the border" (Lazaroff, 1992: 24). Ures was the center of state politics for much of the nineteenth century, but if the community's power is to be revived, the maquilas will have to provide an adequate economic base. Ures was not the only small Sonoran community to find itself hosting a new maquila in 1992; Caborca welcomed three agricultural maquiladoras, and Yécora planned to build a maquiladora sawmill.

Maquiladora-style production has also spread to agriculturally productive parts of this corridor. When the Mexican government changed maquila legislation in 1989 to facilitate agricultural production, it fostered the rise of agro-maquilas that can process crops more cheaply than in the United States, making them more competitive with their foreign counterparts. One example is Basic Vegetable Products, a California-based firm that "assembles" a finished onion from imported seed, then re-exports onion flakes and powders for distribution in the United States. In 1991, it was reported that agro-maquiladoras represented the fastest-growing segment of the $3 billion-a-year maquiladora industry (Millman, 1991), and they were predicted to be the next major economic development in the Sonoran interior in the early nineties (O'Brien, 1990b).

Arizonans preparing for NAFTA at a conference cosponsored by the Denver-based Center for the New West anticipated the "establishment of a trade and transportation corridor that would extend from Edmonton, Alberta, south through Arizona, and on to Mexico City" (Carlile, 1992). Alternatively, a report on attitudes of business and government leaders in Arizona and Mexico envisioned merged Pacific and western corridors. "Arizona is no longer just part of the U.S. Southwest, but also part of Mexico's northwest." They renamed this area with a population of more than 33 million the "Desert Pacific Region." While the capital is Los Angeles, Arizona can play a critical role as a crossing point for traffic heading into the United States from western Mexico (Western, 1992).

Another way to redraw the map is to make Arizona "an important leg of a proposed Rocky Mountain Trade Corridor connecting the Canadian cities of Edmonton and Calgary with Mexico City through major cities in the western United States. This would make an Arizona city, (most likely Tucson) the Brussels (i.e., financial and legal center) of North America" (Waits, 1992). It has also been predicted that Tucson will gain jobs in manufacturing, warehousing, and distribution.

NAFTA supporters have given several reasons why they expect it to stimulate the economy of their industrial corridor. They usually list geography and history first—being at the right place at the right time—and cite common cultural links, since most of Arizona was part of Mexico until

1855. Also, compared to Texas and California, Arizona is less frenetic, has lower wages, and has a more friendly business climate. Such advantages are often promoted by commercial interests such as the Palo Seco real estate corporation. Palo Seco spokesperson Jay Kittle says, "Things are in a state of flux. There are a lot of opportunities but it's a little like musical chairs. A lot of firms are sitting down and there won't be enough chairs for everyone" (Herr, 1992). Many pro-NAFTA businesspeople see Mexicans as potential friends at a time when they need new ones. Peter Longwill, owner of a Tucson-based floor-covering company, put it (with a sarcastic spin), "The lure of new clients in Mexico is the pull; the doldrums of Arizona's economy, the push. Tucson's economy is so wonderful, that we had no choice" (Rosenblum, 1991).

Despite all the promotion of regional interests, it is also clear that life among the saguaros, the giant cactuses whose blossom is the Arizona state flower, is not perfect (Deters, 1991). Many voices from the western corridor say that NAFTA may not have much effect on maquilas or regional development, or that it could even hurt Arizona. Silvers and Pavlakovich (1994) argue that although NAFTA will encourage the movement of industry from the United States to Mexico, Arizona will experience either a small negative impact or a negligible impact from the shift to maquila assembly. They conclude that predictions of positive impacts from maquiladoras under NAFTA may be overly optimistic. Other research predicts that Arizona may lose out to other subregions if the corridor is concretely reinforced by roads and other transportation improvements. In a study of the impact of the extension of Highway I-17 from Alberta to Sonora, called the CANAMEX Corridor, Silvers and Rookley (1993) conclude that Arizona would lose $14.4 million per year in trade, while Utah, Wyoming, Montana, and Washington would gain.

One reason that NAFTA may have little impact on the development of the western corridor is that the historic links between Arizona and Sonora have not been as well developed as they might have been. Phoenix has ignored Mexico, even though it could be its biggest export market. The president of the Arizona-Mexico Commission attributes the hesitancy to do business in Mexico to the midwestern roots of the Valley's Anglo community. "It developed because our people are from Kansas and Nebraska and Michigan and Minnesota. The Mexican is stereotyped in their minds as the guy with the burro" (Young, 1991). Ron Ingersoll, vice president of international operations at First Interstate Bank, says that benefits will be realized in midwestern and northeastern states that have extensive manufacturing industries, but there will be little impact at all on Arizona manufacturers (Edwards, 1991).

One question raised throughout the U.S.-Mexico border region is how many north-south axes will develop to internally connect the new international region. Waits (1992) says that many in Arizona believe it does not have the size or resources of California or Texas, and so may not be as attractive to investors. Products may be more likely to enter the U.S. market through El Paso or San Diego than through Nogales and Tucson. Or it may be that Nogales and other border locations are already beyond their capacity.

Even though Nogales is the third largest port of entry in the United States, its infrastructure is weaker than that of most other border crossings. When the Arizona Economic Council studied its potential to become the gateway to a North American trade corridor, it concluded that the reality of having a new border complex, "One Nogales," was dependent on major investments in highway and rail infrastructure (Waits, 1992). In 1992, Charles Cowan, director of Arizona's Department of Transportation, said his agency had identified about $150 million in road improvements necessary to meet anticipated demand during the next five years along five roads leading to the Mexican border (Carlile, 1992). Unfortunately, the state was $100 million short.

Arizona may not be able to catch up. Its goal of controlling the western industrial corridor may lose out to powers with more resources. Senator DeConcini warned that "Historically, the East has commandeered the U.S.-Canadian trade, and unless our region can improve north-south services, trade will continue to flow on an east-west basis" (Carlile, 1992). Of course, Mexico City would also like to strengthen north-south ties without being subordinated by external powers.

Another prediction is that maquila plants will continue to pollute the environment and endanger health. Water flows north from Nogales, Sonora, to Nogales, Arizona, carrying with it toxic wastes from the maquilas and the dump. The water is treated in Arizona, but the facilities are woefully inadequate. Even after the treatment plant was expanded in 1991, it remained below demand. Nogales health officials warned that a second plant was critical to avoid diseases such as hepatitis, cholera, and tuberculosis

(Pérez, 1991). Maquiladoras may be unenthusiastic about investing in such projects. Carlos de Orduña, general director for Sanyo's manufacturing operations in Tijuana, says, "maquiladoras were set up to save costs for the parent company, so if the cost of doing business rises too high—such as being expected to finance major public infrastructure projects—that could also defeat its mission" (Dower, 1992).

In a 1991 interview, Arizona Economic Council President Scott Eubanks admitted that there had been many economic mistakes in Arizona that have not helped its public-relations image. While committed to strengthening Arizona's economic leadership, he warned that unless they pull together to support regional development, they could lose the Cactus League. While baseball generates funds more though entertainment than industry, this is an apt metaphor for the idea that NAFTA will have little effect on maquilas or development of the western corridor. Spring training in Arizona's Cactus League is aimed at major-league teams based outside the state. Players can be traded, or entire teams moved, at any time if their owners decide another competitive level or location is appropriate.

The Nogales, Sonora, Area as a Research Site

Nogales, Sonora, had a population of 108,000 according to the 1990 census, making it the sixth-largest city in the state of Sonora. Nogales has doubled its size since 1980, and the 1990 figure is undoubtedly an underestimation. Many people probably did not get counted in the census because of the chaotic nature of growth. Without basic infrastructure such as streets, a census taker might not make it to everyone's door. Pérez (1991) says that a more accurate estimate of the population of Nogales, Sonora, is 300,000, and that Nogales, Arizona, has a population of about 20,000. A more accurate number of how many people need servicing on any one day is 50,000, with the influx of tourists, Mexican shoppers, business travelers, and commercial transports. The two communities together are estimated to contain about 350,000 people.

Nogales is important less for its size than for its relationship to other places around it. It is the largest port of entry on the U.S.-Mexico border between Mexicali (the capital of Baja California) on the west, and Juárez, to the east. It is Arizona's largest port of entry. Nogales has never had an economic base of its own, but has always acted as an international port. It forwards agricultural commodities produced in Mexico to salad bowls in the United States and Canada, and passes agricultural machinery and farming supplies from the north to the growers. At least half of the winter produce in the United States enters the country through Nogales, making it the largest border crossing for produce in the United States.

Between December and May 1987, about 1.5 billion tons of produce crossed the Nogales border. In a normal season, 600 vegetable trucks cross daily, and about 3,000 people work in produce-related industries in Nogales, Arizona. In 1992 there were over 200 produce distributors in Nogales, Arizona, many of whom also bankrolled the Mexican farmers who grew the produce.[1]

Because its location on the border between consumers and producers has always been its *raison d'etre*, Nogales has never established much infrastructure that would support industry or population growth. Its local market has never been sufficient to supply the basic necessities at affordable prices, and public services like water, electricity, and drainage remain inadequate. Because its economic ties to the rest of Mexico have never been very strong, except through commercial agriculture, basic services have not been adequately provided by the south.

Manufacturing arrived in the state of Sonora in 1967 with the first maquiladoras in Nogales. One version of the story gives a leading role to R. Campbell Sr., a producer of plastic baskets for strawberries in Arizona and Sonora. He was so impressed by the quality of his Mexican workforce and its low cost that when maquilas first appeared in Tijuana in the 1960s, he decided to bring the idea to Nogales, and obtained permission from the Mexican government to develop an industrial park. When he returned from his flight to Tijuana to learn about maquilas, he said " 'he was getting out of the produce business and into the maquiladora business'" (Jarman, 1992). This switch from an agricultural to an industrial economic base was an early example of trends that would later culminate in what ex-President Salinas was trying to do on a national level in the early nineties with constitutional changes allowing the sale of farmland by Mexican peasants, and with NAFTA.

Salinas was able to attempt this transition at a federal level partly because of the demonstration effect of rapid maquiladora growth in Nogales and other cities all along the border. Locations like Nogales were pioneers in this effort. The Sonoran state government provided incentives to attract multinational corporations, and as part of this program, the first industrial park was built in Nogales in 1971. Industry was attracted to Nogales by the low level of unionization, high social and political stability, and the industrial infrastructure that was being created for them. Eight years after their inception, the maquiladoras were producing more than agriculture and livestock, and they continued to grow (mostly in electronics) with the help of government incentives. Nogales has the distinction of being the birthplace in the early seventies of the shelter concept. When the Nogales industrial park failed to catch on at first, R. Campbell Sr. offered to handle the labor force, warehouse and industrial space, and paperwork for U.S. businesses interested in opening a maquila in the industrial park.

The company he started, known as Collectron of Arizona in the United States, and Sonitrones in Mexico, was the prototype for what is now generically known as a shelter company. It carries out a form of subcontracting in which a foreign company wishing to operate in Mexico supplies materials and components, while the shelter contracts with its own Mexican company to provide plant, labor, and administrative services. By protecting foreign companies from the necessity of legal involvement, shelter companies have made it easier for foreign capital to relocate to Mexico, temporarily or permanently (Sklair, 1989: 48).

Industrial growth in Nogales continued from its inception in 1967 until the economic crisis of 1974–75, when it suffered 4,500 job losses, more than any other border city. People already in severe need of housing and potable water had no other source of employment. Maquiladoras were restored slowly, and their redevelopment followed the ups and downs of the national pattern described above. Thus the number of persons employed in Nogales maquiladoras dropped in 1981 and 1982, and then rose quite steadily until 1989 and 1990, when it dropped noticeably again. In 1990 there were 9,795 people employed in about 69 Nogales maquiladoras.[2]

Arizona benefited less than Texas and Southern California from maquiladora manufacturing because it had not promoted Sonora as actively as its sister states. Instead, the profits have been realized in midwestern and northeastern states where many of the maquilas have head offices. However, Arizona does benefit in some ways. In 1989, 30 percent of all salaries paid by maquiladoras in Nogales, Sonora, was spent on the U.S. side of the border—an exit of capital from Mexico of approximately $19.5 million (Lara Valencia, 1992; Pavlakovic and Kim, 1990). Although maquiladora employees cross the border personally to make their purchases, trading companies have emerged to supply consumer goods approved for importation in 1988 to Mexican retailers (Talarico, 1990).

In 1990, 92 percent of all value added, and 93 percent of workers employed in maquiladoras, were located at Mexico's northern border.[3] The sixth-largest maquiladora center in Mexico, Nogales is nevertheless the one least studied. Something new can be learned here not only because of inattention by previous research, but also because of the community's unique characteristics.

Nogales differs in several ways from the larger maquiladora centers. Many observers say that a relatively pure effect of maquila growth is observable in Nogales, because factors other than industry itself do not have much impact. While it has fewer plants than some other centers, the number of employees per plant is much higher. This is caused by the concentration of larger companies linked to multinational corporations. Their large-scale production continued to make Nogales an important maquiladora center even at the end of the eighties, when the number of plants was decreasing. A 1990 article in the prominent business journal *Expansión* identifying the 100 most important maquiladoras in Mexico included ten from Nogales, two of which were transport-equipment firms and part of the present research.[4]

Comparing maquiladoras in Tijuana and Nogales in the eighties, Sánchez (1990) notes that while growth has been less explosive in Nogales, it has also been more stable. Nogales maquiladoras are more often owned by large U.S.-based corporations than those in Tijuana, and also tend to be older. A higher proportion of maquiladora employees in Nogales are men than in any other border city. Sánchez calls the Nogales Maquiladora Association one of the most closed enclaves throughout the entire border. Plant managers here are more independent from their head offices than those in other locations.

Maquilas employ a greater percentage of the economically active population in Nogales than in all the other large maquiladora centers (more than 50 percent in 1988). Because Nogales's growth in the last generation was stimulated entirely by the maquiladora industry, without the benefit of urban planning or other considerations, it is the place where one can most clearly observe what has been called a "maquiladora culture," in which everyone is accustomed to assembly and riveting (Ramírez, 1988).

More than any other maquiladora center, Nogales has been without effective unions. In 1981, the Confederación de Trabajadores de México

(CTM) signed a contract with 14 of the largest Nogales maquilas without consulting workers, and setting standards below those specified by federal labor law. The changes included defining many job categories as ones where employees could be hired or fired without corporate responsibility, deploying workers to any function within the plant, flexibilizing hours, changing the "day of rest" from Sunday to any other day, and giving companies the exclusive right to determine the speed of machinery and the number of workers needed.

Proposals to reform federal labor law in the same way at the national level surfaced eight years later in 1989 (Lara, 1990). Denman (1990) says that when historians look back from the year 2020, they will recognize that it is impossible to understand the social composition of the state of Sonora in the twenty-first century without seeing that many practices later taken for granted were first consolidated in the automotive maquilas in Nogales in the eighties.

Nogales's lower proportion of women workers does not mean that the effects of gender cannot be studied here. Gender plays a role even within groups whose members are all the same sex. Recently, the proportion of women workers in other maquiladora centers has been decreasing, although women still constitute the majority of the maquiladora workforce. Because the proportion has always been lower in Nogales, we should be able to get a picture of what the decrease in women workers in other centers might mean for them.

The western corridor contains key U.S. industrial centers such as Phoenix, Albuquerque, and Denver. Phoenix, Arizona, is the location of high-tech industrial operations in electronic and transport equipment. This has stimulated development in Tucson, Arizona, and Nogales, Sonora, and in other Mexican communities nearby. Acknowledging that industrial corridors sometimes overlap, Barajas Escamilla notes that Nogales is also the home of companies whose head offices are in California, which she identifies as being in the Pacific corridor.

Another way to define the region served by Nogales is to look at the boundaries created by transportation facilities. The closest international airport is one hour's drive north of Nogales in Tucson, Arizona. Tucson is the city that anchors the immediate region to which Nogales belongs, serves as its northern boundary, and also has most of the existing distribution facilities. Daily flights have connected Tucson to Hermosillo (capital of the state of Sonora), Guaymas, and Mexico City for some time. On the other hand, it was not until 1992 that Phoenix, the Arizona capital and located only a little farther north, announced that airlines would connect it to Mexico City. This innovation occurred largely in anticipation of better communications necessary for NAFTA.

There is also a comparatively good highway that serves as the north-south conduit or axis of the region. It connects Tucson, Ambos Nogales, or the Two Nogaleses (the twin cities on either side of the border), to Imuris, Magdalena, Santa Ana, Hermosillo, Guaymas, Ciudad Obregón, and Navojoa. These last three cities form the southern edge of the region; in the port of Guaymas in the Gulf of California, Japanese supplies are unloaded for the Ford/Mazda joint venture in Hermosillo. Guaymas also supplies Nogales, Sonora, with electricity. The highway is paralleled by a railroad, which takes finished products such as automobiles north through Nogales on their way to markets in the United States and Canada.

Also included in this study is the village of Imuris, the Mexican community closest to Nogales, eighty kilometers south by highway. In 1990 it had a population of 7,000. Its economy was based in agriculture and livestock until 1986, when the only Canadian-owned maquila in Nogales expanded to build a second plant there. Located in a valley where three rivers come together, it had never suffered water scarcity like Nogales, but it also never needed to develop much infrastructure. A few other small maquiladoras have opened in Imuris, but the Canadian-owned operation is the only one of note, and it has totally changed the economy of the village.

In 1980, only 26 percent of the population was classified as urban; in 1990, this figure rose to 70 percent. Before 1986, the majority of the economically active population was engaged in farming and livestock production. Immigration has increased the population, and today, the majority work in industry.

While development in the western corridor and its internal regions has received more attention recently, the focus has been on Hermosillo, where the new maquiladora is predominant. Even though the Ford plant there is not legally a maquiladora, it is understood as part of a second wave of industrial development that increasingly employs high-tech production and new forms of work organization (Shaiken, 1990: 3). Sandoval, who has studied the Ford plant in Hermosillo, believes that the main difference between it and the legal maquilas is its labor force: it employs men who have been very active in their union, whereas the legal maquilas hire more women who have no unions or unions which do not represent them.[5]

Nogales provides a research site in the same corridor that will help round out the picture. In fact, the kind of maquilas found in Nogales are more typical than the Hermosillo operation. Wilson's (1990) research indicates that the traditional maquila doing labor-intensive assembly remains the largest category within the maquiladora sector (44 percent in 1989). She also found that the fastest-growing type of maquila was not the new one, but labor-intensive assembly on long manual lines. The Ford plant in Hermosillo, despite being a new maquila, shares many characteristics of the more typical maquilas such as having a young and relatively inexperienced workforce and high turnover rates (Shaiken and Herzenberg, 1987).

The fieldwork for this study was done in Nogales and Imuris in 1991 in order to bring this relatively unstudied area into better focus. Data were collected on all maquilas (job advertisements), the community of Nogales (household survey), and the ten maquilas doing transport-equipment[6] production (workers' and managers' surveys). A sample of advertisements for maquila jobs throughout the eighties was collected in order to outline the industrial labor market. It is the first data set of its kind, modeled after similar data collected by Carrillo (1991a) for one month in Juárez and Tijuana in 1990. The sample was drawn from the only newspaper in Nogales, Sonora, and all maquila sectors were included. All information in advertisements for maquila jobs appearing for four months in six different years was recorded and analyzed. The results appear in chapter 3. The ads reflected industrial activity beyond the Nogales, Sonora, city limits, with jobs in Magdalena, Agua Prieta, and Imuris.

A unique secondary analysis of data was carried out on the 1988 Encuesta Socioeconomica Anual de La Frontera (Annual Socioeconomic Survey of the Border), referred to as ESAF, which was done in Nogales in 1988. ESAF has been developed by El Colegio de la Frontera Norte (COLEF) in conjunction with the Instituto Nacional de Estadistica Geografía e Información (National Statistical and Geographic Institute), or INEGI, as a systematic way of generating information on the social and economic characteristics of Mexico's northern border (Chande, 1990). The survey has been administered as a stratified, multistage sample survey of households. Areas bounded by natural geographic borders were selected based on whether the majority of dwellings appeared to belong to a high, medium, or low socioeconomic stratum.[7] Blocks were then selected within each area, and the dwellings on those blocks listed for the eventual systematic selection of dwellings. The respondents interviewed in each of these areas were the persons found at home, who were asked to answer questions on housing, the household, characteristics of those normally living in the household, and migration. In Nogales in 1988, interviews were conducted at 571 households, and the sample was weighted to be representative of the entire community. However, Sánchez (1990: 165) is somewhat critical of this database, implying that the sample may have missed the zone called Los Tápiros, which was in the process of invasion in 1986 by 7,000 people, mostly maquiladora workers, who did not have any public services.

Analysis of the ESAF data was used for contextualization and is reported mainly in chapter 4. The strategy for this study was to focus on the workplace rather than the household or community in order to address questions raised about technological paradigms in the transport-equipment sector. Workers' surveys previously conducted in the same cities as the ESAF have benefited by adopting items of established reliability from it, like those used to assess the respondents' age, education, and other background characteristics. I adopted these items and several questions on housing in almost exactly the same form they had been asked in ESAF. A sample survey of direct workers in all ten transport-equipment plants (N = 216) was administered, including items that measured the sociodemographic profile of workers, their labor force experience, migratory history, activities performed on the job, workplace organization and attitudes toward work.[8] The sample of workers was 10 percent of those working in all transport-equipment plants in Nogales and Imuris in 1990, and was stratified by size of plant and gender. Care was taken not to interview more than one worker from a household.

There is no consensus among independent researchers studying maquila workers whether they are best interviewed within plants where they are employed, with the permission of management, or outside the plant, with or without the permission of management. The most important advantage of interviewing inside plants is that there is some possibility of drawing a random sample from management's files on employees. The disadvantage of interviewing workers inside the plant is that they often identify researchers with management and respond in whatever way they think will protect them on the job. In contrast, workers interviewed outside the plant are more likely to give valid responses, but a random sample cannot be selected in this way, and the interviewer has to locate the respondent and find a place for the interview.

My interviews with Nogales workers were conducted both inside and outside the plants. Early in the data collection period, I found responses to be so much better outside the plant that it was worth giving up the possible randomness that might have allowed the use of probability statistics in the analysis of the data. As a result, most of the workers in this study were selected in a non-random fashion outside their plants. The analysis of the data adheres to the caution against generalizing from non-random samples; consequently, tests of statistical significance are not reported. Brannon and Lucker (1989: 42) reported that they also preferred interviewing workers outside maquila plants in Juárez, because within the plants, personnel records were often inaccessible for the drawing of random samples, and confidentiality of respondents' answers was difficult to maintain. Godínez Plascencia (1990: 18) has said that the lack of representativeness is the main weakness of samples of maquila workers.

I also surveyed managers in seven of the ten transport-equipment plants, in interviews that lasted from 30 minutes to five hours, sometimes continuing over several visits and including plant tours and cafeteria lunches. I most often interviewed the general manager, but in some factories, I interviewed production, personnel, and financial managers, depending upon availability and who had easiest access to the information requested. I also spoke to a former leader of the maquila association who had played a leading role in that organization's history, and he was able to speak about the growth of the maquila industry as well as the electronics maquilas he had managed.

Why Study Transport-Equipment Maquiladoras?

Today, Mexican government authorities consider automobile production to be one of the best types of investment because of the dynamism that made it a point of contention in NAFTA negotiations.[9] Former Yucatan Governor Dulce Maria Saura said, "I'd like a car plant, that's the dream of every governor, but it takes time. Our people need work now" (*Economist*, May 1993). The automobile industry's current continent-wide reorganization has greatly affected the economies of Canada, the United States, and Mexico, with Canada and Mexico being competitors for the U.S. market. According to Womack, Jones, and Roos (1990: 266), the Mexican government strategy begun in 1989 has the potential to change the configuration of production for all of North America, with Mexicans producing more for Canadian and U.S. consumption, and also buying more vehicles manufactured in the United States and in the "Canadian Midwest."[10]

This study focuses on auto maquilas rather than some other subsector of the maquila industry for insight into the interrelationship between the forces of maquilization, regional development, continental economic integration through NAFTA, and feminization of the labor force. As noted in the discussion of maquilization, the concept was first used to interpret changes observed in Mexico's auto industry. Many consider the rapid increase in vehicle and parts exports from Mexico to be synonymous with maquiladora growth after the 1983 decree. Scheinman (1990b: 119, 122) shows that in 1988, auto maquilas represented a little more than one-fifth of those employed, and almost a third of the value added in maquiladoras. He thinks the auto industry invested in maquiladoras because it could get around local content rules and also get access to readily available cheap labor.

NAFTA as a state policy facilitated the integration of North American auto production, following years of policies that moved more slowly in this direction. In a prepared statement before Congress in 1991, R. Morris, the director of international trade for the National Association of Manufacturers, suggested as a litmus test for NAFTA "the rule of thumb that if the agreement doesn't work for the American automobile companies it is probably not a good agreement" (cited in Marchand, 1994b). Historically, most of the trade between Canada, the United States, and Mexico has been trade within different parts of the same firm. Automobile firms were the ones most often represented—because the automobile industry makes up the largest part of manufacturing, its competitiveness has become identified with the competitiveness of the entire North American economy.

The Mexican corridor of the auto industry starts in Mexico City (Chrysler), passes through Cuautitlán (Ford), and extends through Silao (General Motors), El Salto (Honda), Aguascalientes (Nissan), Saltillo-Ramos Arizpe (Chrysler and General Motors), and ends in Hermosillo (Ford), which is within easy trucking distance from the border crossing at Nogales. This outline of the Mexican auto corridor by Rozenberg (1994: 37) shows the strategic location of the western industrial corridor, since the two in fact merge. It is no accident that the auto plants located outside of the main auto corridor—Nissan in Cuernavaca and Volkswagen in Puebla—have head offices in countries other than the three NAFTA signatories.

The goal of the integration of the North American auto industry via state policies is to overtake the non–North American competition, and another vehicle for achieving this is lean production. The Mexican automotive sector is usually the showpiece presented as proof that the new paradigm—technologically sophisticated production using participatory self-management techniques—is possible in Mexico. However, the high degree of variation within the industry may mean that the old paradigm remains in strength as well.

Seven of the ten auto-parts maquilas that are the most in-depth focus of the study produce wiring harnesses: octopus-like systems of wires that connect the ignition to all of a vehicle's electrical components. In the largest plants studied, wiring harnesses were assembled on boards that traveled along a semicircular assembly line. Workers repeat the same tasks, such as routing color-coded wires along the pattern of the harness, attaching and joining connectors that protect the terminals at the end of the wires, testing electrical components, placing wires in tubes, and taping the connections. Several other tasks precede production on the line, among them making the boards on which the harness is assembled, cutting the wires that go into the harness, organizing wires into specific size and color lots, delivering them to the line, making connectors in molding machines, and greasing them with a gun. After the harness is produced, it must be tested electrically and manually, and packed for shipping.

Wiring harnesses have been considered low-tech products, and it has been argued that "the move towards centralized control and multiplex wiring in automobiles is likely to eradicate the need for this labor-intensive product" (Hoffman and Kaplinsky, 1988: 108). Whether or not wire-harness production is automated depends on how economical it seems, which is related to technological developments in the industry, as well as NAFTA's effect on other costs in Mexico such as labor and supplies. If it is assessed to be economical, Sklair (1993: 261) predicts that tens of thousands of maquila jobs in Mexico will be wiped out. Another possibility is that Mexico's low wages will make the introduction of new products less cost-effective, thereby stalling modernization. For example, in a report on how the Mexican auto-parts industry can be made more competitive on a world level,

Table 2.1   Major Indicators of Transport-Equipment Plants in Nogales
and Imuris, Sonora, Mexico, 1990

Plant	Labor Force	Mexican Materials	Imported Materials	Value Added	Value of Production
Micro Plant					
Plant A	8	n.d.	n.d.	n.d.	n.d.
Small Plants					
Plant B	97	n.d.	n.d.	n.d.	n.d.
Plant C	85	0.0	2,681.6	817.4	3,499.0
Plant D	60	11.8	1,280.3	406.7	1,687.0
Plant E	47	0.0	252.2	137.8	390.0
Medium Plants					
Plant F	382	0.0	3,817.7	2,132.5	5,950.2
Plant G	376	0.0	2,768.8	1,792.1	4,561.0
Plant H	363	0.3	6,343.4	1,710.7	8,054.1
Large Plants					
Plant I	702	0.0	14,240.0	4,803.3	19,043.4
Plant J	555	0.0	5,328.6	2,325.4	7,654.1

Source: SECOFI, 1990. Concentrados mensuales de la industria maquiladora de exportación.
Mexican Secretariat of Trade and Industry, Subdelegación de Fomento Industrial,
Nogales, Sonora.

Note: Values are in thousands of U.S. dollars. Plants are classified according to size of the
direct labor force.
Micro plants: from 1 to 25 workers
Small plants: from 26 to 99 workers
Medium plants: from 100 to 499 workers
Large plants: 500 or more workers

Booz-Allen and Hamilton and Infotec (1987: 110) recommend that no
changes be made in maquiladora industries, because it is the maquiladoras
that have made Mexico an attractive producer of auto parts.

The number of wiring-harness plants in Mexico has increased. In 1989,
cables for vehicles were the number one manufactured product that Mexico
exported to the United States (Ayala, 1991). Many of them, such as the
G.M. plant in Juárez, have adopted new work rules that are part of just-in-
time organization (Carrillo, 1992). Howes and Markusen's (1993: 16) statement that through flexible production "even some segments of labor-
intensive, low-wage industries are transformed into high-skill, high-wage

industries" also indicates that wire-harness production, although historically done under the old paradigm, is a subsector subject to transformation toward the new one.

The ten auto-part plants in which the most in-depth information was collected are ordered in table 2.1 according to the total personnel employed. They range in size from very small to large, with more than one company in almost every size category. The factories not engaged in wire-harness production were Plant H, which preferred to be listed as producing a vehicle component, and Plants A and C, which produce automobile accessories. Plant C is the only one that manufactures a finished product. All companies are totally owned by foreign capital (from the United States, Canada, and Japan), and the largest is a subsidiary of one of "the Big Three" U.S. automakers. Plants A and B are administered by the shelter company, and Plant D is a subcontractor.

three

CONSTRUCTING THE NOGALES MAQUILADORA LABOR MARKET IN THE EIGHTIES

"I'm hiring whoever comes to my door," said Jorge Tye, a plant manager in No-gales. "Everybody is expanding and there are not enough people." Managers are advertising in the Mexican newspapers for operators, secretaries, security guards and technicians for the plants. (Jones, 1987)

The search for a new labor force, especially on the northern border, has been described as one of the great bottlenecks contributing to the crisis in productivity and quality that has plagued Mexican manufacturing since 1985 (De la Garza and Leyva, 1993: 73). This identification of labor as the source of crisis is prompted by modernization theory, which views labor transfers as the main link between the modern industrial sector of the economy and the traditional agricultural one. If a sufficient number of people with the appropriate values do not shift jobs from the farm to the factory, then the theory predicts that modernization will be blocked (Allahar, 1989: 73).

A labor market is defined as the range of activities and institutions that determine long-run flows of the workforce and employment opportunities. It includes activities of employers and future employees, governments, educational institutions, and unions.[1] Obviously, some of these groups will have more say about how the labor market works than others. Because No-gales has the distinction of allowing investors relative freedom from union and government constraints, we can assume that its investors are the most powerful players in the labor market. To exist at all, the Nogales industrial labor market had to be actively constructed, and those most centrally involved in its early construction were the representatives of investors: that is, managers.

Does Jorge Tye, the plant manager quoted at the beginning of the chapter, expect workers to show up at his door when his plant is located in a place without a historically developed labor force? How far would he travel to hire workers? More important, how far could he go, given the restrictions by upper management and company owners? Would he cross his doorstep to place an ad in the local newspaper? Could he pay new benefits, or raise wages? Would he move his plant to a neighboring community where the labor force had not already been absorbed by maquilas?

A labor market operates as a series of social filters between skill and the wider economy and class structure. To some extent, the labor market dominates the labor process (Thompson, 1984: 80), which means that before people can demonstrate their capabilities—the quality of their work and the level of their productivity—they must first be hired. If the dynamics of the labor market keep them from ever getting certain types of jobs in the first place, they will never be able to demonstrate or develop the skills thought to be a part of those jobs.

The first part of this chapter examines how managers in Nogales built the labor force they now administer. Their subjective understanding of the process, which assumes the modernization perspective, is reflected in the nature of their statements, in the popular press, and in personal interviews. Their individual style and attitudes reflect their expectations of the labor market.

The second half of the chapter reports findings from an analysis of more objective data collected from newspaper advertisements for jobs in maquiladoras during the 1980s. It focuses on seasonal rhythms in the formation of the labor market, adjustments made by plants to deal with absenteeism, the length of time taken to fill a position, and labor-market segmentation.

Managers' Perceptions of Labor Shortage

Employment in maquiladora industries in Nogales, Sonora, rose substantially in the last decade from just under 13,000 in 1980 to more than 18,000 in 1989 (table 3.2). The rate of growth was even higher in Sonora locations with far fewer maquilas, due to companies searching for new "green field" locations (Lara Valencia, 1990: 11). In the eighties, more plants opened in other nearby, smaller locations such as Agua Prieta, Imuris, and Magdalena, and eventually cities farther in the interior, such as Hermosillo and Ciudad

Obregón. Thus, while Nogales remained the site in Sonora with the greatest concentration of maquiladoras, the decade's growth resulted in permeation to other communities.

The U.S. recession caused a decline in 1990 in personnel employed and value added in all Sonora maquiladora cities except Agua Prieta.[2] The contraction in the U.S. economy did eventually affect the labor force in Agua Prieta in March 1992, when 2,500 workers lost their jobs (Ortiz González, 1992)—approximately 40 percent of the labor force there.

However, even at the end of the eighties, in the midst of economic stagnation, the adequate supply and quality of labor were important concerns of industry and the state, which was attempting to facilitate industry. The local Nogales, Sonora, newspaper, *La Voz del Norte,* furnishes a record of the discourse around this issue; articles also appeared farther south in Hermosillo's *El Imparcial.* Local press coverage reveals the importance of labor for the maquiladora industry, and the difficulty managers experienced in bringing the labor force together.

For example, on January 12, 1989, Francisco Molina, the president of the Agua Prieta Maquiladora Association, said companies there faced a deficit of 1,500 workers, which was reducing production (Ponce, 1989). He blamed the government, saying that obsolete housing programs did not satisfy workers' needs. He complained that the taxes collected in communities such as Agua Prieta went to larger cities rather than staying at home to build transportation networks and other essential infrastructure. He called the result "anarchic development."

The situation did not improve in Agua Prieta that year; on November 14, 1989, the same maquiladora association estimated that the demand for labor was between 1,200 and 1,500 workers (Medina, 1989). In this later announcement, Molina blamed inadequate housing not only on the state, but also on the economy and industry itself for demanding so much labor. This recognition of industry's role as a cause of insufficient labor is rare; when it is heard, it is usually heard from state functionaries and union leaders.

In mid-March of 1989, a "crisis" in the Nogales maquiladora industry was announced; the major indicator was a severely inadequate labor supply (Olivares, 1989b). The deficit of workers, set at 2,000, was seen as a serious impediment to companies that were consequently losing production and suffering delays. The head of the Nogales Maquiladora Association blamed the lack of infrastructure for previously established maquilas, and a supersaturation of maquilas on the border in the previous few years. A spokesman for the state agency SECOFI (Secretaría de Comercio y Fomento Industrial) emphasized the high concentration of plants in a few centers, and advised companies to move to more intermediate locations that still had an adequate labor supply (Olivares, 1989a).

In May 1989, the press still characterized the Nogales maquiladora industry as having serious problems hiring enough workers (Romo and Osuna, 1989). It was predicted that companies would not attract enough personnel to meet that year's anticipated growth of 18 percent. The head of the maquiladora association said that at that time, the demand for labor was estimated at 2,700 workers, or 15 percent of the total 18,000 workers then employed in maquila industries in Nogales.

The next year, the problem of insufficient labor was still a major issue in the press, even though it was not quite so bad as it had been. In early January 1990, the head of the maquiladora association of the state of Sonora announced a labor force deficit of approximately 1,000 workers (on average) per month in Nogales maquiladoras (Olivares, 1990). Attributing this to the growth in existing firms, he also acknowledged that it was better than the labor deficit in the previous year, which had been about 2,000 workers per month. He credited the improvement to plant closures, with the fired workers absorbed by other plants.

When I collected the data for this study in 1991, Nogales's maquilas seemed to be in one of the "crisis" periods so typical of the newspaper reports. On my early plant visits, managers in two of the small-sized plants expressed the same concern about the downturn in the business cycle. They pointed to the largest plant in the sample, Plant I, which because of its size, influenced the entire local labor market. Difficulties in the automotive sector of the U.S. economy had caused Plant I to cut back on production. Workers had been fired because there was no work for them, and many had returned to their hometowns after receiving severance pay.

Some managers at smaller plants, like Plant C, said this contributed to "a vacuum of workers when we need them most, like right now." A manager at Plant I attributed the fault for this disruption to federal labor law in Mexico: "Labor is more flexible in the United States because it can be laid off for a week, and then called back. In Mexico, because of the labor law, you can't temporarily lay people off. You have to pay them three months salary, *indemnización*. And then they go back home and you lose your labor force." Workers at other plants also evidenced this sense of crisis when they reported that some of their benefits had been frozen because of the Gulf War. When I conducted my last interviews two months later, Plant I was hiring again and anxieties seemed to have subsided.

For the most part, Nogales managers I interviewed were greatly concerned about sufficiently qualified, available labor. Indeed, staying in operation in Nogales for any length of time meant being able to adapt to "crises" in the labor market. One exception was the manager of Plant A, the microsized plant, in operation only since 1988. It had contracted with the local shelter company to supply the little labor that it used. When the manager gave me a tour, he opened the doors from the foyer and offices to a warehouse-like space full of crates and machines, and with a flourish of his arm, said proudly, "See? No people." The shelter company also supplied all of Plant B's labor.

Neither was Plant E's manager very concerned with maintaining his workforce, perhaps because he was discouraged by the economic downturn and the difficulty this was causing for his operation. He said that even his fellow executives in the larger plants were wondering if they were going to have jobs at the end of the year. Apparently unaware of workers' origins, he asked me if my survey had found most of them coming from the south of Mexico or El Salvador (which chapter 4 shows is not the case). Although he had worked for almost a dozen years in Nogales maquilas, he thought workers left one plant for another for something as trivial as whether or not the plant parking lot had a basketball court.

Issues like the labor shortage are taken very seriously by the Nogales Maquiladora Association, an organization of managers which in April 1991 had members from 60 percent of all Nogales maquilas. Companies run by Sonitrones, the shelter company, did not belong. There were 40 full members (at $200 each) and 20 associate members. Only the president and secretary of the organization were paid. A former leader of the association, an electronics plant manager who still wielded a great deal of influence among managers, said, "We get 20 members out to most meetings, and there is a 10-member board of directors, and many subcommittees. Attendance at meetings increases to almost the total membership whenever there is some problem with unions, customs, the environment, or some other important issue. This maquiladora association is one of the most respected on the border."

An Anglo U.S. national, he said he had been criticized for not hiring Mexican managers. As noted above, the early maquilas hired foreign nationals, usually from the United States, to fill all their technical and managerial jobs, whereas the new maquilas increasingly have Mexican technicians and managers. I found both Mexican and foreign nationals as managers and technicians in transport-equipment plants, and what was considered to be the most appropriate way of being a manager varied by nationality.

The differences in roles I observed among Nogales managers speak to modernization theory, which argues that traditional sectors of society would not be able to modernize without embracing values like the high regard for individual achievement, tolerance for diversity, the use of rational procedures, and the pursuit of utilitarian goals. The theory predicts that if people in traditional societies cling to particularistic relations and kinship obligations, with too much adherence to religious beliefs, economic development will be out of their reach (see Allahar, 1989: 65–70).

Managers who identified themselves as U.S. nationals, and whose first language was English, were more likely to have what the maquiladora association leader called an "international" style. They wore ties to work and were interested in discussing with me what had been in the *Wall Street Journal* that morning that related to their business situation.[3] The leader of the maquila association defined having an "international" style as realizing that the ability to compete with the "sharks" at higher management levels was more important than whether you were talked to with respect.

He recounted a situation in which, as the general manger of an electronics plant, he had needed a new junior manager and could not find one quickly. He convinced a Mexican to be recruited from the shop floor for the job. After a while, the new Mexican manager came to him and said that he did not like the way the general manager was talking to him, because Mexicans talked to each other with greater respect. In order to teach the Mexican manager a lesson, the general manager "took him up" a few levels in the company, and let the higher levels of management "eat him alive" in a meeting. The object of the lesson was to make the point that managers have to do their work the "international" way. "You can't wear your culture on your sleeve. The fact that a manager is Mexican is totally irrelevant to me," the maquila association leader said.

Managers who had adopted an "international" style tended to interpret any difficulties they had in maintaining their labor force in terms of cultural differences. Although several managers expressed this view, the maquila association leader articulated it most clearly as Mexican culture being dominated by the father image. "If a worker's father tells her to come home right in the middle of the week, she does, rather than wait until Saturday. I know because they have come into my office with letters from their fathers saying they have to go home, and I have paid them what is owed and filled out the separation papers." Another cultural trait he pointed to as problematic for developing a labor force with appropriate work habits was the reluctance to separate personal life from work life in Mexico. "I could argue with a person at work and still have a beer with him after work whereas the Mexicans wouldn't do this. They won't offer constructive criticism of each other in meetings either."

He was familiar with several very wealthy Sonoran families. He found the present generation uninterested in operating maquila plants themselves, although they were interested in operating shelter companies. The younger men would have liked to operate maquilas, but the family's money was controlled by the grandfathers, who did not consider maquilas a respectable business. The maquila association leader believed that when this generation's grandchildren had control of the purse strings, they would be industrialists.

The general managers at Plants D and G were both Mexican and took a very personal approach to maintaining their labor force. Both of them emphasized that they were not "jacket and tie"–style managers and that they maintained good communication by working on the shop floor occasionally when needed. They linked their disregard for the formal symbols used by some managers to the fact that they had begun at the bottom of the maquiladora industry and worked their way up.

When the smallest of these two plants had relocated within Nogales, the manager had personally driven 17 of his workers daily in his van to the new location. Eventually, the commuting workers quit, because they considered the new location too far from home. Other workers who lived in a *colonia,* or residential district, only a few minutes walk from the new location were hired. This same manager also authorized payments for workers' long-distance telephone calls and telegrams when they could not get back in time after Christmas or Easter holidays. He interpreted the cause of their absence as inadequate transportation, and he believed this was a justified reason for not being able to get to work. There were handwritten signs in the plant saying, "¡ERES IMPORTANTE!" (YOU ARE IMPORTANT!) to keep self-esteem high.

The manager in the larger and older of these two plants boasted of having solved turnover problems by promoting only from inside his plant. He had written a series of training manuals for all jobs, and he said, "This way, everybody reads from the same sheet of music." He also sent workers and administrative employees to take courses outside the plant at company expense. He believed his own internal education program was superior, but thought the courses were worth the money because employees developed increased confidence when they realized they already knew most of the content of these courses. The efficacy of the management style at Plants D and G was borne out in tours of the plants, where there was evidence of mutual respect and trust.

In all of the plant tours I received, I walked behind the manager who led the way, making it possible for me to observe workers' behavior as the manager approached and after he had passed. Workers from Plants D and G appeared more comfortable with their managers on the shop floor. Their behavior did not change when they were behind the manager's back, as in some other plants. Workers in Plants D and G also seemed more comfortable with my presence, in one case assuming that I worked for the head office. They also approached the manager freely in my presence with news or questions. The fact that what I was observing was a typically Mexican management style is corroborated by DeForest (1994: 34), who says, "Stepping out onto the typical Mexican plant floor, a visitor is immediately impressed by the cordial and good natured atmosphere. This impression is not misleading—characteristically, the Mexican desire is for harmony rather than conflict."

There were undoubtedly other Mexican styles of managing that I did not have an opportunity to observe. The general manager of Plant I was a Mexican national who wore a jacket and tie. Given his attire and the large number of administrative personnel with whom I observed him working, I doubt if he worked on the shop floor when labor was short like the managers of Plants D and G. Unfortunately, I spoke to him only long enough to explain the study and have him authorize the full cooperation of two other senior managers: an Anglo male U.S. national and a Mexican female national. The large size of this plant allows for a greater division of labor and thus more role specialization.

The so-called international-style managers eschewed as paternalistic the payment for long-distance calls from absent workers. They all said it was mandatory that they personally make a few rounds of the shop floor daily, but they clearly thought there were better uses of their time. Their plants had higher rates of absenteeism and turnover.

At Plant H, I observed a middle path between the Mexican and international management orientations—an integration of styles rather than the adoption of one over another. The general manager, an Anglo U.S. national, said that when the plant first opened, it employed more *gringos* than anyone else in Nogales, because there were not enough Mexicans with the skills they needed. They have had to develop and train their own labor force because they have found local education in the technological college to be inadequate. After several years, the heads of production and quality control are Mexican nationals, and every Anglo department head now has a Mexican assistant ready to take over should the department head leave.

There was no question in the general manager's mind that Mexican managers did a better job. "We would be 100 percent better off here with all Mexican managers." In fact, he had subordinated the head of personnel to the head of production (both of whom were Mexican), because the production manager understood workers much better than the personnel staff, who he said defined themselves as a caste above the ordinary worker.

The general manager at Plant C, a Hispanic U.S. national who had worked at U.S. plants owned by his company before coming to Nogales, tried to integrate the two managerial types. Having studied engineering and finance at the post-secondary level, most of his time was actually spent on technocratic tasks. However, he said that "In Mexico they want a father figure, and so I take two or more walks through the plant a day to give workers more or less a pat on the back and to keep up communication. This would not be expected in the United States, but it is here." He also played a leading role in the Border Trade Association, which can influence labor markets at government levels.

What managers say about how they retain their employees is worth noting. As Sklair (1992: 92) has argued, they are part of a "transnationalist class which is gradually changing the ways in which Mexico relates to a global capitalism in the process of reformation." In Nogales, this class is made up of two ethnic groups with different ideas about the best way of managing workers. This biculturalism, or binationalism, is recognized in the structure of the Nogales Maquiladora Association. While all members are very close and share the same attitudes at some levels, the highest-level leader is always a U.S. national, and the next in line is always Mexican.[4]

The advantage of interviewing individual managers is that they illustrate the thinking behind their companies' activities, and it is clear that several different kinds of logic are at work simultaneously. The Mexican style is described as paternalistic and respectful of the individual's dignity. The international style is more oriented toward achieving workplace goals, without regard to workers' responsibilities outside of the plant, and is impersonal in comparison. A disadvantage of personal interviews, however, even with key informants like managers, is that those interviewed may not always present the entire truth in their responses, or may not be aware of the larger picture outside their offices.

Crisis as Myth

With Nogales's post-1960s development as Sonora's largest maquila center, a continuing preoccupation has been the constitution of a labor force of adequate size and quality. Announcements of "crises" in the maquiladora industry mask the fact that this may be the usual state of affairs because of the tendency to boom and bust depending on swings in the U.S. economy. The most commonly heard explanation for insufficient labor is that cities like Nogales cannot support workers' basic needs, and lack minimum infrastructure in housing, water, and transportation. Nogales has a harsh winter climate, but housing is scarce, and what does exist often does not provide adequate shelter in cold weather. When I was collecting data in March and April of 1991, it snowed twice. My experience of being awakened early in the morning by the cold of an overnight snowfall is not uncommon. In November 1989, plant supervisors said that in the cold weather of that period, 10 percent of workers quit their jobs and went home because they were not used to the climate. Supervisors predicted that by mid-winter, workers' absences would increase to 30 percent.[5]

Carrillo et al. (1991: 22–24) do not accept managers' definition of labor as in short supply in their study of the maquila labor force in Tijuana, Juárez, and Monterrey. They explain that there are, and will continue to be, women and immigrants who can work in maquilas.

The soaring expansion of maquiladora activity leads to the assumption that this kind of company sooner or later will be confronted with a situation in which they won't be able to find anyone available to work. However, this preoccupation should be mitigated, since immigration flows are composed mainly of people of working age, principally between 15 and 35 years old. Besides, over 50 percent of women are not part of the economically active population.

On analyzing the economically inactive population, high rates of persons, mainly women, are found who work in the home or are inactive. It was calculated that almost 30 percent of the economically inactive population have sociodemographic characteristics which maquiladora plants prefer in their worker selection policies. Thus, a considerable volume of the population exists which can be integrated into new jobs predicted for the maquila industry.

Carillo and others also predict that in cities like Monterrey that have non-maquiladora industries, there will be a transfer of labor from them to the maquiladoras. Although similar calculations for Nogales have not been performed in this study, their dismissal of a labor shortage is soundly argued and may be applicable to Nogales as well.

The fact that labor of the kind management wants is not immediately available is problematic for the organization of work, the labor process, and the labor market itself. One result is the increase in rates of turnover—the movement of workers from one plant to another in search of better wages and working conditions. Silvers and Lara Valencia (1990: 160) indicated that the turnover rate in Nogales exceeded 15 percent in some months, although it varies by plant. The head of the maquiladora association in Agua Prieta said in November 1989 that the scarcity of workers was causing terrible competition for labor among plants. The problem was felt most acutely by those companies having complete production systems (the new maquilas), because they require more time to train workers. The SECOFI spokesman referred to above said high rates of turnover complicated matters because companies that had spent a great deal on training programs often had to retrain new workers, but might well lose those they had already trained to other companies.

Increased competition for workers on the part of companies is evidenced by offers of new bonuses or benefits, often food, usually tied to attendance.

Companies have also tried other ways to minimize losses in their production processes, especially at the year's end and beginning. Workers are less likely to leave a company just before Christmas, since this would mean losing the annual bonus they are legally due at that time. However, most of them are migrants from more southerly regions, and sensitive to Nogales's inadequate housing. After the holiday, many of them stay with relatives they visited farther south, especially if they can find work there. This leads to the highest rates of absenteeism in January, with an estimate on January 4, 1989, of some plants missing 50 percent of their personnel (Figueroa, 1989a).

Recruitment campaigns constitute one industry response to January's predictable absenteeism and astronomical turnover. Numerous ads are placed on radio and in newspapers in early January. Word of mouth is also an important recruitment strategy, and it is rumored that bus drivers on public transportation routes engage in piracy, informing workers of companies having new and better benefits. Companies may also take precautions by hiring more people than normal before Christmas, and they may give valued workers special permission for longer holidays if they promise to return. Thus, there have been very clear acknowledgments of the problems caused by hiring a migratory labor force which is employed in a city with inadequate infrastructure, and attempts made to restructure the situation.

One industry response to labor shortages that can be characterized as an adjustment in regulation has been to reschedule working hours to take advantage of the workers' greater reliability before Christmas. To avoid the production problems caused by the scarcity of workers in January 1990, Nogales maquiladora industries shut their plants for a longer Christmas vacation than legally required in December 1989, with the agreement that workers would work eight Saturdays before Christmas. Workers were said to be "paying for" a longer holiday by working these extra eight Saturdays. As noted later in chapter 4, this has become institutionalized in some plants, with workers now working extra Saturdays to "pay for" the holidays they are due by law as well.

The Nogales Labor Market

One way of examining the size, structure, and internal components of a labor market is by analyzing job advertisements. Newspaper ads are only one representation of a labor market, since advertising is also done on radio and through "word of mouth." However, newspaper ads have been used to great advantage by government agencies like Statistics Canada to measure shifts in the labor market. Their Help-Wanted Index is considered an early indicator of general economic activity, since changes in advertising requirements occur early in a business cycle (McKitrick, 1989: 23). And since, as discussed in chapter 4, 95 percent of the population in Nogales is literate, it can be assumed that newspapers are an accessible source of information for most people looking for work.

A recent study analyzing ads for maquila jobs from a month of Juárez newspapers and another month of Tijuana newspapers in 1990 led to findings about other border locations that are sufficiently interesting to encourage a more extensive replication here (Carrillo, 1991a, 101–107). The greatest demand in the Juárez and Tijuana ads was for jobs as technicians, supervisors, and engineers. This is consistent with the dual-technology thesis that a second wave of more technologically sophisticated maquilas is becoming the norm. However, it is not clear whether the number of ads, or the number of jobs available in the ads, was calculated. One ad usually offers several positions. This study lengthens the time period for observation to the entire decade of the eighties, assuming that a larger sample will allow a more complete and accurate picture of the labor market.

An advantage of using ads as a source of information is that they are more easily observed than communication through word of mouth or radio. They also give clearer indications of managers' preferences for certain kinds of labor than can be found in other sources of information, such as surveys in which managers are asked to report to an interviewer about their behavior or the behavior of their company. Managers might or might not report to an interviewer that they preferred certain kinds of labor for particular jobs, depending on their perception of the social acceptability of their views. Stronger evidence for the preference, or lack of preference, for certain kinds of labor can be found when companies place advertisements that reflect their marketing strategy for certain kinds of labor.

The newspaper from which ads were sampled was *La Voz del Norte*, the only Spanish-language daily in Nogales and the surrounding region. The years 1980, 1983, 1985, 1987, 1989, and 1990 were chosen for two reasons—to detect trends over the decade, and because they were years for which the newspaper's archives were complete. This decade was chosen for study because it would allow observation of the effects of the most recent changes in maquiladoras. As noted in chapter 1, government policy toward the maquiladoras changed dramatically in the early eighties, when state policies began to facilitate maquiladora growth in order to strengthen the country's economy and contribute to national development.

Four months were selected from each year to test the hypothesis that there are seasonal variations in the demand for labor. January and February were hypothesized to be months in which more jobs would be advertised, while September and October were expected to have fewer jobs advertised and a more stable labor market. It was also hypothesized that it would take longer to fill jobs in January and February than in September and October. Every job advertised was coded, along with the number of positions available, prerequisites, incentives, length of time the ad ran, and any other information present.[6]

A tally of the number of jobs advertised in Nogales provides data for comparison with the national level. An increase in number of ads indicates a shortage in the supply of, or increased demand for, labor of the type management prefers and/or needs. The prerequisites advertised for different jobs more fully elaborate how management attempts to constitute its labor force. While the employees hired may not necessarily receive all incentives advertised, the ones that appear in the paper do indicate sources of indirect pay and the needs that are thought to motivate workers, what Rubery (1987) and Tarling (1987) call the configuration of disadvantage found in the labor market.

Table 3.1 shows the number and kind of jobs advertised in the periods sampled. Under "Jobs Advertised," the number and percentage of times a job title appeared in ads are reported as indicators of the supply of available jobs. The most frequently occurring job titles were supervisors (16 percent), followed by secretaries (13.1 percent) and operators (12.8 percent). However, simply counting the number of times a job title appears underestimates the number of jobs available in this labor market, and the distribution of different types of jobs, since for all job titles except skilled administrative assistants, more than one position often needed to be filled. Ads for unskilled production personnel sought an average of 26 persons per ad, whereas ads for skilled production, administrative, and control personnel sought one to two persons per ad on average.

Table 3.1   Maquiladora Employment as Advertised in Nogales and Region by Job for Selected Periods, 1980–1990

Job Titles	Jobs Advertised		Positions Available	
	No.	%	No.	%
Unskilled Production Personnel				
Operators	45	12.8	1,672	78.2
Other	21	6.0	55	2.6
Skilled Production Personnel				
Mechanics	16	4.2	26	1.2
Technicians	35	10.0	85	4.0
Engineers	33	9.4	42	2.0
Skilled Administrative Personnel				
Secretaries	46	13.1	52	2.4
Assistants	12	3.4	12	0.6
Security Guards	21	6.0	34	1.6
Dispatchers	6	1.7	8	0.4
Other	41	11.7	46	2.2
Skilled Control Personnel				
Supervisors	56	16.0	80	3.7
Managers	18	5.1	24	1.1
Total[a]	351	100.0	2,137	100.0

Source: La Voz del Norte in Nogales, Sonora.

[a] There is one case for which information on the job title is missing.

The column entitled "Positions Available" shows the product of the number of job titles times the number of positions required to be filled.[7] This gives a more accurate picture of how plentiful the supply of jobs is. In the case of operators (78 percent), the job with the most positions, it looks like the demand for labor that is expressed in the review of news reports from above from 1989. Carrillo (1991b: 39) found that in February 1990, the vast majority of positions for maquila employees in Tijuana and Juárez was for unskilled workers (77 percent).

This evidence from three different industrial corridors that the type of labor overwhelmingly in demand is unskilled supports Barajas Escamilla's

(1989b) argument that what Mexican maquiladora centers primarily do is perform labor-intensive aspects of production for industrial centers in the United States. The particular form of their integration means that they do not have many jobs of the high quality that would be identified as part of the primary labor market, that is, requiring substantial human capital and paying well, which are predicted to be more plentiful in the new maquila. Instead, the jobs available are those mostly identified with secondary labor markets and the old maquila.

The number of ads and jobs broken down over the decade and compared to fluctuations in actual maquiladora employment in Nogales reveals a relative parallel between advertising and employment. This is shown in table 3.2, which compares the number of jobs advertised to the number of positions available and the number of workers employed between 1980 and 1989. The personnel employed in maquiladora industries in Nogales increased throughout the decade. While there is a plateau in growth of workers employed between 1980 and 1983, the largest leaps are between 1983 and 1985 (12 percent) and 1985 and 1987 (16 percent). After 1987, the rate of growth is less steep at 10 percent. This confirms that maquiladora employment in Nogales follows the national pattern described in chapter 1, with a decrease during the recession in the early part of the decade, a boom in mid-decade, and a decline toward the decade's end.

When total employment made its biggest gains of 12 percent and 16 percent between the years 1983, 1985, and 1987, so did jobs advertised, with gains of 69 percent and 62 percent. And when the rate of employment increase began to decline in 1989, the number of jobs advertised beat a hasty retreat to 1985 levels. This pattern is also evident in the number of positions available, with the biggest leap coming early, between 1980, when 39 positions were available, and 1983, when 321 positions were available. The number of jobs advertised and positions available dropped by about the same rate between 1987 and 1989. The figures for 1989 are congruent with the interpretation cited above that the problem of insufficient labor was not as bad that year as in 1988 because although most plants expanded, some had closed. Although ads and positions available in ads dropped, maquiladora employment in 1989 still increased by 10 percent, which might well reflect the fact that some plants closed, making workers available for the others, which continued to expand. The supply of labor would meet the demand without advertisement in such a situation.

Table 3.2   Changes over Time in Advertisement and Employment for
Maquiladora Workers in Nogales and Region, 1980–1989

Year	Jobs Advertised	% Change	Positions Available	% Change	Workers Employed	% Change
1980	32	—	39	—	12,784	—
1983	39	22	321	723	12,784	0
1985	66	69	546	70	14,268	12
1987	107	62	665	22	16,588	16
1989	64	–40	420	–37	18,202	10

Source: La Voz del Norte and SECOFI in Nogales, Sonora.

There is also evidence of Nogales being an important center in this industrial corridor, with plants either expanding from Nogales to nearby locations or trying to draw labor from elsewhere and remain in Nogales. While
97 percent of all jobs advertised were in Nogales plants, a little more than
7 percent of these offered free transportation from Magdalena, over an
hour's bus ride away, as an incentive. The company placing these ads was
looking for operators with experience in industrial sewing. Another company with plants in both Nogales and Magdalena advertised for a driver in
Nogales and a production planner in Magdalena in the same ad. A little
more than 2 percent of positions available were located in Agua Prieta and
Magdalena, with the company advertising these positions looking for an industrial engineer, general supervisor, line supervisor, dispatcher, computer
operator, and production operators. Less than 1 percent of all positions advertised were in both Nogales and Imuris, with the company looking for a
personnel coordinator and engineers who would work in both plants. This
company also offered free transportation as an incentive.

The Search for Maquiladora Labor

The undifferentiated nature of the largest group of positions available is
demonstrated by the dearth of terms used in ads to describe the desired type
of workers. Unskilled production personnel were referred to in the ads as
"operators," "workers," "cleaning employees," and "concierge," with one
ad simply stating a need for "female personnel." While only these few types
of jobs are listed in the unskilled production category, there were many more

types in each of the other categories, so that the skill level of a job category and its internal differentiation are inversely related. Twenty-three different job titles appeared in the skilled-production category, including five kinds of mechanics, five types of technicians, and seven differently named engineers. Thirty-seven different job titles appeared in the skilled-administration category. The twenty-six job titles in the skilled-control category included ten differently named supervisors and eleven kinds of managers. For the few people who get jobs in the these three skilled categories, the labor process may vary in stimulating ways.

Chapter 1 traced the development of maquiladora industries from their inception at the national level, with the fourth period from 1983 to 1989 characterized by a boom in maquiladoras and a change in their labor force to more highly segmented skill categories with a greater majority of personnel in unskilled jobs (aspects of maquiladorization). Table 3.3, which shows changes over time for both direct and indirect workers employed, and ads for their jobs, gives evidence of these same qualitative changes in the classification of labor occurring simultaneously at the local Nogales level. In 1980, the end of the third period, there were the fewest number of jobs advertised (32) for the fewest number of positions (39) of any year. It is also noteworthy that all of these ads were for indirect personnel classified as skilled. Thus, there was no shortage of operators in 1980.

While the need for indirect personnel is responsible for the increase in the number of ads, the need for direct personnel is responsible for the explosion in the number of positions available. In 1983, positions advertised for indirect personnel were only 18 percent (48/273) of positions advertised for direct personnel. This high ratio of direct to indirect positions available varies little for all years thereafter, even for 1989, when the decline began. While the increase in jobs advertised and positions available in 1985 and 1987 reflects the maquiladora boom in the mid-eighties, the overwhelming demand for mainly unskilled production personnel is characteristic of the nature of the maquiladorization process. Most of the jobs advertised in this boom were for undifferentiated, low-level work, which has come to dominate the Nogales labor market.

Six of the ten transport-equipment plants where workers and managers were surveyed placed ads during the months sampled. These were plants identified in table 1.1 as C, F, H, I, and J—the larger assembly plants and the one manufacturing plant. Of all jobs advertised in this sample, 16 per-

Table 3.3 Changes over Time in Advertisement and Employment for
Direct and Indirect Workers, 1980–1989

	Jobs Advertised		Positions Available		Workers Employed	
Year	Direct	Indirect	Direct	Indirect	Direct	Indirect
1980	—	32	—	39	10,638	2,146
1983	7	32	273	48	10,461	2,287
1985	18	48	452	94	11,617	2,651
1987	20	87	557	108	13,365	3,223
1989	18	46	366	54	14,575	3,627

Source: La Voz del Norte and SECOFI in Nogales, Sonora.

cent were by plants in the transport-equipment sector. One-third of all jobs in the sample of ads were in the machine-assembly sector of maquiladoras, 17 percent in textiles, and 14 percent in other manufacturing.

There was also a clear seasonal variation in the placement of ads. January had the greatest number of positions available (34 percent or 731/2,137, in table 3.4). This supports the hypothesis guiding sample selection that January would be the time of year with the highest demand for labor. However, February had the fewest (18 percent or 373/2,137) positions available, indicating that the supply of labor is high at that time and that the problem caused by workers not returning after the Christmas break is solved more quickly than was hypothesized. By February, either new workers have been hired, or workers on the job before Christmas have come back. September and October had the same proportion of jobs advertised: approximately 24 percent.

January showed the highest number of positions available because, as is clear in table 3.4, it was the month with the greatest number of ads for unskilled production and skilled administrative personnel. Even though the proportion of positions advertised for unskilled production personnel was just as high in February and September as it was in January, a higher absolute number of unskilled production personnel was advertised for in January. On the other hand, positions available for skilled production and control personnel were more likely to appear in October than any other month sampled. Since the high number of ads appearing in January indicates the

Table 3.4   Seasonal Variations in the Demand for Labor in Nogales and Region, Selected Periods, 1980–1989

Type of Position Advertised	Jan.	Feb.	Sept.	Oct.	Total
Unskilled Production	626	333	433	336	1,728
Skilled Production	27	10	28	88	153
Skilled Administrative	54	21	29	48	152
Skilled Control	24	9	23	48	104
Total	731	373	513	520	2,137

Source: La Voz del Norte in Nogales, Sonora.

high turnover at this time of year, it is clear that this is mainly true for unskilled production personnel and not other types of jobs. Some of the more qualitative content of the ads also leads to the conclusion that companies expend great effort in January maintaining the unskilled productive sectors of their labor forces. For example, an ad for workers to do industrial sewing, which ran from January 2 to 11, 1985, included an invitation for all women workers already with the company to continue in their jobs.

Advertisements start to appear later in January than for other months, on the 15th day, on average; normally the first day a job is advertised is the 9th or 10th day, on average.[8] The years 1987 and 1989 are the ones in which ads appear latest in January, thus empirically reflecting the new form of regulation adopted in the industry around holidays. Jobs are probably advertised later in January than other months because management is expecting workers to return and therefore waits before placing ads. As noted at the beginning of this chapter, there has been an extralegal institutionalization of the custom of working Saturdays before Christmas, aimed at minimizing possible loss of production time from rotation, turnover, and absenteeism after the break. This may mean that everyone expects to take a holiday until mid-January, even though it legally ends long before that.

Another important characteristic of the Nogales labor market is the length of time it takes to fill a job, operationalized here by the number of days a job was advertised. The job with the longest average running time was dispatcher, with a mean of 12 days. The second-longest running time was for technicians, with a mean of 10 days, and the third-longest, operators, with a mean running time of more than 7 days. The length of time it took to fill a job also varied depending on the subsector of the maquiladora industry, with jobs in shoes and leather being advertised the longest (13 days on average), followed by jobs in textiles and transport-equipment (9 days each).

As indicated in table 3.1, only 8 dispatchers' jobs were advertised throughout the whole decade of the sample, so a more comprehensive picture of the labor market emerges by looking at the broader category of work in which dispatchers fall—skilled administrative personnel. In fact, as table 3.5 shows, ads for skilled administrative personnel have the lowest average for days run. Unskilled production jobs were advertised for the longest period, followed by skilled production jobs, and skilled control jobs. Since the largest difference in the means presented in table 3.5 is between

Table 3.5   Average Number of Days Advertisements Ran by Type of Maquiladora Job, as Advertised in Nogales and Region, Selected Periods, 1980–1990

Personnel	Days	N
Unskilled Production	8.23	1,728
Skilled Production	8.05	153
Skilled Administrative	5.45	152
Skilled Control	6.90	103
Total	7.95	2,136

Analysis of Variance	
Between Groups SS	1,192.86 (3 d.f.)
Within Groups SS	81,502.27 (2,132 d.f.)
Total SS	82,695.13 (2,135 d.f.)
Between Groups MS	397.62
Within Groups MS	38.23
F	10.40*
η^2	.01

Source: Data from *La Voz del Norte* in Nogales, Sonora.

*$p < 001$. d.f. = degrees of freedom.

unskilled production personnel and skilled administrative personnel, it is clear that administrators' jobs are easier to fill than workers' jobs.

If these broad occupational categories are compared to social classes, unskilled production personnel come closest to Poulantzas' conceptualization of the working class as those who produce surplus value but have no control over the labor process or other workers.[9] The generalization in the literature, based on studies of Hermosillo and other areas with more technologically sophisticated production, is that skilled production personnel are the most difficult to find in Mexico. This study shows that in other, more typical areas, like Nogales, it is working-class personnel who are most sought after by industry through newspaper advertising throughout the eighties.

Is the Labor Market a Free Market?

In the last resort it does not matter to capital whether it is employing men or women—capital is not sexist (nor racist, for that matter) though it does use sexism (and racism) to suit its purposes, which are the production of profits and the accumulation of private wealth. . . . They [the maquila industry] employed women because it was quite naturally assumed, in terms of sexual stereotypes in both the U.S. and Mexico, that women could be constrained within the work place to adapt themselves to the image of the 'ideal' worker that the industry wished to create, better and faster than men. Once the image of the 'ideal' maquila worker is institutionalized and accepted by the working class along the border, the need to employ women in preference to men diminishes, and the job opportunities for docile, undemanding, nimble-fingered, nonunion and unmilitant men open up. (Sklair, 1989: 172–173)

Although manager Jorge Tye's words, quoted at the beginning of this chapter, express a willingness to hire anyone coming to the factory door, we assume that there were more prerequisites for any job advertised than appeared in a newspaper ad, and that even those jobs without prerequisites listed would entail the applicant fulfilling certain requirements. Nevertheless, even with a measure that undoubtedly underestimates the number of requirements necessary to get a job, 73 percent of all positions available specified one or more prerequisites. The wide-ranging requirements included gender, marital status, age, professional qualifications, skill, education, experience, hours or shifts to be worked, immediate availability, applicant's community rootedness and/or mobility, bilingual linguistic ability, attitude, personal characteristics, recommendations, and legal qualifications.

Of the fifteen different prerequisites listed, the one most frequently attached to a position was gender (38.8 percent). A little more than two-thirds of all jobs specifying gender prefer women. This is followed by experience (24.4 percent), and almost half of the positions stipulating this prerequisite asked generally for "experience related to the job," while about one-fifth asked for a specific amount of time ranging from one to five years. Hours or shifts to be worked was the next most frequently listed prerequisite (22 percent), with one-third of those positions specifying three rotating shifts, and a little less than half specifying two rotating shifts. Other requirements regarding hours specified that the successful applicant would have to work a special shift, be available to work overtime, or be flexible in their hours.

The frequency with which other prerequisites appeared dropped substantially in comparison to those profiled above. Only 7.3 percent of all positions advertised required a particular skill, like knowledge of a certain production process or the ability to operate certain machinery. Almost 6 percent of all positions specified some age requirement, almost all of which set 18 years as a minimum age. The same proportion, almost 6 percent, specified that applicants had to start work immediately. A little over 5 percent of positions required bilingual personnel, and a quarter of these even specified that the applicant should be from 50 percent to 100 percent proficient in English. Just over 3 per cent of all positions required the applicant to have a certain attitude or personal characteristic, such as being self-motivated, honest, desiring to improve, good or excellent appearance, responsible, or dynamic. About the same number of positions (2.3 percent) wanted applicants who were settled in the Nogales community, or, alternatively, could commute to other nearby locations. Less than 1 percent of all positions specified legal or professional qualifications, letters of recommendation, or marital status as prerequisites for employment.

These requirements can be interpreted in terms of at least two conceptual frameworks explaining how people end up with the jobs they do. The human capital model assumes that labor-force participants freely compete for jobs in one open labor market and would consider the most important variables determining occupational attainment to be professional and legal qualifications, skill, education, experience, language ability, and recommendations. Labor-market segmentation, dual economy, and job competition models are much more likely to argue that the labor market is not so free or open, but is structured by factors over which individual job seekers have much less control, such as gender, marital status, age, hours or shifts to be worked, whether or not one can be ready to work immediately, and community rootedness or mobility (Bustamante, 1979).

The fact that gender, an ascriptive characteristic, tops the list of prerequisites at 38.8 percent and is so far above achieved characteristics such as skill (7.3 percent) and education (1.5 percent) supports the idea that those who place the ads use gender to structure the labor market, and that gender is more important in affecting occupational attainment than the other variables considered by the human-capital model. Experience, a human capital indicator, is also very important—it was the second-most frequently listed prerequisite; however, there is a negative correlation of 0.3 between gender and experience. Less than 7 percent of the positions advertised that had a gender requirement asked that the applicant also have experience. There are also some interesting relationships between gender and hours/shifts available, with jobs where women were preferred being much more likely to specify the shifts available (31 percent versus 19 percent).

These patterns observed among the prerequisites warrant further investigation in order to empirically test the hypothesis that the prerequisites fall into two groups, based on the human-capital and segmentation theories of occupational attainment. The high frequency with which gender is specified as a requirement (which is a preference for women two-thirds of the time) and its interaction with other prerequisites is especially intriguing because some observers, like Sklair, cited above, have suggested that the sex of workers is irrelevant to capital.

To test the hypothesis that prerequisites were interrelated with each other so as to constitute two categories based on human-capital and structural-segmentation models, we used a well-known classification technique called cluster analysis.[10] The question addressed by clustering the prerequisites is which of them tend to appear together, attached to the same position, considering the way in which they co-vary in the sample as a whole. Cluster analysis begins by treating each prerequisite variable separately, and then links them together on the basis of their similarity, until they are all united in one group.

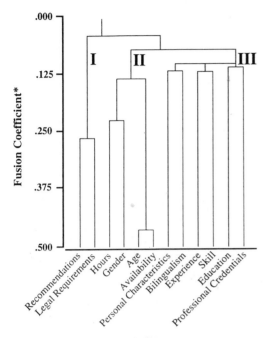

Figure 3.1   Single-Linkage Tree Diagram of Prerequisites in Maquiladora Job Advertisements, Nogales and Region, Selected Periods, 1980–1990. *Source:* Data collected from *La Voz del Norte* in Nogales, Sonora. *Analysis is based on a Jaccard similarity coefficient matrix (Sneath and Sokal, 1973).

The single-linkage tree diagram in figure 3.1 lists the prerequisites across the horizontal axis at the bottom, with the vertical lines rising from it representing branches, and the horizontal lines between them indicating at what point they are joined. The shorter the vertical lines stemming from a prerequisite, the more similar are the elements joined in a branch, or the more likely they are to appear together. The tree diagram can be interpreted in terms of three clusters, which support the hypothesis that prerequisites are configured into human-capital and structural clusters, as well as yielding an unexpected cluster made up of the legal qualifications and letters of recommendation (indicated by cluster I in figure 3.1). The legal requirements observed were having a particular kind of passport, being recognized to carry out transactions with customs authorities, and no previous prison record. The second cluster (II) consists of hours to be worked, gender, age,

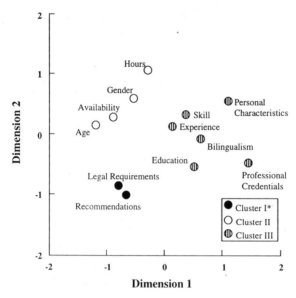

Figure 3.2   Multidimensional Scaling Scatterplot of Three-Cluster Solution for Maquiladora Job Prerequisites, Nogales and Region, Selected Periods, 1980–1990. *Source:* Data collected from *La Voz del Norte* in Nogales, Sonora. *Cluster membership refers to the three-cluster solution to the tree diagram in figure 3.1. Analysis is based on a Jaccard similarity coefficient matrix (Schiffman, Reynolds, and Young, 1981).

and immediate availability for work, and fits the structural conceptualization. It also contains some of the prerequisites that tend to most often occur together, particularly age and immediate availability for work. The third cluster (III) fits the human-capital conceptualization, containing experience, skill, personal attributes, language ability, education, and professional qualifications. Given that the vertical branches of this part of the tree are the longest, and do not come together until quite late in the clustering process, it is clear that these occur together less often than prerequisites in the other two clusters. This cluster solution is represented more clearly with a multi-dimensional scaling scatterplot (Sneath and Sokal, 1973; Schiffman et al., 1981) as shown in figure 3.2, where all three clusters clearly separate from each other.

Unfortunately, there were not enough observations for all prerequisites every year to test the exact process by which these constellations for employment requirements emerged over the decade. It is noteworthy that the prerequisites of age, immediate availability, recommendations, and legal requirements were not listed for any jobs in the first two years of observation (1980 and 1983), and that age, recommendations, and legal requirements were not listed for any jobs in the third year of observation (1985). Thus, the unexpected first cluster identified above, made up of recommendations and legal requirements, emerges only in the second half of the decade. The absence in 1980 and 1983 of the requirement for labor to be immediately available is congruent with the characterization of the decade as a boom that began with a recession.

Next, labor-market structure was mapped out in more detail by relating the clustered prerequisites to type of job and subsector within the maquiladora industry. To assess how prerequisites from the three clusters might be differentially related to various types of jobs, each of the three types of requirements was summed for every position advertised, and then averaged by broad job type. Table 3.6 indicates that unskilled production jobs were different from all others in that they asked applicants for significantly fewer human-capital requirements and significantly more structural requirements than skilled production, administrative, and control jobs. Table 3.7 shows that subsectors of the maquiladora industry were inversely related with regard to the structural and human-capital prerequisites for work. Jobs in transport-equipment, electrical, and other manufacturing subsectors asked for more structural prerequisites than jobs in textiles and sporting goods, which in turn asked for more structural prerequisites than jobs making furniture, shoes, and other leather goods. On the other hand, the furniture, textiles and 'other' manufacturing subsectors asked for more human-capital prerequisites than manufacturers of shoes and leather, transport equipment, sporting, and electrical goods.

Job type has a stronger effect on the level of structural prerequisites than subsector of industry, but there is an interaction between job type and subsector as they influence structural prerequisites. For example, if a company in the transport-equipment sector advertised a skilled control job, then the structural prerequisites were high. In all other subsectors, however, skilled control positions were associated with relatively few structural prerequisites. Job type also has a stronger effect on human-capital prerequisites than subsector, and there is an interaction between the two here as well. While skilled control jobs asked for the highest number of human-capital prereq-

Table 3.6   Average Number of Prerequisites by Type of Maquiladora Job and Type of Prerequisite, as Advertised in Nogales and Region, Selected Periods, 1980–1990

Personnel	Structural	Human Capital	Good Past Behavior	N
Unskilled Production	.823	.275	.002	1,728
Skilled Production	.196	.719	.007	153
Skilled Administrative	.605	1.099	.132	152
Skilled Control	.087	1.000	.029	104

Analysis of Variance

Between Groups SS	103.94 (3 d.f.)	154.26 (3 d.f.)	2.37 (3 d.f.)	
Within Groups SS	1,388.47 (2,133 d.f.)	884.87 (2,133 d.f.)	32.27 (2,133 d.f.)	
Total SS	1,492.41 (2,136 d.f.)	1,039.13 (2,136 d.f.)	39.64 (2,136 d.f.)	
Between Groups MS	34.65	51.42	.79	
Within Groups MS	.65	.42	.02	
F	53.22*	123.95*	45.16*	
η^2	.07	.15	.06	

Source: Data from *La Voz del Norte* in Nogales, Sonora.

*$p < 001$. d.f. = degrees of freedom.

uisites, this was not equally true in all subsectors of maquiladora industries, especially transport equipment, which had fewer human-capital prerequisites than any other subsector.

Job Incentives as Indicators of Social and Economic Disadvantage

All maquiladora workers are entitled to certain benefits under federal labor law, although as the previous chapter indicated, plants have signed contracts with unions that often set lower labor standards. Companies stress their distribution of legally required benefits in advertisements because not all companies, in fact, dispense them. Until a maquiladora has officially registered with the government, it can get away with not paying taxes or benefits to workers. Failure to register is more frequent with smaller maquiladoras or those located in rural regions away from the immediate border.

Workers may be too intimidated or too poorly informed to insist that they receive their benefits. Once a maquiladora is officially registered with the government, it must enroll its full-time workers with the *Instituto Méxicano del Seguro Social* (IMSS). It must pay all of the subscription costs for workers earning the minimum wage, and half for those earning more. Even maquiladoras that are officially registered usually wait a month or more

Table 3.7   Average Number of Prerequisites by Subsector of Industry and Type of Prerequisite, as Advertised in Nogales and Region, Selected Periods, 1980–1990

Subsector	Structural	Human Capital	Good Past Behavior
Textiles	.55	.68	.00
Shoes and Other Leather	.01	.51	.00
Furniture	.24	2.30	.00
Transport Equipment	1.07	.29	.01
Sporting Goods	.57	.29	.01
Electrical	.84	.18	.04
Other Maquila Mfg.	1.51	.29	.02
Total	.73	.39	.01

Analysis of Variance

Between Groups SS	380.05 (6 d.f.)	114.33 (6 d.f.)	—
Within Groups SS	1,095.03 (2,056 d.f.)	862.28 (2,056 d.f.)	—
Total SS	1,475.08 (2,062 d.f.)	976.61 (2,062 d.f.)	—
Between Groups MS	63.34	19.06	—
Within Groups MS	.53	.42	—
F	118.93*	45.43*	—
η^2	.26	.12	—

Source: Data from *La Voz del Norte* in Nogales, Sonora.

*$p < 001$. d.f. = degrees of freedom.

before enrolling an employee with the IMSS. Workers earning above the minimum wage pay the other half of IMSS costs. The actual coverage costs vary according to the wages earned, and the health and safety dangers inherent in the job, with better-paid, more dangerous jobs having higher IMSS rates.

According to federal labor law at the time these data were collected, all full-time maquila workers should have been insured for treatment of work accidents and illness contracted from job conditions. Pregnant employees were legally allowed six weeks' leave before and after their delivery and were guaranteed their jobs back after this period, with two half-hour breaks for breast feeding once they returned to work. For every full week worked (i.e., forty-eight hours in six days), employees were guaranteed at least one day off with pay, and if they worked the seventh day, employees were entitled to extra remuneration. If the seventh day's holiday was not a Sunday, the worker was to get paid 25 percent extra. A worker could be legally required to work up to three hours' overtime, three times a week, at double the usual rate. If overtime exceeded three hours for each of three days, the worker was to be paid three times the regular wage. After one year, a worker was entitled to six days' paid vacation at 125 percent of his/her wage; after the second year, eight days at 125 percent; after the third year, ten days at 125 percent, with increments following seniority. Workers with one year's seniority were also entitled under law to a Christmas bonus to be paid before the twentieth of December, equivalent to 15 days' wages. If a worker had put in less than one year, he or she was entitled to whatever proportion of the Christmas bonus their seniority represented.

Incentives for maquiladora jobs appeared far less often in *La Voz del Norte* than did job requirements. Only 41 percent of all advertised positions listed at least one incentive, whereas almost 75 percent of all positions specified prerequisites. A total of twenty different incentives were observed for the positions advertised, which when ranked from the highest frequency to the lowest included benefits additional to those required by law (24 percent), subsidized cafeteria (13 percent), free or subsidized transportation (13 percent), minimum professional salary (9 percent), production bonus (9 percent), wages above the minimum required by law (9 percent), salary according to aptitude (5 percent), good work environment (3 percent), attendance bonus (3 percent), opportunities for upward mobility (3 percent), free medical consultation (2 percent), social, religious, or sports events (2 percent), permanent contract (2 percent), assistance with buying furniture (1 percent), and life insurance (0.1 percent).[11] Although only listed for one job each and not even one-tenth of a percentage point, personal loans and "benefits according to federal labor law" were also observed as incentives.

To test for relationships among the incentives, a cluster analysis was performed on those which appeared often enough to have a substantial presence.[12] As the tree diagram in figure 3.3 indicates, two clusters emerged. One contained assistance with buying furniture, possibilities for advancement within the company, salary according to aptitude, benefits in addition to those required by law, and excellent working conditions. The other contained minimum professional wages, the production bonus, transportation bonus, subsidized cafeteria, and the attendance bonus. The incentive "wages above the minimum" did not cluster with either of the other two groups. The jobs with this last incentive were almost all unskilled production jobs.

As discussed previously, the vast majority of jobs advertised were characteristic of a secondary-labor market, which Rubery (1987: 80) says "is an extensive hierarchy of jobs and of productivities of workers that are rewarded at a relatively homogeneous and low pay level. The factor that workers most have in common in this sector is social and economic disadvantage." The first cluster contains food and transportation incentives, which appear with productivity, attendance, and the minimum professional salary, and links workers' output directly to their social and economic disadvantage. It was hypothesized that this cluster of incentives would be more related to unskilled production jobs than other jobs. The second cluster contains incentives (furniture, benefits additional to the legal ones, open salary, opportunities to move up, etc.) that are not as necessary for survival, and in Nogales might be considered perquisites.

They are clearly aimed at maintaining the employee through better pay and promotion. It was hypothesized that incentives in this second cluster would not be offered for unskilled production jobs as often as they would be for other, more-skilled types of jobs.

These hypotheses were supported, as the bar graph in figure 3.4 shows. Unskilled production jobs had significantly fewer incentives from the second cluster than skilled production and administrative jobs. On the other

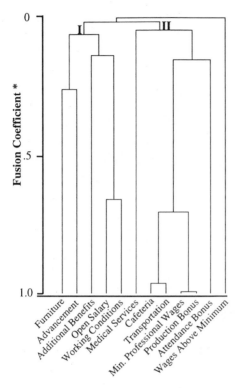

Figure 3.3   Average-Linkage Tree Diagram of Incentives in Maquiladora Job
Advertisements, Nogales and Region, Selected Periods, 1980–1990. *Source:* Data
collected from *La Voz del Norte* in Nogales, Sonora. *Analysis is based on a
Jaccard similarity coefficent matrix (Sneath and Sokal, 1973).

hand, unskilled production jobs had significantly more incentives from the
first cluster than all other kinds of jobs. As noted above, when "wages
above the minimum" were offered as an incentive, it was almost always for
unskilled production jobs.

These findings from the analysis of incentives have reinforced dimensions of labor-market segmentation already identified as primary and secondary sectors. Sinclair (1991: 8) argues that "In a context of deskilling and
the 'homogenization' of workers, the separation of the labor market into a
hierarchical primary sector, within which workers are provided with incentives, and an unstable secondary sector, is said to be functional to capitalism. . . . [S]uch divisions prevent workers from uniting to strengthen their

bargaining position." In Nogales, where the industrial labor force is being constituted for the first time in this population's history, both primary and secondary sectors were offered incentives, but of different kinds.

To reflect the different kinds of incentives, the cluster made up of subsidized cafeteria, transportation, minimum professional wages, medical services, and the production and attendance bonuses, which were found to be associated with unskilled production jobs, is called secondary. The other cluster of incentives, made up of open salary, excellent working conditions, benefits additional to the law, upward mobility, and assistance with furniture, which were found to be associated less often with unskilled jobs than skilled ones, is called primary. While Nogales maquiladoras try to use incentives to attract and keep personnel in all types of jobs, incentives associated more with skilled jobs (including production, administrative, and control personnel) allow for the creation of a more privileged group that is employed with greater security.

Primary incentives appeared to be a more permanent force shaping the labor market in comparison to secondary incentives. Primary incentives

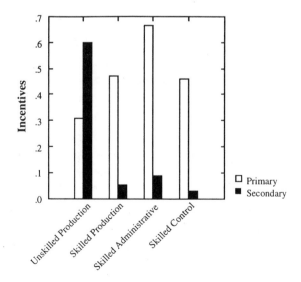

Figure 3.4   Primary and Secondary Labor-Market Incentives by Type of Maquiladora Job Advertised. *Source:* Data collected from *La Voz del Norte* in Nogales, Sonora.

were advertised for jobs in each of the six years in the decade for which data were collected. No secondary incentives were observed at the beginning of the decade (1980) or at its end (1990), when maquiladora industries were in relative decline. Secondary labor-market incentives were highest in 1985 and 1987, at the height of the boom.

The months in which particular kinds of incentives appeared are congruent with the findings reported above on the seasonal variation in the demand for labor. While there were more incentives advertised in January than any other month, primary labor-market incentives were found to appear less often in January, while secondary labor-market incentives appeared more often in January than other months. The incentive "wages above the minimum," which did not cluster with either primary or secondary incentives but was almost always offered with unskilled production jobs, appeared twice as often in January as in other months. This confirms that the high turnover in January is mainly due to the absence of personnel in unskilled jobs.

Gender Segmentation in the Labor Market

The boom in Nogales maquiladora industries during the eighties has meant an explosion in the demand for labor, most notably in unskilled production. Workers were recruited into unskilled production jobs on the basis of ascribed characteristics, such as age and gender, and into skilled jobs on the basis of achieved characteristics such as experience and education. Also used to structure the labor market were incentives such as open salary scales, opportunities for upward mobility, and excellent working conditions, offered in order to create a small primary-labor market. A larger secondary-labor market was built with such incentives as minimum professional wages, production and attendance bonuses, and subsidized cafeteria and transportation.

While cluster-analysis techniques outline the structure of the labor market in terms of the coherence between types of requirements and incentives carried by different jobs, it is important not to obscure the fact that one of the most important dynamics was one of the structural criteria: gender. As Milkman (1987: 5) has argued, sex segregation should not be seen as just one of many divisions among workers. This section examines the relationships between the preference for hiring women and other variables.

It is clear that if "in the last resort it does not matter to capital whether it is employing men or women," as Sklair (1989: 172) argued, capital in Nogales has certainly not reached "the last resort." The fact that almost 40 percent of jobs advertised stated a gender preference indicates that it *does* matter to Nogales capital. This call by capital for women workers is lower than their actual rate of participation in the Nogales labor force. In 1987, Nogales, Sonora, was second from the lowest in the ratio of men to women employed among direct workers at 44/56. The lowest ratios of all locations were other, smaller towns in Sonora, which had a ratio of 49 men to 51 women (Sareigo Rodríguez, 1990: 21). If the level of women employed in other maquiladora centers continues to decline, moving closer to Nogales rates, future research should investigate whether the opportunities for them will be limited in the same way as women's opportunities are limited by the Nogales labor market.

Jobs for which women are required were not spread randomly throughout the job hierarchy. Table 3.8 shows gender prerequisites listed for the positions available in broad job categories. A glance at the total column on the right indicates that 64 percent (535/830) of the times that gender was specified as a prerequisite for a job, the gender preferred was women. None of these jobs which management would prefer to be filled by women are in the skilled production or control categories, but almost 89 percent (475/535) are unskilled production personnel. As the few job titles named above for unskilled production personnel indicated, the term "feminine personnel" was used synonymously with unskilled production personnel. It is not uncommon in any maquiladora center to see this phrase on "Help Wanted" signs placed in front of factories. Perhaps Nogales is more similar to other locations with respect to the gender of unskilled workers than previously believed. Carrillo (1991a) found that women were preferred as operators and men as technicians in the month of ads he collected from Juárez. The Tijuana ads called for both men and women operators.

The remainder of the positions in which females are preferred is in the skilled administrative category, of which 40 of 60 positions were secretarial. These jobs were also the ones where candidates' personal characteristics were specified most often. More than two-thirds of the ads that specified particular personal characteristics required women with good or excellent appearance for secretarial positions. Besides having to be physically attractive, women applying for secretarial positions were to be responsible,

Table 3.8   Gender Prerequisites of Positions Available in Nogales and Region by Job Type

	Job Categories				
	Unskilled Production	Skilled Production	Skilled Admin.	Skilled Control	Total
Gender Not Specified	976	143	88	100	1,307
Women	475	0	60	0	535
Men	0	4	0	0	4
Both, Either/Or	277	6	4	4	291
Total	1,728	153	152	104	2,137

Source: La Voz del Norte in Nogales, Sonora.

honest, and perseverant. Interestingly enough, they were never required to have prerequisites from the third cluster, described above as "good past behavior," which included letters of recommendation, legal recognition by customs authorities, and no previous prison record. Thus, skilled female administrative personnel (i.e., secretaries) provide a kind of security for their employers that is perceived to depend more on their personality and other ascribed characteristics than for male personnel who carry out similar tasks (e.g., security guards) and are required to exhibit more achieved kinds of prerequisites.

If unskilled production jobs are equated with a secondary sector of the labor market, and other skilled jobs are seen to form a primary sector, it is clear that gender segmentation exists within both sectors. This conclusion is based on the kinds of job advertisements that specifically asked for women as shown in table 3.8. When women were called into this labor market, most of them were intended to fill the least-skilled and lowest-paying jobs, with a very small niche also available in skilled clerical jobs. However, clerical work may not fit very well into the primary/secondary split of dual labor-market theory (Walby, 1988: 19). It has been classified in this study as skilled administrative personnel, a category that also includes assistants, security guards, and dispatchers. If secretaries are not included in the secondary sector, then the small niche observed for women becomes almost invisible (20/2,137 jobs).

Some evidence suggests that this segmentation may be attached to an incipient wage gap between male and female unskilled workers. "Wages above the minimum" were offered as an incentive for some jobs in unskilled production, but unskilled production jobs that preferred women were significantly less likely to offer "wages above the minimum" as an incentive than unskilled production jobs that did not prefer women.

Gender segmentation can be further delineated by the interaction of the gender prerequisite with other prerequisites such as requirements for personal characteristics and hours. Jobs for which women were explicitly preferred were limited to the day and afternoon shifts, and were not the same jobs that required applicants to work all three shifts, or work a special shift. The limitation of hours for women workers may represent management's acknowledgment of the connection between women's work in and outside of the home.

Unskilled production jobs that prefer women have significantly fewer human-capital prerequisites and secondary incentives than unskilled production jobs that do not prefer women. While different subsectors within maquila industries varied in their preference for women workers, textiles was not the only subsector which preferred them, as might be expected. Of all jobs specifying a preference for women, 40 percent were in fact in textiles, but 29 percent were in the assembly of sports machinery, equipment, and articles, and another 20 percent fell into the "other manufacturing" category within maquiladoras.

Conclusion

Managers in Nogales transport-equipment and electronics plants indicate that there are important differences in the way a maquila can approach the formation of its labor force, especially at the managerial and administrative levels. Mexican managers and administrative personnel are highly visible in Nogales maquilas, unlike the early days when few rose above the level of supervisor. However, if the nationality of people holding the best maquila jobs is assumed to be indicative of the new maquila (George, 1990: 224), then Nogales firms do not fit this model either. Even in Plant H, where every U.S. manager had a Mexican deputy, and where the general manager stated that the plant would be much better off with 100 percent Mexican managers, I observed technicians from the United States operating machinery that had come from the head office. I observed more heterogeneity in the makeup of administrative and managerial personnel than dualism.

Alternative management styles are often framed in terms of cultural differences between "international" and Mexican approaches. These approaches echo assumptions from modernization theory that traditional cultures are impediments to development. One of the managerial leaders of this community believes that the more personal style of Mexican managers and the way they recognize status prevents them from being effective at the upper ranks of the corporation, which are usually located in the United States and governed by more impersonal, individualistic norms associated with the Anglo culture. The preference for Anglo normative orientations is institutionalized in the Nogales Maquiladora Association, which is structured with a U.S. national as the most prominent leader and a Mexican national as the second in command.

Although the managerial leader who named his preferred management style "international" was no longer president of the maquila association, he was highly respected and followed by many other managers I interviewed. On the other hand, there is evidence on a more general level that recognition of and adaptation to difference is growing, as opposed to the assimilation assumed necessary by modernization theory. In the *Academy of Management Executive,* DeForest (1994: 34) explains how the expectations of employers' responsibilities toward workers developed historically in Mexico and advises that "Americans respect the employer's admittedly paternalistic social obligation."

While the subjective understanding of these relationships may be articulated in cultural terms, the analysis of ads makes visible a tentative outline of a labor market with a particularly identifiable structure. The dimensions of this outline will be traced here in conclusion, as well as being compared in later chapters with information about the workers who really get hired. The job advertised most often was that of unskilled production operator. Among the small proportion of skilled jobs, many required great specialization, while the majority of unskilled jobs were quite simply described. In the eighties, unskilled workers were the hardest for companies to find, perhaps because the demand for them was so high.

The dual-technology thesis, that more technologically sophisticated maquilas which prefer to hire men are becoming the norm, is not supported by the findings reported in this chapter. The skilled jobs that would be necessary to work with advanced technology are a very small proportion in comparison to the number of unskilled jobs. There is a small (one-fifth) primary sector of the labor market, with a much larger (four-fifths) secondary sector, both of which can be defined in terms of job requirements and incentives. Both of these sectors are segmented by gender, with a preference for females in a significant proportion of jobs.

The call for workers extended past Nogales to Magdalena, Agua Prieta, and Imuris. Plants have adjusted to high absenteeism after Christmas by getting their employees to work overtime before the holiday, increasing their ads in January, and finally, waiting for their people to return. By the end of the decade, however, much of the demand had tapered off, and post-holiday absenteeism, which occurs when the weather can be very cold, is not as great a problem.

The Nogales labor market channels most of the women it seeks into jobs that are low waged and considered low skilled. This is similar to the situation in the early maquilas, except that women workers sought in Nogales ads were not often required to be single. Marital status was not listed as a prerequisite in many ads. Tiano's (1994: 92) managerial respondents in the Mexicali electronics and clothing sectors had also changed their preferences from younger to older women between the early eighties and 1990.

The larger context outside the factory supports gender inequality and plays a role in labor-market construction by allowing the institutionalization of selective recruiting practices. The Mexican state shares the responsibility for permitting job advertisement by gender with the private sector that places the ads. The province of Ontario in Canada, where two of the transport-equipment plants studied originated, made it illegal in 1970 to place job advertisements in newspapers that stated a gender preference. The goal of Ontario's Women's Equal Opportunities Act was to reduce gender segmentation created in the labor market, since it was identified as an important cause of gender inequality in the workplace (MacFarlane, Kopinak, and Dewdney, 1971). It has been transplanted to Mexico, however, in a form that reinforces systemic gender inequality there.

This chapter contains analyses of data from two sources: in-depth interviews with transport-equipment and electronics plant managers in 1991, and a survey of all maquiladora job advertisements throughout the eighties. Leaders of maquila associations throughout Sonora are quoted as spokespersons for the whole industry. The ads also cover the entire maquila industry but do not include the service part of the Nogales economy. Less than one-fifth of the ads sampled were from the transport-equipment sector, but great differences were not detected between maquila sectors.

four

ON THE HOME FRONT: WORKERS, HOUSEHOLDS, AND COMMUNITY

E. P. Thompson (1965: 9) insisted on using the word "making" in the title of his book *The Making of the English Working Class* in order to emphasize that class formation is "an active process which owes as much to agency as to conditioning. The working class did not rise like the sun at an appointed time. It was present at its own making." Thompson warns that classes never arise in exactly the same way in different times and places. We cannot assume that the making of the Mexican working class is the same as the making of the English working class. However, commentators such as Valle Baeza (1992) have made some useful comparisons, having observed that by 1980, the proportion of people working for a wage in Mexico had grown to 60 percent.

Because communities like Nogales were much less developed before the maquiladora industry, it is often mistakenly assumed that the industry created them. The previous chapter looked at the role of managers as active agents in the formation of the Nogales-area labor market. This chapter focuses on workers, who are much more numerous and central in the industrial process. Managers favoring an "international" style viewed Mexican workers' tendency to fuse work and personal life as problematic.

As this chapter shows, workers often came to Nogales primarily to find paid work to help support their families. In bringing industrial capitalism to northern Sonora and other border locations, maquiladoras have enlarged the public sphere workplace that values individualism. Workers have the legal right to sell their labor to the employer of their choice. In contrast, the relevant economic unit in the agricultural economy from which most workers came is the household. In this private sphere, workers pool incomes and redistribute them according to prevailing norms regarding age and gender. In most developing societies, survival of the majority depends on the interdependence of roles within the family. For example, let us look at how one worker links her participation in the labor force to her family responsibilities.

As she answered a question about how much seniority she had, Lupe, a nineteen-year-old maquila worker from Guasave, told us a great deal about her background.[1] Located just north of Sinaloa's capital, Culiacán, Guasave anchors one of the three largest agricultural valleys in that state. Together, these three valleys grow most of the produce that is exported to the United States through Nogales. Although Lupe was born in nearby Orange Station, she had always lived in Guasave because her family could not make a living in Orange Station. In the mid-eighties, mechanized technology was introduced in agriculture, and many of the people who had previously worked in farming lost their jobs. While some still work in fishing and farming around Guasave, many have migrated to Nogales or Tijuana to look for work.

When Lupe finished her six years in primary school, she needed money but could not find regular employment. At sixteen, after working mainly around the house, she decided to come to Nogales with women friends to find work. Guasave is at least 16 hours away by bus, but the trip is often longer because there are many stops along the way.

Lupe was hired as an operator in Plant F. She was settling in, but she knew that other members of her family back home were still having a difficult time. After nine months of work, she asked the plant for permission for a leave of absence so that she could go home and help her family. When the plant refused, she quit and returned to Guasave to help her younger brother collect his things and move to Nogales with her. He sells souvenirs in one of the many tourist shops that line the border, but his pay is not secure because he earns only a commission on what he sells.

When the two returned to Nogales, Lupe was again hired as an operator at Plant F. She worked steadily for another year, and again asked for a leave of absence, this time to go home for her mother, who was in her late forties. Once again denied a leave, she quit in order to go home and help her mother move back to Nogales with her.

On their return, she got her old job at Plant F back. When we met her, she had been working steadily there for a year and two months. In all of the time she had worked at Plant F, she had done the same job, putting circuits into connectors on the assembly line. She liked this job, but she wanted to be able to earn more money, since hers was the main income supporting

herself, her brother, and mother. Her total weekly income, including bonuses, was 98,000 old pesos (U.S. $33.00).[2] At the time of the interview,
her brother's earnings were poor, because rumors that Operation Desert
Storm might close the border made tourists afraid to cross. The three of
them lived together in a small, one-bedroom dwelling, which they rented
for 100,000 old pesos (U.S. $25) a month.

Lupe wished she could get the regular seniority bonus—usually increased at her plant every three months. However, she had twice lost all of
her seniority when she had had to quit to bring family members from
Guasave. Even if the plant recognized her previous seniority, it would no
longer matter, because with the Persian Gulf crisis, they had frozen seniority bonuses.

Lupe is like many Mexican workers who have led their families northward in search of work, and whose progress on the job has been influenced
both by company policy and by the composition of their families and the
economic situation at home. A better understanding of their situation can be
found in answers to the following questions: Who are the people who get
the maquila jobs advertised in the newspaper? Where did they come from,
and why? Who else do they live with in Nogales and Imuris, and under
what conditions? Are they likely to move elsewhere in the future?

Nogales-Area Maquila Workers: A Demographic Profile

Nogales maquila workers were found to be the same age as maquila workers studied previously, but they tended to be younger than the city's population at large. While 66 percent of maquila workers were between the ages
of 15 and 23 years, only 23 percent of the general Nogales population was
between 15 and 24 years old. It is likely that people in this age group were
over-represented in the maquiladora labor force because, like Lupe, they
were working to help support younger and older family members with less
earning power.

The average age of a Nogales maquila worker was 22.8 years; half of
them were 21 or younger. However, in using average and median ages,
there is a danger that the statistics will gloss over the exact distribution
across different age groups. In fact, one-third of transport-equipment workers were very young—between 15 and 19 years old. According to Articles
173 and 174 of Mexico's federal labor law, it is illegal to hire anyone under

18 years of age. However, minors from 14 to 18 can be hired with the written permission of parents or guardians. In the early days of the BIP, minors were hired in maquilas only during school vacation periods, but hiring minors soon became common year-round.

The young age of transport-equipment workers is an important characteristic of the labor force. Young workers are likely to be quite flexible in adapting to work processes, a highly prized characteristic in the new paradigm. For the individual worker, it often means that education has been curtailed by the need to seek paid employment. Orantes Gálvez (1987) found that young Nogales maquiladora workers often studied at night, but sometimes only two hours every third day. This would make it difficult to build up what we have called "human capital" in the last chapter, leaving them little competitive edge in the labor market.

More than half the transport-equipment workers (58 percent) had achieved educational levels higher than primary school. Primary school in Mexico is equivalent to the first six grades of elementary school in the United States. However, 9 percent reported that they did not have any schooling or did not complete primary school. Comparative rates available for the general Nogales community show that for those six years old or more, 5 percent were illiterate and 43 percent had some secondary (junior high in the United States) or more. Although transport-equipment workers appeared to be better educated than the general Nogales population, it should not be overlooked that 9 percent had enough formal education to be only half literate.

Younger workers tended to be better educated than older workers. Although there was no association between gender and education within either the labor force or the general community, a small but interesting difference was observed among workers when marital status was also considered. Unpartnered women had more education than unpartnered men, but among the partnered, the opposite was true.

Youth can be a source of vulnerability for workers, especially when they are living far away from their families. A 16-year-old male worker interviewed at Plant B when the day shift ended said he had migrated to Nogales from Navojoa, in the south of Sonora, because of the difficulty of getting a job there. He lived in a rented room in the dormitories operated by the shelter company for 44,000 old pesos a month (U.S. $14.66), and he sent money home to his family so that his younger siblings could attend school.

He sounded rather homesick when he said, "What I miss about my home-town are the sunrises and the smell of green grass and the flour tortillas my Mom would make for me. I am sometimes scared when I see other workers all drugged up on marijuana. I now see that living at the border can be dangerous, but the good thing is that my mother gave me good advice, telling me that I shouldn't go around doing things like smoking dope." There is very little, if any, green grass in Nogales, because of its desert geography. Its location between two hills means that the sunrise is only visible after the morning shift in the windowless factories has begun. Workers were sometimes observed smoking marijuana when they came out of the plants at the end of shift, which is what the worker quoted above was pointing out to the interviewer. It was obvious that his "hometown" had a very different daily schedule than the one he followed in Nogales.

A large majority of the workers surveyed were not married. Over two-thirds of workers had an unpartnered marital status—single, widowed, separated, or divorced. Important turning points occurred at ages 21 and 30. Those younger than 21 were unpartnered more than expected by chance; those over 30 were partnered more often than expected. The older workers were more likely to have children; no one under 18 had children. Workers tended to be unpartnered more often than the general Nogales population, in which only half of all persons over 12 years were unpartnered; this rate was the same for both men and women. Women workers (74 percent) were more likely than men workers (65 percent) to be unpartnered.

Most workers' entrance into the labor market coincided with their first maquila job. Workers were asked if they had done anything to help cover family costs in the month before their first maquila job. Almost two-thirds said that they had not; a little less than half did housework, and more than a third studied. The remainder of those who were not contributing to family expenses before their first maquila job reported being unemployed, but in the formal labor market.

Workers at Home

The picture of workers as individuals is hardly sketched when the effects of their membership in groups such as households become important in understanding their situations.[3] Workers' households ranged in size from one to 13, with an average of 4.5 persons per household. When compared with the size of households in the general Nogales community, this is between the average number of people per household in the middle (4.6) and upper (4.3) socioeconomic strata. Over a third of transport-equipment workers lived in small households of three people or less, and cumulatively, 72 percent lived in households of five or fewer people.

It is important to distinguish between household and family. People who are not kin may live in the same household. Table 4.1 shows how often men and women workers headed their households, and when they were not heads, their relationship to the head. Most workers were either heads of households (87) or the children of heads of households (75); together, people in these two roles constituted 75 percent of the workers interviewed. On the other hand, almost 7 percent of workers (15) reported that they were not related to the head of the household. If we assume that the heads of households were related to the people they lived with, then most of the workers' households were families.[4]

The formation of workers' families is related to the type of employment available to them. If the dual-technology thesis were to be supported, then the male workers in the transport-equipment labor force would be expected to have skilled jobs that allow them to earn higher wages than their female coworkers. Women's lesser wage-earning ability would designate them as supplementary wage earners within the household.

This kind of household has been named the family consumer economy, and is based on men earning a wage that will support the family, and women's decreasing participation in the labor force (Tilly and Scott, 1978). If men can earn a family wage, families may decide to send only their male members to work outside the home. Women specialize in unpaid work in the home that supports men's work—they feed and clothe the family and create an environment in which male workers can rest in order to go back to work.

However, as Heyman (1991) points out in his study of Agua Prieta, the family consumer economy, modeled on industrial development in Europe, may be impossible in this situation given low Mexican wages and pricing of U.S. consumer goods in dollars. The decline in real wages was a very important reality in Nogales throughout the eighties and will be examined in more detail in chapter 6. The maquila-worker household typical of places like Agua Prieta and Nogales may be closer to the family wage economy, in which most workers are children of the head of the household (especially

Table 4.1   Gender of Respondent by Head of Household, or Family
Relationship to Head of Household

Sex of Respondent	Relation to Head of Household						
	Head	Spouse	Child	Sibling	Other Relative	Not Related	Total
Female	22	14	39	6	5	4	90
Male	65	0	36	9	3	11	124
Total	87	14	75	15	8	15	214

Source: Survey of workers in Nogales and Imuris, Sonora, 1991.

female children) who contribute part of their income to the household. "A
family consumer economy lacking a historical basis in rising adult male
wages . . . simply pushes 'working children' harder" (Heyman, 1991: 176).

Heyman (1991: 171) found the families he studied in Agua Prieta were
an amalgamation of the family-wage/consumer-economy models. The majority of male maquiladora employees in his 1986 survey were the sole
financial supporters of their households, and men had greater access to
maquila jobs like supervisor and mechanic, which paid more than the minimum wage. He identified two types of workers in households he studied:
female working children, and married males who usually headed their
households and were the only source of wages. Since Nogales and Agua
Prieta are in such close geographic proximity and—as the ads analyzed in
chapter 2 showed—have overlapping labor markets, we might expect the
same findings in Nogales.

However, Heyman's findings were not entirely replicated in this study.
The analysis of maquila ads in the previous chapter confirms the greater
access for men to better jobs, which Heyman found. But the primary sector that was discovered was very small. Chapter 5 reveals that the numbers
of technicians, who are better paid than operators, decreased in Nogales
transport-equipment maquilas during the decade of the eighties. This makes
it difficult for the average male head of household to earn higher wages,
since better jobs are not that plentiful.

The two main types of workers in Agua Prieta, female working children
and married males who headed their households and were the only source
of wages, constituted only 26 percent of workers interviewed in Nogales.

Both men and women workers who headed their households in the Nogales area earned the same as workers in any other family role, except workers who were sons of the head of household. They tended to earn less than other working family members. Workers who headed their households were more likely to be the sole wage earner, regardless of whether they were men (40 percent) or women (43 percent), than workers who were spouses, sons, or daughters in the household. While the finding that sons earn less than heads of households increases working daughters' importance in the household by comparison, table 4.1 shows that male and female workers were equally likely to be children of the head of their household. This differs from Heyman's finding that male children were less likely than female children to be direct workers in maquilas.

Table 4.1 shows that 75 percent of all heads of households are male. This is higher than the 1979 rate of male headship of maquila households in Juárez reported by Staudt (1986) but is consistent with the fact that Nogales has a lower proportion of women in the maquiladora labor force than Juárez. Part of the explanation for the over-representation of men as heads of households can be found in the presence of 15 male single-person households where the respondent had by definition to be the head. There are good reasons to assume that most of the 14 wives could potentially have shared the headship of their households.[5] If they are added into the group of female heads, at the same time as the single-person households are subtracted, we get male and female heads at rates closer to what would be expected by chance. Males were over-represented as heads of households in Nogales-area transport-equipment maquilas because they were more likely to live in single-person households, and because wives were more likely to defer to their husbands when asked who was the head of the household.

This does not mean that female workers universally deferred to men. One 33-year-old woman said that she was the head of her six-person household, which had one other income contributor—her common-law spouse, who she said earned the minimum wage as a day laborer when he could, but who was presently unemployed and generally did not have the personality to be the head of the household. Another 16-year-old woman with one month's seniority at her present workplace said her mother was the head of the household. Her father, a mechanic, was too unreliable to have a dependable income. Together, she and her mother, who also worked in a maquila, stabilized the household economy.

In the larger Nogales community, even more of the households were headed by men (80 percent), but evidence suggests that the position of head of household is disassociated with earning power; 16 percent of those named heads of households earned absolutely no income. Where heads of households did earn an income, the ratio of their income to the average income of other economically active household members was .97, indicating that heads of households earned the same, on average, as other wage earners in their household.

With little variation in earnings, the status of head of household is linked to age and gender, in ways characteristic of patriarchal societies. The family is not structured according to the economic rationale of capitalism. For example, a woman worker aged 35, who was single and had no children and earned the only income in her household, said that she was not the head of her household, but the daughter of the head of the household. The only other person in her household was an over-45 male who was her father.

Unlike Heyman's finding of an amalgamated family wage and consumer economy, this study of Nogales transport-equipment workers finds little support for the family consumer economy because of the flatness of wages among direct workers.[6] While some transport-equipment workers in the Nogales area must have lived in households headed by men who were the sole support because they earned higher wages, this is not the general situation among direct workers. Because direct workers are the largest group in the Nogales labor market, their situation is more typical than other occupational groups like technicians and administrative personnel, who are classified as indirect labor. The family wage economy is more typical in Nogales. As many wage earners as possible are in the labor force, regardless of whether they are children or parents. However, as the remainder of this section will show, this type of wage-earning household is not universal. There are variations in household structure depending on the gender of the workers in the household.

In most workers' households, income for living expenses comes from more than one person. Women workers were the only income earners in multiple-person households more often (15 percent) than men workers (9 percent), when single-person households are not included in the calculations. Survival for multiple-person households with only one income must be a constant struggle, given how increasingly difficult it has become for most people in Mexico to make ends meet. Real wages in the last 14 years have plummeted, as a direct result of state policy opening the country economically, according to Orozco Orozco (1991). In 1991, the buying power of the minimum wage corresponded to a third of what it had been in 1982. The minimum wage set by the federal government in Mexico only buys about a quarter of the basic necessities for a typical worker's family, so that the average worker has to have at least four minimum wages earned in the household just to meet basic needs.

The sample of workers was divided into subgroups based on the gender of wage earners in the household. Table 4.2 lists a number of economic indicators for the entire sample, women workers, men workers, and workers whose households had same- and opposite-sex workers. All workers earned an average income of 553,000 old pesos (U.S. $184) per month—twice the minimum wage at the time the survey was administered, and 40 percent more than earned by Lupe, whose situation introduced this chapter. Twice the minimum wage has been set as the line between Mexico's "absolute poor" and those even less fortunate. Of Mexico's economically active population, 49 percent are absolutely poor, earning between two and five minimum wages; 43 percent of the economically active earn only one to two minimum wages (Rodríguez Gómez, 1992). The first column of table 4.2 shows that 64 percent of the average worker's household was economically active, with an average household size of 4.5. There are thus 2.8 economically active persons in the household of the average worker.

Regardless of the worker's gender or that of other wage earners in the household, the worker earned almost exactly the same as the average of all other wage earners in the household (see table 4.2, the ratio of the worker's income to the average household income, third row from the bottom). Given that the average worker earns twice the minimum wage, with all workers in a household earning about the same amount, 2.8 economically active persons in a household would bring home more than five minimum wages. This is congruent with Orozco Orozco's argument that the minimum wage set by the Mexican government only covers about a quarter of the basic necessities of the typical worker's family, placing them on the borderline of what was identified above as the "absolute poor" in Mexico.

The fact that most workers earned the same wage has implications for household strategies for survival. In this economic environment, it would seem that the best strategy for the household as an income-pooling unit would be to increase its size to take advantage of economies of scale, and send as many wage earners as possible into the labor force, regardless of the potential wage earner's gender or position in the family. In this situation, women's work outside the home is absolutely essential, not supplementary, to the household's subsistence. This pattern is observed in other border cities as well. Young and Christopherson (1986) showed that households in Juárez in 1979 increased their resources by adding an adult who worked in a maquiladora or took over household duties to free the wife/mother to work in a maquiladora.

While this strategy may be the best one for the household as a group, it may not benefit all household members equally. As Benería and Roldán (1987: 122) have demonstrated, it cannot be assumed that households are monolithic with a single corporative interest. The majority of husbands in the households they studied kept some of their income for themselves, and sometimes even "borrowed" from pooled funds, while wives contributed all of their earnings to pooled funds. If this were also the case in the No-gales area, then perhaps the large household sending the maximum number of members into the labor force would be the best strategy for husbands, but not for their wives or children. However, if the internal household dy-namics that Benería and Roldán found were operating in the Nogales area, they would stimulate female family members' work outside the home to make up for potentially pooled funds that husbands kept for their own use.

The middle section of table 4.2 shows a number of ratios that measure what proportion of the household is economically active, the proportion of maquila workers in a household, and maquiladora workers as a proportion of economically active household members. The ratio of economically ac-tive persons per household does not differ much for the average male and female worker. The greatest difference is between workers from households with both male and female wage earners (.68) and workers from house-holds with female wage earners only (.55). It is not surprising that the monthly incomes of the total household for these two groups are the fur-thest apart, with households including both male and female wage earners having the highest mean monthly incomes (1,889,500 old pesos, or U.S. $629.83) and households with only female wage earners having the lowest mean monthly incomes (811,600 old pesos or U.S. $270.53). The differ-ence in monthly income available per person in these two households is 99,400 old pesos or U.S. $33.13. As noted above, however, this study did not investigate whether household income was, in fact, divided equally

Table 4.2   Economic Structure of Households by Gender of Wage
Earner(s)

	Entire Sample (N = 216)	Female Respondents (N = 90)	Male Respondents (N = 123)
Mean Monthly Incomes[a]			
Respondents[b]	553.00	537.20	564.50
Economically Active Household			
Members	603.90	594.40	614.60
All Household Members	381.10	370.30	389.00
Total Household	1,528.60	1,596.40	1,479.00
Household Economic Activity Ratios			
Economically Active Persons Per			
Household	.64	.62	.65
Maquiladora Workers Per			
Household	.53	.47	.57
Maquiladora Workers Per			
Economically Active Household			
Members	.81	.75	.85
Ratios of Respondent's Income			
Over Other Household Incomes			
Respondent's Income Per Mean			
Household Income	.98	1.01	.96
Respondent's Income Per Total			
Household Income	.52	.48	.55
Mean Household Size	4.50	4.70	4.30

Source: Survey of workers in Nogales and Imuris, Sonora, 1991.

[a] Income is reported in thousands of old pesos. When the data were collected, 3,000 old pesos were worth a little more than U.S. $1.

[b] Respondents' monthly income is calculated in the manner conventionalized by Mexican unions. Weekly income (including benefit and overtime pay) is multiplied by 52 and divided by 12.

among all household members. Given the age and gender dynamics at work in naming the head of the household discussed above, it is likely that household income is not equally divided.

The last three columns in table 4.2 indicate which type of household might serve as the best income-pooling unit. A household with both male

Table 4.2   *(Continued)*

| | Households With | |
Mixed-Sex Wage Earners (N = 125)	Female Wage Earners (N = 25)	Male Wage Earners (N = 66)
536.80	539.20	589.10
599.70	547.00	640.10
401.40	302.00	371.60
1,889.50	811.60	1,104.80
.68	.55	.61
.52	.50	.55
.74	.93	.90
.99	.99	.96
.35	.80	.73
5.10	3.20	3.70

and female wage earners may be the best strategy, since in this type of household we find the highest total household and per capita incomes, and the least dependence on respondent's income. The less the household depends on any individual's income, the less it is likely to suffer if that income is lost. Workers in households with income from many wage earners are probably also freer to switch jobs. Households with both male and female wage earners also have the lowest proportion of economically active members working in maquilas, so that they are not as dependent on an industry in which their jobs might disappear on short notice.

The most precarious households were those like Lupe's, with only female wage earners. Workers in such households earn the least, at 539,200 old pesos (U.S. $179.73) per month, and the average income of the other wage earners in their household was also the lowest, at 547,000 old pesos (U.S. $182.33) per month. Their households had the lowest proportion of members who were bringing in wages (.55), and the greatest reliance of the household on the maquiladora industry (.93) and on the worker's income (.80). However, if Benería and Roldán's findings about redistribution of income within the household are applicable in the Nogales area, women who have only other women workers in their household may have more control over this smaller income than women who work in households with both male and female wage earners.

Men workers living in households with other male wage earners appeared to be better off than women workers in households with other female wage earners. They earned more, on average, (589,100 old pesos or U.S. $196.37) than the average worker from households with only women workers or workers of both sexes. Their households also had the highest average income of economically active members (640,100 old pesos or U.S. $213.37).

Many more workers from households with only male, or only female, wage earners said they were the heads of their households than workers from households with male and female wage earners. Not counting single-person households, 52 percent of workers from households with only women wage earners reported being heads, compared to 32 percent in households with only male wage earners, and 26 percent in households with mixed-sex wage earners. Respondents from households with only women wage earners also reported being single parents much more often (36 percent) than respondents from households with only male wage earners (9 percent), or households with men and women wage earners (7 percent).[7] If we omit single-person households, 60 percent of all workers surveyed in households with only female wage earners were the sole wage earners, but 35 percent of workers surveyed from households with only male wage earners were the only wage earners. By definition, no workers from mixed-wage earner households could be sole wage earners.

Even though the maquiladora industry serves as the economic base for the Nogales area, maquiladora workers' households and those of the larger population differ. Maquiladora households are somewhat smaller than households in the general population, and have more people between the ages of 15 and 24. Maquiladora households contain more people with an unpartnered marital status than the general population, and males may not head maquiladora households as often as in the general population. The maquiladora household is probably better off than the general community households because more of its members are economically active. The finding that at least 75 percent of the other wage earners in the household (besides the worker surveyed) also worked in maquiladoras probably makes for a sharing at home of information about the workplace and the growth of a proletarian culture.

Migration and Maquiladoras

Theoretical frameworks used to understand economic integration also have implications for levels and types of migration. From the NIDL perspective, capital's movement within the old paradigm is explained in terms of neo- or peripheral Fordism: the search for cheap labor to do simple assembly jobs. It implies that migration (especially international) would not be stemmed by transnationalization, because much of the employment made available was not sufficient to sustain workers and their families. Thus they would have to migrate to other locations where they might earn more. Models of flexible specialization developed within the new paradigm have argued that the kinds of jobs transplanted are not only the less skilled ones, but also those that require more training and pay more than basic assembly. Consequently, while intra-regional migration within a country such as Mexico might increase when people move to work for new investors, they are not expected to migrate out of the country as often because of the fact that some "better" jobs are made available. The push-pull forces that some demographers believe to be at the root of migration would still operate within a country whose economy had been opened, but their effect would be lessened beyond its borders because foreign investment would make pay for work available at home comparable to work available outside the country. As interfacing areas between countries, borders are predicted by both the old and new paradigms to receive more migrants.

Although migrants were not preferred as workers in the early days of the maquiladora program, the boom of the eighties increased the importance of migration for supplying labor to maquiladoras at the border. Most of the workers and general population surveyed in Nogales are migrants. Only a fifth of workers reported that they were born in the community where they worked. Migrants had also arrived fairly recently. It had been a little more than five years, on average, since the last time they had moved to the Nogales area; their mean age at arrival was a little over 18 years. Thus, the growth of maquilas in the eighties was, if fact, a magnet that drew migration to Nogales.

Maquila workers' birthplaces make a difference in their personal situations. Those who were born where they worked came from households that were larger (6) than the ones of those who were not born there (4), so that the native worker probably has a more solid support structure at home. Migrants may be able to compensate for less household support with their own personal job experience; half of them had been economically active before their first maquila job, as compared to a quarter of natives who had been economically active. The maquila industry tends to hire more housewives than students from the community that hosts the plant, and more students than housewives from other areas. This is probably because housewives tend to work in their home communities, continuing to do housework after they begin to work outside the home.

The fact that so many workers were migrants probably also means that they were still related to households in other places. Although the questionnaire did not specifically ask if workers contributed money to any other households, two volunteered the information that they sent money home; in one case, the money was meant to pay for the education of siblings, and in the other case, it was sent to the worker's mother. Four workers also said that their households received income contributions from relatives working on the U.S. side of the border. I suspect that this level of income entering and leaving the household is an under-representation, and I predict that more in-depth research would reveal more monetary links to other households.

Workers who migrated tended to come from areas relatively close to the Nogales area, which would contribute to strong ties between them and the families they left. Four-fifths (81 percent) of them came from the same region of Mexico: the northwest, which includes the states of Baja California, Baja California Sur, Nayarit, Sinaloa, and Sonora. None of the workers interviewed came from Baja California Sur, and only one from Baja California, reinforcing the geographic outline of the western industrial corridor in chapter 2.[8]

Only 9 percent of Nogales-area workers came from the northern region (Coahuila, Chihuahua, Durango, and Nuevo León), with the remainder coming from the west, south-central, and other regions. Migrant workers in the Nogales area were more likely to come from their own region of Mexico than was true of migrants in the general population in Tijuana, Juárez, and Nuevo Laredo (González Ramírez, 1990). Nogales, like Juárez, is a center of intra-regional migration. Unlike Tijuana, it does not draw much of its population from other regions.

While men and women workers were equally likely to be migrants, women were more likely to come from closer locations. Over half (57 percent) of women workers who had migrated had previously resided in other Sonora locations, whereas only 40 percent of men workers who had migrated did. Men were more likely than women to have come from Sinaloa or Nayarit. Workers like Lupe, described at the beginning of this chapter, are often disadvantaged by being migrants. The migration process is not usually completed in one move. It may take them away from the workplace repeatedly, cutting down on seniority and making it more difficult for them to learn new skills.

Because there are fewer migrants, Imuris, an interior location with only one maquila, has a more stable labor force. There were far fewer workers who reported migrating to Imuris (50 percent) than Nogales (80 percent). Migrants who worked in Imuris were also more likely to come from Sonora (80 percent) than migrants who worked in Nogales (40 percent). Nogales workers were more likely than Imuris workers to have done maquiladora work elsewhere in Sonora before moving to their workplace.

The reasons migrants were uprooted were overwhelmingly economic. Almost two-thirds came for greater employment and earning opportunities, with only a quarter saying they had moved for family reasons. In a 1978 survey of workers in several border cities including Nogales, Seligson and Williams (1981: 81) found the opposite—that family-related reasons were far more significant than maquila employment in migrants' motivations.

However, they predicted that the latter would become more important due to the economic crunch in Mexico and growth in jobs available. Their prediction is confirmed here.

Gender differences among workers in their motivations for migrating were not large, but women migrated for family reasons slightly more often than men. On the other hand, 12 percent of male migrants (but only 1 percent of female migrants) reported being motivated by some kind of wanderlust (adventure, "to see what it was like," curiosity). The wanderers tended to be either distant or nonrelatives of the head of their household, or to live in single-person households.

Workers' motivations were mostly economic because there really was no other source of income or subsistence for them in their place of origin. A man who had migrated to Imuris with his brothers to work in the maquila said, "We'd work in something else if there was any opportunity, but if the maquiladora wasn't here, we'd have to sell things in the street." A 19-year-old woman worker said she had migrated with her female cousin from Durango, where she had been doing housework. She came to work in the maquila in Imuris because, "Where we come from there are no jobs, only cleaning houses or sweeping stores. We came here because there are more job opportunities. I regret leaving school because I would like to be promoted and have a well paid job." The house she shared with four others appeared to be one of the best constructed in Imuris. They were proud of an oven that a family member had built behind the house of cement, block, and clay, which was just like the one they had had in Durango.

Even though workers had migrated for economic reasons, their journeys had taken them only as far as the international border. Few had crossed, and few had migrated to the Nogales area with the intention of crossing. Only two had been employed in the United States in the month before their first maquila job. A 21-year-old woman working in Imuris, who commuted daily from an *ejido* adjacent to the village and had previously worked in two Nogales maquilas, said that before her first maquila job she had worked in Tucson in a private home caring for children. An 18-year-old man reported that he had migrated from Veracruz, in the northeast, to Nogales with the intention of crossing illegally into the United States. He succeeded in doing this through a hole in the fence, migrated to Los Angeles, was employed in McDonald's, and bought a false social security card there. After all this, he had returned to Nogales, because he said that gringos treat Mexicans very badly, and that the lifestyle in the United States does not suit Mexicans. He expressed satisfaction with his job as an operator in a Nogales plant making wiring harnesses. He hoped to acquire skills in his workplace and be promoted to supply keeper. The secretary at Plant H said she had legally migrated to work in California for part of a year, but she had come home because it was too expensive to live there.

One of the issues that received much attention in NAFTA debates and will continue to be highly salient is whether or not the increased investment that a free trade agreement offers will keep Mexicans working at home rather than migrating to the United States. Cornelius and Martin (1991) have argued that growth in maquiladoras would not increase migration to the United States, since they have always drawn the bulk of their workforce from within the states in which they are located. Most migrants to the United States tend to come from farther away than the border and bypass it entirely. Included among employment reasons for migrating in the 1991 survey was moving to Nogales or Imuris in order to work in the United States, but it is noteworthy that only two workers in the entire sample said that they had done this.

In 1991, Nogales maquiladora workers did not express any strong desire to migrate to the United States. In a 1989 survey of workers in Nogales and two other Sonora border locations, Lara Valencia (1991) also found that a negligible percentage of workers said that working in the United States was the reason they had moved to Nogales. He argued that because of the development of the maquiladora industry, border cities within Mexico have become the preferred destination for migrants.

As Seligson and Williams (1981: 84) have pointed out, different findings may emerge from samples of Mexicans in the United States who have migrated, as opposed to samples of industrial workers or rural peasants in Mexico. They suggest that dissatisfied male workers are likely to migrate to the United States, legally or illegally. From the findings in this study, I predict that the wanderers—males who had come to Nogales for adventure— would be the most likely to cross the border and head north. However, in a San Diego County study, Solórzano-Torres (1987: 54) argues that there may be a relationship between maquila employment and the undocumented immigration of Mexican women to the United States, since she found that of those women who had worked in Mexico prior to moving to the United States, almost two-thirds had worked in maquilas.

The migration of Mexicans to the United States may depend not so much on their location within Mexico but on the resources available to them. De los Angeles Crummett (1985: 12) found in her study of Calvillo, Aguascalientes, that migration to the United States predominated among the middle peasantry, and that the poorest peasants migrated only within Mexico because their precarious economic base restricted international migration. It may be that maquila employment will provide more of an economic base from which they can consider migration north of the border. However, international migration will also depend on the welcome in the receiving host society. The few workers in this study who had tried migrating to the United States did not find it very warm. If this chilly reception continues, then growth of better jobs in the new maquila may adequately satisfy basic needs and reduce international migration.

Among the 38 percent of Nogales-area workers who had helped pay family expenses in some way before their first maquila job, the largest group (28 percent) were agricultural workers, followed by commercial salespersons (19 percent), trade apprentices and assistants (16 percent), manual industrial laborers (11 percent), and domestics (7 percent). These frequencies are the same for both migrants and non-migrants. When maquila workers do have labor-force experience, it is in marginal, poorly paid, and/or seasonal occupations. If most maquiladora jobs disappeared—in their old and new forms—because of continued recession in the United States or some new economic or political crisis, there would probably be little reason for workers to return permanently to their original communities, which they left for lack of employment. There would be more reason to go north in search of jobs and higher wages. By this reasoning, the existence of the maquilas on the border does absorb labor that might otherwise move northward.

Housing and Living Conditions

Nogales's recent population explosion has led to an acute shortage of housing and services. In the housing crisis, demand has grown out of all proportion to supply, which is restricted by insufficient building and financing (Camberos Castro and Barojas, 1988). Things had been improving between 1970 and 1985, when more families had water, sewerage, and electricity, but by the end of the decade, housing conditions had deteriorated. In three years, between 1986 and 1989, 20 new residential districts appeared in No-gales. Most dwellings were built by the migrants themselves. Even from outside, they were visibly inadequate as basic shelter (Lara Valencia, 1991).

Table 4.3 demonstrates how Nogales area transport-equipment workers compared to the larger community on a number of variables indicative of housing quality. Almost two-thirds (62 percent) of workers, almost three-quarters (72.6 percent) of the larger community, and four-fifths (81 percent) of the lower stratum said they owned their housing.[9] The fact that home ownership increases as one moves down the socioeconomic scale indicates that most people in Nogales cannot afford to rent. Instead, they build their own dwellings, often out of scrap material discarded from the maquilas.

A look at irregularities in home ownership provides a better appreciation of the housing situation. Camberos Castro and Barojas (1988) say that the maquiladora program, with its demand for the building of industrial parks, has led to land speculation and raised the cost of housing construction. Ille-gal activities such as the invasion of idle land are linked to low wages, which make rental housing a luxury. Invasions, however, do not necessarily mean free land; in some cases, the owners appear after settlement has taken place, and negotiate long-term payment. In 1985, a thousand families in-vaded idle land. The settlement became Colonia Los Tápiros and by 1990 had a population of 8,000 people (Tolan, 1990). In 1986, another 200 fami-lies staged an invasion in another area, and again in 1989, 150 people moved onto empty hills on government land to form Colonia Emiliano Zapata, which by 1990 had more than 2,000 inhabitants.

The quality of workers' housing can be evaluated with standards previ-ously used in Nogales and other Mexican locations. Coplamar (Camberos Castro and Barojas, 1988) sets two persons per room as the level at which overcrowding occurs. Table 4.3 shows that the average home of transport-equipment workers is overcrowded by this standard, although the average home in the larger Nogales population and the lower-stratum home are not. Inadequate dwellings are defined as those constructed of materials such as cardboard, mud, and sheet metal, and table 4.3 indicates that 36 percent of workers fell in that category with non-durable walls, and 13 percent with earthen floors. Other evidence of inadequate living conditions includes the absence of running water for 19 percent of workers, absence off sewer-age for 41 percent, and lack of electricity for 23 percent. With an average of 0.3 rooms per dwelling available for purposes other than bedrooms,

Table 4.3   Quality of Housing of Nogales and Imuris Transport-Equipment Workers in Community Context

Housing Characteristics	Transport-Equipment Workers 1991	Nogales 1988	Nogales Lower Stratum 1988
Percentage of Home Owners	62.0	72.6	81.0
Mean No. of Persons/Household	4.4	4.6	5.2
Mean No. of Rooms[a]/Household	2.2	2.9	2.3
Mean No. of Persons/Room	2.0	1.3	1.6
Mean No. of Bedrooms/Household	1.9	2.0	1.8
Mean No. of Persons/Bedroom	2.0	2.0	2.5
Percentage Without Running Water[b]	19.0	12.7	19.9
Percentage Without Sewerage	40.7	19.4	53.7
Percentage Without Electricity	23.1	8.7	36.6
Percentage Without Durable Walls	36.4	27.1	52.3
Percentage Earthen Floors	12.5	11.3	40.3

Source: Survey of workers in 1991 and secondary analysis of socioeconomic community survey in 1988.

[a]Excludes kitchens, bathrooms, hallways.
[b]Running water was considered available when it was within the dwelling or on the lot outside the dwelling.

kitchens, bathrooms, or hallways, not only is there no 'free' space, but overcrowding is the norm.

Some maquiladoras pointed to their own services as supplementary to poor community services. Plant C installed showers for workers to discourage them from leaving for other plants. Camberos Castro and Barojas (1988) suggest that maquiladoras should go further than this in their assistance with workers' poor living conditions, and contribute from their profits more than what is available through Infonavit (government-subsidized housing) to a special fund for housing construction.

Although table 4.3 paints a bleak picture, its reporting of summary statistics such as percentages and averages glosses over important variations in workers' living conditions, discovered through a cluster analysis of the housing items in the workers' survey. Three factors were found to divide workers into two groups with regard to housing. The most strongly differentiating factor combined the availability of electricity and durability of walls, the second factor differentiated respondents by whether they had running water and sewerage, and the third on the amount of 'free' space. Thirty-one percent of workers fell into the bottom cluster, which had the worst housing. These housing variations allow comparisons that help to understand how maquiladora workers manage their existence in Nogales.

Workers improve the quality of their housing by sharing resources with others. Those with the worst housing had smaller households and were also more likely (31 percent) to report that they contributed the only income to the household, in comparison with those who had better housing (14 percent). When those with the poorest housing did have others who contributed to the household, their contributions tended to be lower than for those who had better housing. This provides further evidence that the household mediates the effects of the economy. Inadequate housing is also one of the costs of migration for workers, since of those who were born where they worked, 17 percent had the worst housing, but of those born elsewhere, 36 percent suffered these conditions.

Conclusion

Biological reproduction and migration are alternative ways of constituting a labor force, and the household is an important structure facilitating either option. While Mexico as a country has no difficulty in biologically reproducing itself, the economic restructuring of the eighties—which culminated in NAFTA—meant that for many Mexicans, employment was available at home less often than it used to be. Journalists such as Lovera and Chousal (1993: 10) have observed that the media have been used by the state as vehicles "for convincing people to change their reproductive behavior, to control or encourage migration—like migration toward the northern border—and it has been those media . . . which propagate the idea that it would be a better life with a small family, without questioning what women or couples want."

This chapter has shown that the individuals who get the Nogales and Imuris transport-equipment jobs advertised in the newspaper actively organize their lives outside of work to take the most advantage of whatever opportunity maquila employment offers. Many have left their families and traveled from Nayarit, Sinaloa, and from locations within Sonora to work at the border. Most of them come from within the western industrial corridor, rather than outside of it. Even though most were not employed before their first maquila job, or worked marginally in agriculture, they now comprise an industrial labor force that this corridor internally generates. (The central corridor also generates its own maquila labor force, but the Pacific corridor does not.)

Workers organize themselves into households which attempt to mediate some of the sharpest difficulties of the economy. The household is especially important in this attempted mediation due to the absence, as shown in chapter 6, of effective trade-union organizations that might help defend workers' rights and represent their interests. The others with whom workers undertake the active organization of their lives are in most cases members of their families.

Given Mexico's economic crisis in the eighties, and the concomitant drop in real wages, the average maquiladora worker's household must be seen as an organization promoting family survival, rather than one whose goal is to accumulate consumer goods. The goal of subsistence is accomplished better by some maquila households than others, and the optimum form seems to be a household with both men and women wage earners, as opposed to a household with only male wage earners or only female wage earners. Households with both male and female wage earners had the highest total household and per capita incomes, the least dependence on the income of any one worker, and the lowest proportion of economically active members working in maquilas. They were also larger than households that had only male or only female workers, indicating that the slogan used by family-planning promoters that "between fewer burros, there are more cobs of corn" is not necessarily a valid assumption (Welti, 1993: 17).

While Nogales has one of the lowest proportions of women in its maquila labor force of any maquiladora center, the wages of women transport-equipment workers were found to be about the same as anyone else's wages in their households. Women workers who identified themselves as wives or daughters of the head of the household in which they lived were definitely not supplementary wage earners, as is often assumed. Women workers also headed their own households, and sometimes could not count on any income brought home by men. Households without any economic support from men probably provide for the most precarious existence.

Perhaps if maquiladoras paid workers higher wages, there would be more reason for workers to separate their work life from their family life, as suggested by the maquiladora association leader in chapter 3. As shown in chapter 6, however, such a wage increase would have to be quite substantial to make up for the drop in real wages that occurred in the eighties. Even if wages did increase to a level that could provide the material possibility for living independently from family, Mexicans might very well not choose such a lifestyle, since there is strong cultural support for family economies. This chapter has shown that at present, this question is not dependent on culture, as many managers indicated, but on the material basis that would make it a possibility. Maquiladoras do not pay workers enough for them to put work before family even if they valued their work more highly than their families, which, in general, they do not.

While household organization enhances the well-being of the family group as a unit, it may also create and maintain inequalities structured internally on the basis of age and gender. Other authors have argued that women maquila workers are subordinated by their families. Although redistribution of income within the household was not specifically investigated in this study, I think there is no doubt that the household is one site of women's subordination. The fact that some men said they had migrated because of curiosity or for excitement, whereas women never gave such a reason for migrating, is an indication of the greater choices available to men for acting outside of family structures. The household, however, is not the only source of women's subordination. Chapter 3 showed how this happened with gender segmentation in the labor market, and chapter 5 will investigate how it happens in the workplace.

Even those households with both men and women wage earners, the best type of household for pooling income, often failed to meet basic standards set by Mexicans for decent living. Evidence for this is the finding that the average maquila household in Nogales, including all wage earners, only brought together enough income to be considered "absolutely poor" by prevailing standards. Moreover, many of the households evaluated as having achieved an effective structure for group survival share housing that is overcrowded, built of inadequate materials, and poorly serviced by utilities like water and electricity.

In general, employment in Nogales transport-equipment maquilas does not serve workers very well. If the dual-technology thesis were becoming a reality, more workers would be expected to live in households that were accumulating consumer goods rather than merely surviving. Also, more workers would be expected to have better housing due to an increase in skilled jobs, which should be better rewarded.

The existence of the border to stop migration means that maquila workers' main cross-border travel is for shopping to take advantage of lower prices, greater variety, and better quality in the United States. Most Nogales workers buy their groceries and other basic supplies in the United States in dollar-denominated values (Lara Valencia, 1992). With little to spend, they are limited to stores in the immediate Nogales area. They may, however, consider more permanent trips farther into the United States if maquila employment provides them with enough resources. On the other hand, higher wages might help Mexicans establish a better standard of living south of the border and root them there. In the final chapter, we will look at the effect of the crisis of 1994–95 on migration in the western corridor.

TECHNOLOGY AND THE ORGANIZATION OF WORK

Is Mexico a potential site for high-tech production or does its comparative advantage lie in labor-intensive low-tech operations? . . . [T]he U.S.-Mexican border no longer represents a barrier to high-tech production. (Shaiken, 1994: 39)

Spokesmen for the industry also believe that automation in newly established maquiladoras is changing the composition of the labor force and, therefore, the definition of what constitutes a desirable employee. That may be partly true; nevertheless, unskilled and semi-skilled jobs still predominate in the maquila industry. (Fernández Kelly, 1987: 159)

One of the arguments in favor of industrial restructuring is that computerized, numerically controlled machine tools and flexible manufacturing systems will play a key role in restoring U.S. competitiveness in world markets (Kelley, 1989: 235). The dual-technology thesis holds that this technology has been incorporated into the second wave of electronic and automotive maquilas in Mexico because it allows workers to reprogram machinery quickly and flexibly, thereby reducing labor costs (Ramírez and Fuentes Flores, 1989). Much published work on maquila development in the 1990s falls within the new paradigm, making flexible production the *sine qua non* of successful future industrial competition. This claim is based on the fact that lean production, requiring skilled workers who are involved in the labor process, is less wasteful of material and human resources than mass production.

There is a circularity here: by assuming that flexibility is inevitable, the new paradigm may influence methodological decisions, which in turn make it appear so. For example, Carrillo and Ramírez (1992: 57–58) studied direct workers' involvement in the labor process, and activities related to the organization of work, in plants in Tijuana, Monterrey, and Juárez. The observations were statistically weighted to represent 358 plants, the largest representative sample in this area of research. In order to interpret findings arising from measures of the social organization of work, they dichotomized them into only two categories, which they called "greater flexibility" and "less flexibility."[1] Plants with greater flexibility were defined as those where direct workers participated in more than 30 percent of the types of involvement and work organization they measured. Using this yardstick, they found 27 percent of the plants to have greater flexibility; the remaining 73 percent had less flexibility.

This methodology is problematic because it makes it impossible to discover something other than flexibility. If all forms of work organization are assumed to be flexible to some degree, then the concept will shed no light on the variations. The idea of flexibility was introduced into the Mexican maquila literature at the end of the eighties, when its usefulness was already being questioned elsewhere. Gertler (1988: 45), for example, cites British evidence which "views 'flexibilization' as an ideology propagated by firm owners as a desirable future end state, and supported by conservative (and paradoxically some radical) academics, pro-business political forces and governments in order to assist the private sector in achieving this goal."

In the quotations that open the chapter, Shaiken counterposes the alternatives envisioned by the old and the new paradigms, and recognizes that the U.S.-Mexico border no longer impedes the technological aspects of the new paradigm. Fernández Kelly acknowledges this as well, but says the social relationship between workers and technology maintains the low-skill aspects of the old paradigm. This chapter shows that while Nogales-area transport-equipment maquilas often incorporate microelectronic technology, they do not use the flexible forms of work organization anticipated by the new paradigm. For a number of reasons, most managers do not believe that the adoption of advanced technology is cost effective or advisable. If work is not intensified through the introduction of more advanced technology, what are the alternatives? What is the quality of workers' jobs? What are their prospects for new skill acquisition and upward mobility?

The Cost-Ineffectiveness of Advanced Technology

At the time of this study, six of the ten transport-equipment maquilas in the Nogales area had recently introduced microelectronic-based automation.

In all cases, this meant bringing in equipment to improve product quality through electronic diagnosis and testing. At Plant I, for example, microelectronics were used to predict the possibility of shorts in a wiring harness. This equipment is programmable, so that the computer is simply resequenced for a new model. Previously, any change meant dismantling the connections and installing new wires. Another example comes from the annual report of Plant C's parent corporation: "all divisions are automotive oriented. They focus on equipment which is capital intensive. All products involve hydraulic, pneumatic or electrical power."

Asked if they had difficulty obtaining the most cost-effective technology, a Plant I manager cited bureaucratic problems within the company, which had limited resources but unlimited wants. "When the cost of labor is so low in Mexico, does it pay to invest in new technology?" he asked rhetorically. "Mechanical equipment can produce better quality than a human can, but it's not necessarily cost effective to use it."

When microelectronic technology has been introduced, infrastructure has often been inadequate to support it. "Brown outs" and electrical power surges have caused Plant I to fail, especially during the monsoon season in July and August. One of the managers I interviewed half-jokingly speculated that the wires carrying electricity in Sonora did not seem to be totally waterproof. Some of the new equipment at Plant I had been destroyed, or as he put it, "fried."

While I was collecting data in March and April 1991, the electricity in Nogales, Sonora, went out on several occasions because of high winds. During an interview with the general manager from Plant C, the power suddenly went off. The office darkened, muffled cheers arose from the shop floor, and he ran off to see to the problem. The electricity usually goes out about once a month, for about 45 seconds at a time. In the stormy season, however, it has gone down for as much as a day and a half. Electricity comes to the Nogales-area maquilas from Guaymas, and "we have no control over it," the manager said, throwing up his hands in frustration. He had installed a satellite dish on the roof, so he could at least call out when all the lines were down. Nogales is not the only point on the border where maquilas have taken the initiative to reinforce infrastructure for their needs. In Juárez, by 1988, some firms had their own satellite communication networks and electronic generators to prevent disruption of telephone communications, especially in sensitive electronic applications (George, 1990: 230).

Plant C is the only one in our sample that makes its entire product in Nogales, albeit with imported materials. Although it does not use statistical process control (SPC), operations are computerized at the administrative level. The computers in the Nogales plant are networked to the head office in the United States, where everything starts. The head office brings new products on line and markets them. Once they get sales orders, 90-day contracts are signed, and computer technology is used to set production and work schedules. During the 90-day period, the buyer is permitted to change some of the product's specifications, so it is important to maintain constant contact between head office and the Nogales plant. Electricity failures complicate administration of the production process, which may explain why none of the other plants studied had their computers networked into the foreign parent company. As Sklair (1993: 256) says, "While the control system for the factory of the future is 'computer integrated manufacturing,' this is still some way off for practical purposes." Despite their use of microelectronic technology, Nogales transport-equipment maquilas are not among Mexico's most technologically sophisticated. Hermosillo remains an "island of automation" at the southern end of the western corridor (Shaiken, 1990: 122).

One manager at Plant I said he did not think high-tech companies could successfully move to Mexico. When I asked about Ford in Hermosillo, he said he did not think they were so successful, because they had "union problems." While this negative sentiment might have been related to Ford's position as his company's competitor, it does not mask his company's rejection of most characteristics of the new paradigm. His response shows that some administrators of Mexican maquilas, and undoubtedly their superiors at U.S head offices, have chosen not to ride the second wave, fearing they might crash against the rocks and shoals of labor relations, inadequate infrastructure, or other problems.

At first, the general manager at Plant H hedged, saying "I don't know" when asked whether his plant was using the most cost-effective technology. He said he knew of more sophisticated technology they might be using (their machinery was twenty years old), but they were concerned they "might never be able to pay for it." Also, he did not think people with experience in maintaining newer machinery were available in Mexico. Plant H gets technological assistance from its corporation's head office in the United States in the form of machinery, and personnel to train Mexican workers in how to use and maintain it. The general manager said Nogales was very different from Hermosillo, where they have the latest technology and better educational programs.

It is evident that Plant H has been designated as a site within its multinational firm for low-wage production. This is clear from their account of how the level of technology is decided. Wages are the least expensive component of their production costs. They have avoided newer technology because they would not "be able to pay for it." Although machinery often comes from the firm's U.S. plants, the ability to pay for better equipment would have to be generated by extracting value from labor in Mexico. Higher wages would make their present operation cost ineffective. Thus, the adoption of more sophisticated technology that would transfer more skills is out of the question because of policies originating within this firm, which stretches across multiple borders.

The maquiladora association leader, who managed an electronics plant, explained why Nogales was not at the technological cutting edge in this way:

Author: What has your experience been with the implementation of automated technology in Mexico?

Maquila Association Leader: You would only do it when it's cost effective. As long as you could do something more cheaply by hand, why would you go out and buy a million-dollar machine? Anything is possible with Mexican labor. It may take them more training and time, but they can learn anything. If you show them how to do something, they will copy it exactly and keep doing it the way you showed them. They are different from American workers in that they will not make a decision to change things themselves. If something goes wrong on a unit that an American worker is using, the American worker will take a hammer and try to fix it. The Mexican worker will not take the initiative, but will wait until he is told what to do.

It is evident from the managers' accounts that the use of advanced technology in Mexican maquilas is restricted by the low cost of labor, lack of confidence in Mexican workers' ability to maintain it, and uncertainty over labor relations. While microelectronic technology has been adopted in many Nogales transport-equipment maquilas to test for quality and to identify defects, it is not embraced as a panacea in the way that the new paradigm suggests. The inability to reliably deliver electricity to support microelectronic technology also diminishes its attractiveness. These findings, and the maquila association leader's view that Mexican workers follow instructions exactly but are reluctant to innovate, keep Nogales transport-equipment maquilas outside of the new paradigm of production. This is consistent with Sklair's (1993: 256) prediction that "technology tends to advance by small increments because the more you want to invest, the higher up the company you need to go. . . . It is certainly the case that the theoretical or even practical existence of new technology is a necessary but by no means sufficient condition for its use in production. Offshore sourcing in cheap labor zones in general and the maquila industry in particular bear eloquent testimony to the truth of this proposition. NAFTA as proposed will not necessarily alter this." Although investment in microelectronic technology with flexible forms of work organization might be most fruitful in the long run, more immediate profits may be preferred by investors.

Dual Technology

Sklair (1993: 248) has suggested that the 1980s' trend toward upgrading personnel will increase with NAFTA, which would be consistent with the new paradigm. González-Aréchiga (1989b), who says profound changes in the maquiladora industry have led to a second wave, uses the ratio of technicians to direct workers to test for dual technology.[2] The assumption of this measure is that technological sophistication will mean more technicians per direct worker. Using the ratio as a kind of barometer, researchers have come up with a variety of findings which indicate that while technicians may have increased as a proportion of the maquila labor force nationally, there is tremendous variation within Mexico.

   Barajas Escamilla (1989b) showed that the ratio of technicians to workers at the national level increased between 1975 and 1986 from 10.2 technicians for every 100 direct workers, to 14.8 technicians. González-Aréchiga (1989b: 28) argued that Tijuana contained the two kinds of electronic- and auto-part maquilas suggested by the dual-technology thesis. On the other hand, Arteaga G., Carrillo, and Micheli T.'s study (1989) of G.M. maquilas found no change in the relation between direct and indirect workers. Eighty percent of employees were direct workers, 4 percent technicians, and 15 percent administrative staff. We will now look at whether the internal variation in Nogales-area transport-equipment maquilas fits the notion that there is a dichotomy separating maquilas into old and new.

Table 5.1 shows the ratio of direct workers to technicians in Nogales-area transport-equipment plants from 1982 to 1990. To support the dual-technology thesis, this table should show some plants with a high ratio of workers to technicians, and others with a discernibly lower ratio. If a second wave of maquilas is emerging, the ratio of direct workers to technicians should substantially decrease in at least some plants over time.

In fact, table 5.1 does reveal two levels at which direct workers relate to technicians. The most dramatic change visible in this table is at Plants J and F, which make wiring harnesses and are owned by the same company. Both plants drastically reduced the number of technicians in comparison to workers between 1989 and 1990, although they were among the plants which had had the fewest technicians before 1989 as well. Even if common ownership of these plants meant that they shared some of their technicians, the average of their ratio of workers to technicians is still 45.8—more workers per technician than any other plant in the sample. Among those plants with lower ratios of workers to technicians, evidence indicates a slight decrease in the ratio of workers to technicians over time, especially at Plant I, which is the most similar to Plant J.

The technological dualism discovered in the Nogales area is the opposite of what the dual-technology thesis predicted. Rather than increasing the proportion of technicians, some plants got rid of almost all their technicians.

Plants I and J provide a good basis for comparison because they are in the same size category and both make wiring harnesses. The huge gap in their ratios of workers to technicians by 1990 (3.7 at Plant I and 59.2 at Plant J) indicates the discretion available to companies in how they produce the same product. This prerogative is more closely associated with technological heterogeneity than dualism.

What happened at Plants F and J between 1989 and 1990 to reduce the number of technicians they employed? The Canadian company that owns these plants has recently reorganized its operations. The Mexican general manager at Plant F had held his position for less than a year after being hired to replace the previous Anglo-American manager, who had disagreed with the owner about how production should be organized. A worker at Plant F said that the company had lost a client the previous year because of too many defects. The new manager had an academic background, having

Table 5.1 Ratio of Direct Workers to Technicians in the Transport-Equipment Industry in Nogales and Imuris, Sonora, Mexico, 1982–1990

Plant	1982	1983	1984	1985	1986	1987	1988	1989	1990
Plant A[a]	n.d.	n.d.	n.d.	n.d.	n.d.	n.d.	n.d.	4.0	1.7
Plant B[b]	n.d.	n.d.	n.d.	n.d.	n.d.	n.d.	n.d.	n.d.	n.d.
Plant C	1.1	1.5	2.6	2.1	3.4	8.0	4.9	5.5	5.3
Plant D[c]	n.d.	n.d.	n.d.	n.d.	n.d.	n.d.	n.d.	0.0	10.4
Plant E	0.0	8.0	6.2	6.5	10.7	14.8	5.9	5.8	5.4
Plant F	22.0	20.4	2.7	4.0	6.6	4.4	18.4	14.1	32.4
Plant G	13.7	14.1	8.3	8.3	8.7	8.8	3.8	7.0	3.8
Plant H	9.8	12.3	12.6	12.2	13.0	11.0	11.4	16.6	16.4
Plant I[d]	n.d.	10.8	18.3	14.8	7.6	5.3	6.2	4.5	3.7
Plant J[e]	n.d.	n.d.	n.d.	n.d.	2.8	18.1	17.7	14.2	59.2

Source: SECOFI, 1990. Concentrados mensuales de la industria maquiladora de exportación. Mexican Secretariat of Trade and Industry, Subdelegación de Fomento Industrial, Nogales, Sonora.

[a] Plant A began operations in 1989.
[b] Plant B began operations in 1989, and the shelter that services it reports all data to SECOFI in the aggregate.
[c] Plant D began operations in 1989.
[d] Plant I began operations in 1983.
[e] Plant J began operations in 1986.

taught in the technological college for seven years. He told me he was well aware of the new paradigm.

Workers had observed Canadian personnel who were sent to Nogales in 1989 for a review; the results included a lot of *jefes* (bosses) losing their jobs, and promises to workers of better conditions. In 1991, however, workers told us that working conditions had not improved. Walmsley (1992: 20) says that in 1988, the company "repatriated" 75 jobs from the Nogales, Sonora, plant to another one it owned in Tillsonburg, Ontario, Canada, because:

> The customer, a giant U.S. electronics company, was so annoyed with the Mexican plant's defect rate and the two weeks lost in shipping time that it was prepared to buy instead from a U.S. or Canadian plant, even if it meant paying more for the product. . . . the company's chairman, CEO and majority owner [said]: "There is an argument for manufacturing in Canada in certain instances. Tillsonburg is becoming the brains of our operation and our facilities in Mexico couldn't exist without it. We found that with smaller manufacturing runs and more technical work, we could do it better here."

Carrillo (1989a: 109–110) says that one of the central questions at the beginning of the eighties in maquiladora research was whether assembly operations in low-wage zones would return to their countries of origin due to automation. By the end of the decade, it had been demonstrated that Mexican maquilas could be automated, and researchers were asking whether they would survive the transition to post-Fordism or flexible specialization. The statement of the CEO of the company owning Plants F and J, that "with smaller manufacturing runs and more technical work, we could do it better here" (i.e., in Canada) suggests that these two maquilas did not survive the transition. The company's Tillsonburg, Ontario, plant, and perhaps others like it, may follow the new paradigm of flexible specialization, but its Mexican maquilas are not to be trusted to do the same. Further research would be useful to investigate whether the Tillsonburg plant represents the maquila transplanted from the south to the north. This would include asking whether any of the characteristics of maquilization (lower real wages, an increasing feminization of the labor force, an increasing proportion of workers classified as unskilled, and a non-union orientation) were adopted at the Canadian production site.

De-skilling—or Downward Job Classification?

How could Plants F and J continue production without their technicians? Were the tasks that were formerly carried out by technicians no longer done in the Nogales area, or were they done by others not classified as technicians? What exactly does it mean for the labor process at Plants F and J if the "brains" of their operations are in Tillsonburg? Does this drain the number of skilled jobs available for Mexican workers?

The findings of two other recent studies help put these questions in context. One cause of high ratios of direct workers to technicians is the introduction of the new-paradigm labor process. Multitasking and multiskilling of direct workers reduces the number of job categories in any plant to two categories—skilled and unskilled—with most jobs considered unskilled. Carrillo (1988) studied skill levels in two Mexican automotive plants owned by the same company. One plant developed under import-substitution policies, and the other under export-led development policies. In the plant developed under export-led development policies, practices in the new labor process (for example, work teams of multiskilled workers) had led to the disappearance of technicians' jobs in maintenance and quality control. This is especially interesting since INEGI's definition of technicians (cited above) specifies quality-control inspectors as skilled workers.

Although technicians' jobs had disappeared, Carrillo concluded that the skills needed to perform these jobs had not. The skills were still carried out by direct workers, in quality circles and work teams. The status associated with job titles and remuneration was not consistent with skilled work, as it would have been if they were classified as technicians. There is reason to believe that this phenomenon may not be limited to automated work: "In the majority of U.S. [owned] autopart maquiladoras which are labor intensive, like the ones assembling upholstery or harnesses, work teams are the central form of change in the organization of work. The teams have the same importance in Hermosillo, Chihuahua or Saltillo" (Carrillo, 1988: 461).

A subsequent study used the largest representative sample of maquila workers in three different subsectors in Monterrey, Tijuana, and Juárez. Carrillo and Contreras (1992) found that the greater the restructuring, the lower the skill level of direct workers.[3] Electronics, which was the most restructured, had the highest proportion (three quarters) of unskilled workers. Auto parts, which had also undergone substantial restructuring, had the highest proportion of semiskilled workers. Clothing, which was the least restructured, had equal proportions of unskilled, semiskilled, skilled, and highly skilled workers.

These findings did not support the assumption of the new paradigm that higher levels of technology—such as those found in electronic maquilas—correspond to a higher skill profile among workers. In fact, just the opposite was found to be true. The garment subsector, with the least advanced technology, had the highest proportion of skilled workers. Carrillo and Contreras (1992) attribute this to the fact that organizational transformations of the most restructured maquila sectors designate all segments of workers at low skill levels. By contrast, a more traditional maquila-industry subsector such as clothing, which was not restructured, attributes greater skill to its labor force. This is powerful evidence of the degree to which the recognition of skill is socially constructed.

There is mounting evidence that the type of flexibility implemented in Mexico has been more unilateral than consensual, especially in the export-maquila industries in the north (De la Garza and Leyva, 1993: 76, 77). The process of maquilization is linked to the adoption of lean production systems through this unilateral implementation. Multiskilling and/or multi-tasking of workers in groups under lean production methods is one way to reclassify jobs downwards, so that workers doing them get less pay and status than they would in the more traditional Mexican industries.

The managerial responses presented so far in this chapter indicate that Nogales-area transport-equipment maquilas more closely resemble the old paradigm than the new. The two studies discussed above suggest that aspects of the new paradigm, such as work teams and quality circles, might increase the ratio of workers to technicians. I did not find this to be the case. None of the transport-equipment maquilas in the Nogales area have implemented work teams or quality circles as part of the new labor process. There were some workers' groups and rotation (described below), but conditions fell short of the new-paradigm forecasts.

At Plant C, for example, workers are organized into modules of nine, but these groups did not have the power to control or change the labor process as the new paradigm would predict. All of the workers in a module learn the production process in that area and can be rotated. From management's point of view there are two advantages: it is helpful when someone absent must be replaced on short notice, and it reduces workers' boredom.

Plant H did not practice systematic rotation of direct workers across different jobs. A universal operator, who is just below the level of supervisor, headed every production line; this person knew every job on the line completely, including quality control. The universal operator played the largest role in training new direct workers. The general manager said that it was one of his ambitions to do away with the job classification of quality-control inspector and institute inspection by the universal operator.

Plant I assembles wire harnesses developed by the company in the United States, where all decisions about suppliers are made as well. "They just send us the blueprints," said the Anglo-American financial services manager, who had worked for this company in Nogales for eight years, and before that in the United States. He said that all the wire-harness plants of his company have gradually been moving to Mexico; the last U.S. plant had closed the previous year. Because of its size and longevity, managers in other Nogales transport-equipment plants often referred to Plant I as a model.

The personnel manager at Plant I, a Mexican woman, identified seven different job classifications within the plant's direct labor force. The first five of these were low-skilled production operators, high-skilled electronic analyzers, medium-skilled molding-machine operators, high-skilled board assemblers, and medium-skilled quality-control inspectors. After labeling quality-control inspectors as direct labor, the personnel manager admitted that they really were indirect workers but were treated as direct workers at this plant.

Plant I does not practice rotation of employees across different jobs except for low-skilled production operators, who are rotated within their job classification but not to other direct-worker classifications. Thus, this plant features a high division of labor rather than multitasking; every line has a person in charge of repair, and another in charge of maintenance. Rotation is used to solve problems of absenteeism. There were two job classifications among technicians: high-skilled maintenance mechanics and electronic technicians. There was no systematic rotation of technicians.

Plant I also had a program to implement quality production that organized workers into teams of 15. Each team was measured monthly on the quality of its product, its members' adherence to work rules, and absenteeism. The best team was awarded a free meal in the cafeteria, T-shirts, and special mention in the company newsletter. The personnel manager said these methods were very effective ways of improving quality, because workers perform better under strong peer pressure. "If someone doesn't pull their weight, they'll kill them," she said. These are different from the quality-control circles developed by the Japanese: they are twice as large, workers cannot voluntarily opt in and out of participation, and they are controlled by management (Shaiken and Brown, 1991: 35). Thus they do not represent the empowerment of workers that is supposed to characterize the new labor process.

Before coming to Plant D, the Mexican general manager had worked for 15 years as a quality-control manager in another company. His small plant had two quality-control inspectors; his goal was to have zero defects and no quality-control inspectors. In his view, every operator should be his or her own inspector.

Plant A, the smallest in the sample, and the one with the lowest ratio of technicians to direct workers (see table 5.1), began operations in Nogales in 1989. This Japanese-owned plant was established in Mexico to access the U.S. market. The Japanese general manager ranked training and skill of workers as the most important factors in an optimum labor-force profile. He said the skill level of Mexican workers was generally not very high. He ranked flexibility and adaptability of the labor force second in importance, stability third, and cost fourth. Given the micro size of this plant, questions about teamwork and quality circles were not relevant. The Plant A manager showed no interest in developing his own labor force in the future, because he felt that all of his labor needs were met by the shelter company. Although this is only one example of a Japanese-owned plant that does not use management methods originating in that country, the findings were consistent with those of Shaiken and Browne (1991). Their study of 13 Japanese-owned plants throughout Mexico found the labor process to be more consistent with the old paradigm than the new. Taddei Bringas and Sandoval Godoy (1993) found that 15 Japanese-owned maquilas in Tijuana and the Ford plant in Hermosillo had implemented a kind of Japanization that used a seriously limited version of the new paradigm. However, managers thought that their Mexican workers had shown a great ability to assimilate Japanese techniques when given the opportunity. This study showed that technically skilled workers who participated in groups that sought higher productivity and quality were subject to a great degree of social control.

They had few channels though which they could air their frustrations regarding wage rigidity, changes in the labor process, and flexibility in general.

Transport-equipment workers in the Nogales area said they were very involved in quality-control activities. However, there was no evidence of quality-control circles as the new paradigm would predict (i.e., collective coordination of production to implement better methods). Three-quarters of the workers in each plant reported that during a normal work day, they carried out some activity related to quality control. A third of the workers who said they did some work to control quality "checked" the product in an unspecified way. Another quarter of them said they checked it visually. A small number (3 percent) reported using a "hands-on" method of quality control, like the "pull test" on harnesses. A few more (6 percent) said they used a manual measuring instrument like a tape measure or gauge.

A small proportion of workers in the sample (3 percent) operated the new microelectronic technology. Their jobs involved a high degree of skill. For example, a 26-year-old man at Plant F said it was his job to program the computers to make the material for the circuits. Once this material had been produced, he put it on a tray and took it to the line. Another regular part of his job was to produce the SPC graphs, which he delivered to quality-control specialists.

While the importance of quality had clearly been impressed on these workers, they were not empowered participants in the work process. The worker who programmed computers and drew graphs said that any problems on the production line were solved by a decision of the supervisor or engineer; they were the bosses, and in order not to have problems, it was better for them to decide.

I encountered one example of new-paradigm practices, which later reverted to mass-production techniques. The general manager from Plant G said he used to train direct workers in multiple skills and rotate them across jobs. He said he had to stop when the company's main client insisted they use a form of SPC, which assessed the number of rotation-caused errors to be too high. "Someone who's rotated is more likely to make a mistake, which will send the graph of defects soaring up." Now, when direct workers are hired, the manager sees that they are trained on one job, like soldering. If they do not do it well, he trains them on another job, continuing in this way until they find a job the worker does well. The result is that direct workers at Plant G are permanently placed in jobs they perform well. These are specialized into 15 categories, which are not given distinct titles. Workers at this plant do not carry out their jobs in teams, although seven of them serve on a health and safety committee. These findings support Kaplinsky's (1994: 344) argument that production systems have homeostatic features that make them return to the ways things used to be done, and that mass-production systems can reassert their former logic. The general manager of Plant G was confident that he could have achieved very high quality with rotation across jobs, but he had been prevented by the plant owner's acquiescence to a U.S.-based client. Only the 12 technicians in this plant were rotated across different jobs, since this did not affect the rate of defects measured by SPC techniques.

Zero inventory and SPC were the only new-paradigm practices found in Nogales-area transport-equipment maquilas. Most managers said that except for generic components, which are cheap and used in large numbers, they keep very little inventory on hand, but follow just-in-time production methods instead. For example, Plant C only kept finished products as stock for about 24 hours on average. The general manager at Plant D did not keep much finished inventory on hand. He said that if he did and found a problem, he would have to go through all the inventory to correct it. "Better to do it right the first time and send them all to the buyer," he said.[4] Plant I maintained absolutely no inventory of finished goods. Instead, goods were warehoused on trailers and on their way to being installed. Within two weeks of being produced at Plant I, a harness was installed as part of a vehicle in the United States. Almost all the plants in the sample used some variation of SPC. Some relied on the technical college to train their employees in its use; others thought such training was inadequate and provided their own.

Carrillo (1988) found reclassification of maintenance and quality-control jobs downward, from the technician to the direct worker, was the result of the implementation of work teams. This study of the Nogales area shows that this can also happen without the new-paradigm work team or quality circles. The unilaterality that De la Garza and Leyva said accompanies implementation of the new paradigm in Mexico has always been part of the old paradigm. In more developed economies, it was mitigated by workers' organizations, which sometimes made the labor process more of a two-way street, if not a consensus. The modules at Plant C were organized to cope with absenteeism, not to involve workers in the labor process. The competitive teams at Plant I lateralized conflict so it would occur between workers and be harnessed to improve production, displacing any conflict that might arise between workers and management. The health and safety committee at Plant G is also quite consistent with the old paradigm. At Plant H, universal operators are multiskilled but remain at the level of an operator, defined as direct labor, even though they are legally defined as within the purview of technicians.

Except at Plant G, the prevailing unilaterality also allowed all managers I interviewed to collapse quality control into the direct labor force, or to plan to do so in the future. This does not indicate de-skilling but rather downgrading the job classification in which skilled work is done to permit lower status and wages. As a phenomenon, it is characteristic of peripheral Fordism: areas outside of the highly industrialized world have weaker unions, which are less able to defend workers' rights. It is also significant that most quality-control inspectors in the plants studied were women. The compliance associated with women's roles undoubtedly makes it easier to give them less credit for their work than is their due.

Workers' Acquisition of "Skilled" Jobs through Specialization

All workers interviewed were asked to name their job title and describe all the activities they carried out on a normal work day. The latter was an open-ended question; interviewers asked whether work was manually, mechanically, and/or electrically done, what tools and equipment were used, and what the worker did with the tools and equipment. There was much more variation in the workers' versions of their job titles than those given by managers, or in the newspaper advertisements discussed in chapter 3. Forty-four percent of the job titles identified by workers consisted of different kinds of operators. Tapers (those working with electrical tape) comprised 13 percent of the job titles; other job titles made up the remaining 43 percent. This large number of categories identified by direct workers makes it clear that they do not perceive themselves as limited to the two job classifications predicted by maquilization.

Among the 43 percent who were neither operators nor tapers were five quality-control inspectors, four mechanics, and three maintenance and repair workers. Workers' self-identification as direct workers mirrors the tendencies of managers (described above) to downgrade what is defined as technicians' work. All the mechanics and maintenance and repair workers were men; all but one of the quality-control inspectors were women. More than half of these workers with downgraded classifications worked for Plants F and J, which had moved production back to the north-central part of the continent because of high defect rates. In the Nogales area, this removal of jobs has truncated workers' job ladders. Even though people are still doing skilled work, there is little opportunity for formal recognition of their performance, or upward mobility.

Workers' jobs were coded as having high, medium, or low skill, in accordance with the labeling given by managers.[5] Using this classification method, four-fifths of the workers surveyed had jobs ranked as low skilled; one-fifth had medium- or high-skilled jobs. Direct operators and tapers were more likely (65 percent) to have low-skilled jobs than workers having other job titles (35 percent).

Almost two-thirds (61 percent) did all their work by hand, using absolutely no tools or machinery. A much smaller proportion (28 percent) used machines, which were not evaluated as terribly difficult to operate (for example, solderers, riveters, drills, voltmeters, spray guns, molding machines, and compression guns). More than a tenth (11 percent) used machines that required more knowledge and training (for example, cutting and testing machines that were computer programmed). Managers classified jobs that required only manual work as low skilled; those which required any kind of machine were more likely to be classified as medium or high skilled. Operators and tapers tended to do only manual work more often than expected, whereas those with other jobs tended to use machinery more often than expected.

Production operators with jobs that managers labeled low skilled most often gave the following job titles: routers, blockers, assemblers, clippers, and tapers. As indicated above, in a few workplaces, operators were regularly rotated through some of these jobs to prevent boredom. Other operators had always done the same job. Plant I, for example, uses more than 7,000 different components in the manufacture of their wiring harnesses. Many of these are quite small—several fit into the palm of a hand. It is important, if tedious, to keep all of the tiny pieces coordinated. One 24-year-old man at Plant I had worked there for two and a half years as a sorting operator. In a normal day, he separated different types of material such as wires of different lengths and qualities, connectors, clips, tape, and glue into separate bins.

One 19-year-old "blocker" said she inserts "the wires into connectors, which are pieces of plastic which have little channels to hold the wires. Afterwards, I cover the cables with tape, and put them on the line. Then I put the spacers, which are small plastic insulators, on with a metal strip. This is all done manually." A "router" said she took the wires delivered to her by the materials distributor, untangled them, laid them out on the board with the shape of the harness traced on it, and routed the wires along the posts in the board to the connectors. Routing involves manually stringing the appropriate wires to other wires with which they will later be connected with glue, molding, or some other means, depending on the operation. The wires are sometimes put into small hoses or tubes.

An "assembling operator" said, "I get the material as it is circulated around the production line to my position. I assemble the spider, which is inserting thirteen points of wire into connectors on the board. You have to do it accurately and quickly." Taping involved wrapping electrical tape around a wire, or several wires, from one end to the other. Sometimes a spiral motion was used to cover the length of a set of wires. In another operation, two sets of wires were connected to form a Y-shape, with a knot taped like a baby's diaper. In some cases, the worker put the appropriate wires together and inserted them into a taping machine, which applied the tape with uniform pressure along the whole harness.

A "machine operator" said he performed more skilled tasks than those already described. "I put the cable into the machine that cuts it and rivets it. We have to change the blades, dies, and cables in the machine too. Then I have to put tags on each type of material. I have to program the computer, and arrange the cables in boxes by fifties." A "mechanic operator" said, "First, I check the cutting machine to make sure that the measurement that is required is the correct one. If it's not the right one, I correct it on the computer. Then I put the wiring in the rollers where it's cut to pieces. I start the machine with a computer." These two workers in cutting had each received four weeks of training, since mistakes can be expensive. As the general manager from Plant G said, "A harness costs $1,200 to cut, and if you cut eight of them wrong, that's a big waste."

How do workers come to hold more- or less-skilled jobs in Nogales transport-equipment maquilas? There was little association between whether a worker had a skilled job and factors that predated entry into the plant where interviewed. There were no age differences between those with low-, medium-, or high-skilled jobs. Fifty-seven percent of workers with low-skilled jobs had more than a primary school education, as compared to 63 percent of workers with medium- or high-skilled jobs, showing a weak association between skill and education in the expected direction. Workers with low-skilled jobs were also as likely as workers with medium- and high-skilled jobs to have worked in other maquiladoras before their present job. Half of the workers employed at each skill level had previous maquila experience. However, experienced workers tended to have had the same average number of previous jobs and the same average seniority at those jobs, regardless of the skill level of the job they held when interviewed.

Although three-quarters of all workers had received some training for the job, there was no association between the skill level of the job and a worker's training (or lack of training). Neither was there much association between length of training time and the skill level of their job. Workers received an average of seventeen days of training for the job they held at the time of the interview.[6] Those with low-skilled jobs had been trained for only two days less, on average. However, workers with high- and medium-skilled jobs were more likely (57 percent) than workers with low-skilled jobs (24 percent) to have always had the same job at their present plant. Workers with high- and medium-skilled jobs also tended to have more seniority than workers with low-skilled jobs. This suggests that workers acquire skilled jobs through specialization in the same job at the same plant. This is in keeping with the old paradigm, in which jobs are specialized, as opposed to the new paradigm, in which workers become more skilled by learning several tasks.

Regardless of the skill label attached to their jobs, some workers believed they had improved their situation by having had more than one job sequentially at their plant. A little less than a third (30 percent) of all workers had held a job other than their present one at their place of work. Half of these had held one other job besides their present one; one-fifth had held two other jobs, and another fifth, three other jobs. Only one-fifth of those who had held more than one job had received any training for their previous job(s). Three-quarters of those having had another job besides their present one believed that this change within the plant had meant some improvement for them. The most frequently cited benefit from changing jobs was an increase in wages (40 percent), followed by learning more (19 percent), more comfortable work (17 percent), and finishing work earlier (9 percent).

Of those who had previously worked a different job in the same plant but had not benefited by any improvement, almost two-thirds worked in Plants F and J, which had sent production jobs back north. Some, in fact, experienced downward mobility. For example, a male production operator at Plant J had previously worked as the assistant to the head of his line, but he had only worked this other job temporarily before the line disappeared. A male taping operator at Plant J used to work as a quality-control inspector before the production which he inspected was stopped. Thus, evidence suggests that the transfer of jobs northward was accompanied by a drain of some better work.

Skill level of a job is strongly related to gender of the worker holding that job. Men are more likely to have high- and medium-skilled jobs (25 percent) than women (10 percent). One reason is that men gained more skill with seniority, whereas women did not (as illustrated in table 5.2). Another explanation is that women tended to be direct operators more often (55 percent) than men (36 percent), and most managers label direct operator positions as low skilled. Women are also more likely (68 percent) than men (56 percent) to have jobs that require only manual labor, which managers classified as low skilled.

As shown in the job advertisements in chapter 2, women are recruited for these low-skilled jobs purposely. Although training was not associated with skill for the sample as a whole, the lack of training for women contributed importantly to their having less-skilled jobs. Slightly fewer women (70 percent) received any training whatsoever for their present job than men (77 percent). However, there were huge gender differences among workers who did receive training for their present job. Women received an average of eight days of training, while men received almost three times more: twenty-two days on average. Thus, women workers are not only segmented into the lowest level of work from the outset, they were far less likely to benefit from any technology transfer that might result from training, or to move up by acquiring skills.

Managers' attitudes play a large part in explaining workplace discrimination against women. Heyman (1991: 170) said that men had better jobs than women in Agua Prieta maquilas because the informal education they gained by tinkering with cars "dovetailed with factory management ideas about appropriate training and job placement for men versus women." In the case of wiring harnesses, I found that while some managers thought women's informal education also prepared them for factory work, this did not help women workers. One manager said that he always asked potential women workers if they knew how to sew, and if they said yes, they were hired. He equated the detailed work of threading wires with the skills women gained in sewing. The job of threading the wires, or routing, is considered low skilled and is at the bottom of the pay scale.

The manager's notions of women's temperament also contributed to his judgment about the kind of work they should do. He thought women had more patience than men to do seated, detailed, specialized tasks. Similarly, a manager at Plant I said that while production operators had low skill, they needed to have dexterity. "That's why we have a lot of women working here. They have nimble fingers," he said, echoing countless managers of the traditional, or early, maquilas.

On the other hand, the manager at Plant C accounted for the fact that only 7 percent of direct workers in his plant were women by saying that the technology was too dangerous for them. Women might get into accidents from the metal at the cutting machines and presses, and the company would be liable, he argued. In this context, it is interesting that one of the male workers interviewed at Plant C thought this work was too dangerous for him as well. He was particularly apprehensive of the sharp metal that was cut in the presses, and he considered his job to be very dangerous. The manager at Plant C also believed painters should be men, but did not elaborate why.

Other research has linked a preponderance of unskilled workers with microelectronic technology used to test for electrical defects. Computer feedback systems allow for the abolition of a separate quality-control job and have been important in improving technical control, which was the original purpose of the assembly line layout (Brown, 1992: 199). In a study of 37 electronic maquilas in Tijuana, Barajas Escamilla (1992) found that computer testing to verify quality was being used to support women's manual work by improving its quality and productivity. Despite the fact that this more sophisticated technology has been introduced, highly labor-intensive work activities are still predominant, with the result that development of workers' manual skills and acute physical sensibilities is an essential characteristic of the preferred labor force. Barajas Escamilla demonstrates that productivity is raised through the simultaneous gender segmentation of the

Table 5.2 Skill Level by Gender, Controlling for Seniority

	First Quartile[a]				Second Quartile				Third Quartile				Fourth Quartile				Total			
	Men		Women		Men		Women		Men		Women		Men		Women		Men		Women	
	N	(%)	N	(%)	N	(%)	N	(%)	N	(%)	N	(%)	N	(%)	N	(%)	N	(%)	N	(%)
Low-Skilled	27	(90)	21	(87)	19	(63)	18	(90)	28	(87)	20	(95)	17	(59)	18	(82)	91	(75)	77	(89)
Medium- and High-Skilled	3	(10)	3	(13)	11	(37)	2	(10)	4	(13)	1	(5)	12	(41)	4	(18)	30	(25)	10	(11)
Total	30	(100)	24	(100)	30	(100)	20	(100)	32	(100)	21	(100)	29	(100)	22	(100)	121	(100)	87	(100)
																			N = 208	

Source: Survey of workers in Nogales and Imuris, Sonora, 1991.

[a]The quartile distribution for seniority is as follows: first quartile = 0–9 months; second quartile = 10–22.5 months; third quartile = 23–32 months; fourth quartile = 33 or more months.

productive process, introduction of advanced technology, and maintenance of low salaries. The feminization of the labor force is inherent in the new maquila and the process of maquilization. A comparison of Barajas Escamilla's findings on the relationship between gender, skill, and technology with the results from this study show that limiting the opportunities of women through gender segmentation is not something that takes place only in the western corridor but is a characteristic of the present restructuring of maquiladoras.

The Importance of Extended Work Hours

If transport-equipment maquilas in Nogales and Imuris have not developed according to the new paradigm, which depends primarily on the use of more advanced technology and the new labor process, then how else can their expansion during the eighties be understood? The history of capitalism demonstrates that before technological advance led to growth, surplus was generated by lengthening the working day, intensifying labor, and expanding the labor force. Describing early capitalism, Marx (1887: 382) said, "The lengthening of the working day . . . allows of production on an extended scale without any alteration in the amount of capital laid out on machinery and buildings. Not only is there, therefore, an increase of surplus-value, but the outlay necessary to obtain it diminishes." Similarly, Lara Valencia has suggested that there is a certain amount of elasticity of the working day in contemporary Nogales.[7]

Federal labor law intensifies work in the north by requiring a 48-hour working week as opposed to 40 hours in the center of Mexico. Although the 48 hours are supposed to fit a six-day week, multinational corporations have "gringo-ized" the week, as the maquila association leader called it, by collapsing the 48 hours into five days. Thus, the legal working day from Monday to Friday is nine and a half hours long, and if Saturday is worked, it is worked overtime. During the period in which I was collecting data, the amount of time that plants were actually keeping workers at the workplace varied from a low of nine hours per day to a high of ten hours and twelve minutes. The plant that fell below the nine-and-a-half-hour legal standard was a plant that had cut back production because of the recession. Those above the legal standard included unpaid time the workers spent at the plant for lunch and breaks. The electronics manager who labeled the adjustment in hours "gringo-izing" said that they had tried working two shifts in his plant, but public transportation was so bad in Nogales that the workers could not get home at night. If they worked overtime into the evening, the plant hired taxis or buses to take the workers home, so management preferred to have them work Saturdays to avoid the cost of transportation.

The modification of working hours by foreign multinationals is not well thought of by Mexican workers and others who try to articulate their point of view. In 1989, García, a leader of one of the left-wing parties in Sonora, criticized the requirement that maquiladora workers work legal holidays. He accused the foreign-owned maquilas of violating workers' constitutional rights by not allowing them to form unions and by making them work May 1, when Mexicans traditionally celebrate Labor Day (Figueroa, 1989a). That year, the government inspector in charge of protecting workers' rights was accused of incompetence because he did nothing when senior maquila executives threatened workers who participated in national labor celebrations rather than showing up for work. The inspector in question said that he could not do anything for workers in this case because the law was not perfectly clear on this point. This is curious, since in other parts of Mexico, this federal law has not been found to be ambiguous. Without representation by unions or protection by government officials, however, the decision about whether, or when, workers are entitled to legal holidays is made by management, and workers have no say (Borquez R., 1989).

Later in 1989, Figueroa (1989b) said Nogales maquiladora workers would enjoy a 16-day Christmas vacation (longer than required by law) because they had worked for eight consecutive Saturdays before the holidays. Some of the effects of this change on labor-market dynamics were reported in chapter 2. Managers announced that this innovation had been agreed upon. They approved it because their companies would not experience a production deficit, since workers had worked on Saturdays for two months ahead. Workers approved it because many of them wanted time to travel, to visit their families in Sonora and Sinaloa.

Since 1989, this practice has been extended to cover other legal holidays; in some plants, such as the one in Imuris, workers have to work overtime in order to get legal holidays off. In our 1991 interviews, before and after the legal holiday on Easter weekend, we found that some workers strongly disagreed with this practice but had little choice. More than one person said that they did not think it was fair that they should have to work

Saturdays in order to, as they said, "pay for" their legal holidays (in this case Good Friday). An Imuris worker said, "I do not agree with them forcing us to work Saturdays in order to pay for our vacation days. What do you understand vacation days to be? I should not have to work those days in order to enjoy the vacation time that I have, but they don't like it when I talk about this, so I get called into personnel sometimes."

In the Nogales area, the length of the working day and week is related to policies of managers and owners—workers have no say except to vote with their feet by working somewhere else if they can. The company in which workers complained most about having to "pay for" their holidays by working Saturdays (and sometimes Sundays also) was in Imuris, which has few, if any, alternative sources of paid employment. If a company wanted to intensify the labor process through extension of the working week, or manipulation of holidays, this would be easier in a place like Imuris. However, there is undoubtedly some interaction between city location and company policy, since the same company that owns Plant J in Imuris also owns Plant F in Nogales, and workers in the latter also reported irregularities around holidays. A Plant F worker said, "For the last vacation we took, they made us sign memos so that they wouldn't have to pay us for the days we were out. The majority of workers say nothing and whatever management says should be done, is done." As demonstrated in chapter 2, the company that owns Plants F and J has advertised for personnel coordinators and engineers who will work in both plants, with transportation provided by the company. At the management level, there is a great deal in common. A worker at Plant J planned to quit and go back to farming in the countryside, which he preferred to maquila work. He said, "The bosses tell us that by law we have to work overtime when there is overtime, nine hours minimum. They pay us 2,000 pesos per hour for overtime. We work three hours extra daily, and sometimes Saturday and Sunday. We have to sign a sheet to work overtime. If we can't justify not working overtime, they suspend us for a whole day the next week, and we miss the attendance bonus, cafeteria bonus, and grocery pay. That means you lose 40,000 pesos for missing one day."

There was a wide range in the number of hours workers said they had to put in at their plants in the week before they were interviewed. The lowest average number of hours, at Plant H, was 46; the highest, at Plant G, was 55. This 9-hour difference is not explained by the way the legal holiday fell, but by the policy of the manager at Plant H, and the owner at Plant G. This became clear to me when I conducted the managerial interviews, which for both plants took place after collecting data from workers.

Plant H is a large multinational with subsidiaries all over the world. Its general manager is a senior executive who appeared to enjoy more autonomy than other managers in relation to the head office. He told me that in 1984, he had devised a plan whereby workers who finished the production expected to take 48 hours in only 45 could go home early and still be paid for the full 48 hours. He said that the plan quickly became a success. Workers were happy to leave early, and management was satisfied with productivity and quality.

In Plant G, on the other hand, the manager was younger and had no administrative experience with his company outside of Nogales. He had worked his way up through the ranks and believed that people did not work well under pressure. His plant was the one that I felt was the most genuinely cooperative, which I attributed to his democratic style of leadership.

While I was interviewing the Plant G manager, the owner called. The owner told the manager that he would be there in ten days with clients, and he ordered six prototypes of each of three new models for the clients' inspection. The manager told the owner it was impossible to have six done in such a short time, but said he could have at least one of each ready if they worked overtime. He later told me that this was a negotiating ploy. In reality, he thought he could have three of each done. He had advised the owner against overtime work, because workers had already done a great deal in the previous few weeks. The owner insisted they work overtime, and the manager was very distraught when he got off the phone. The personnel manager was very supportive of the general manager. She said that if necessary, they would sleep on the tables in the cafeteria to get the work done on time.

At the end of my visit to this plant, the general manager once again said that people did not work well under pressure, although it is clear that this belief of his did not always make a difference. I had a sense that because he was such a good manager, he would get his labor force to work this extra time for him. The owner, who lived half a continent away and was reputed to be tight-fisted, could not have gotten the same results himself, but could order them with one brief phone call. The manager appeared to be in a contradictory class location—he controlled workers, but was himself controlled by the owner.

Another modification by multinationals in workers' use of time is what they do when work is completed (if, indeed, work is ever completed at their plants). Almost two-thirds of workers said that there was a quota or minimum production standard in their job. It was noteworthy that when quotas were not used, the reason was attributed to the machinery. For example, a manager at Plant I said there is no quota for molding-machine operators because "you can only go as fast as the machine."

Asked what they did after they had met the quota and before the end of their shift, workers' responses form a continuum from plant to plant. At the low end is Plant G, where workers can stop working but must stay in the plant. Next are Plants B and I, where workers must do some other work if needed (without extra pay), but extra work was not often needed. At Plant I, this was probably because the production quota had been reduced due to cutbacks in production resulting from the recession in the United States. The policy at Plants D, H, and C is that workers are to continue doing direct labor until the end of their shift. As noted above, if workers at Plant H complete expected production early, the end of the shift comes sooner. At Plant F, the quota was raised to 110 percent. Before workers can call it a day and go home, they have to do 10 percent more work than required by the quota. If workers finish all the work necessary to reach the quota, which rarely happens, they must sweep or pick up material that has dropped. At the highest end of the continuum is Plant J, where workers must help other workers until everyone has met the quota; then they are allowed to go home early. This seldom happens, because the quota is constantly being increased: if the workers reach a level above the quota, that becomes the new quota in the future. When they have been able to leave early, it has been five minutes before the end of the shift. The quota is not an individual one but a collective one.

On this last dimension, Plants F and J were found to have the most extended labor process. The company's recent loss of an important client because of too many defects had resulted in changes that increased conflict between management and workers. A worker at Plant F said:

When we don't meet the 110 percent production quota, we are forced to stay at the plant. Some supervisors make the operators sweep the line and pick up material that's on the floor. If we say no, they threaten to send us to the personnel department. There they tell us that there are no other laws besides the maquila laws. Maybe this is so because there are no unions in the maquilas and workers are afraid of confronting management and losing the fight. For example, many workers were fired, but seniority was not taken into account. We complained to the personnel department and they answered that we could complain all we wanted but that there was no other law than the maquila law and that no one can tell them anything, because if they do the plants could leave.

This is a good example of how unilaterality operates at the level of the shop floor, and of how the absence of consensus and worker empowerment places Nogales transport-equipment maquilas some distance from the new paradigm. These Nogales and Imuris workers are threatened with losing their jobs unless they agree to broaden job definitions to include cleaning, and to losing their seniority when production loss leads to firings. As noted earlier, this company had already make good on the threat by moving some of the jobs back to Canada.

This is a clear example of workers in the north and south of the continent being played off against each other. Labor opponents of NAFTA have always pointed to this kind of whipsawing as one of the main problems with free trade. Time will tell whether labor unions will be able to use the "parallel" labor accord, appended to NAFTA in 1993, to protect workers' rights. As shown in the next chapter, unions in the Gulf corridor had, in the past, been sufficiently effective to limit the working week to 40 hours. The power of strong union leaders in Matamoros has been eroded, however, and in 1993, some plants began shifting from a 40- to a 48-hour week. When Sony imposed a six-day work week at one of its maquilas in Nuevo Laredo, Tamaulipas, in January 1994, workers peacefully demonstrated to show their opposition. Women workers in particular objected to the six-day work week because it prevents them from fulfilling family responsibilities. The AFL-CIO has charged that they were assaulted by police during this protest.

The National Administrative Office (NAO) was created after NAFTA took effect to investigate labor complaints. Four U.S. and Mexican labor rights organizations filed a complaint with NAO in the United States, claiming that Sony was breaking Mexican labor regulations by imposing a six-day work week. It was expected that the complaint against Sony would not be processed by the NAO, which had failed to process earlier cases brought before it, arguing that this was not the appropriate forum.[8] However, the NAO surprised many when it ruled in favor of the complaint against Sony, concluding that workers probably had been dismissed for union organization, and that the independent choice of union representation had been blocked. U.S. Labor Secretary R. Reich requested that the Mexican government ensure that Mexico's labor laws be observed (Dombey, 1995f).

Conclusion

This chapter has shown that only two aspects of the new paradigm have been introduced in Nogales-area transport-equipment maquilas: zero inventory and SPC (statistical process control). Use of the most advanced technology was not considered cost effective because these maquilas are centers of cost reduction for the firms that own them. The only evidence supporting the dual-technology thesis was the drastic reduction of the number of technicians at some plants after production was transferred back to the other side of the border.

Four-fifths of workers have jobs classified as low skilled by managers. However, in several of the plants studied, there are tendencies to downgrade the skill level of jobs, so that this is probably an overestimation used to keep wages low. Workers with medium- or high-skilled jobs acquired them by specializing in the same job within one plant. Women workers had more low-skilled jobs than expected because they received less training than men, and moved up over time to better jobs less often than men.

We did not observe work teams, quality circles, or rotation of multi-skilled workers through several different jobs except in one plant, which rotated technicians only. In some cases, workers were organized into some groups to make them work harder through competition with each other, to alleviate their boredom, and to help management cope with absenteeism. About a quarter of the workers interviewed felt they had improved their work situation by having held more than one job sequentially at their plant.

The changes that have taken place, or which are in the process of being carried out in these plants, do not intensify work through technological means or through the re-skilling and empowerment of workers. Instead, workers and managers describe a situation that harkens back to the transition between handicraft production and manufacturing. The first factories in Britain, which brought workers using hand tools together into socialized production, sustained their profits in the face of competition by extending and intensifying the working day, and by lowering real wages by employing large numbers of women and children. This chapter has provided strong evidence of the extension of the working day and week. When the maquila association leader said that managers had gringo-ized the Mexican working week by getting workers to work 48 hours in five days instead of six, his usage of the term was quite limited. The standard work week north of the border is 40 hours in five days, not 48. Other methods used to extend working time include getting workers to "pay for" their holidays by making them work substitute Saturdays for legal holidays, imposing overtime, and raising production quotas. The degree to which hours of work have been extended in Nogales-area transport-equipment plants varied according to managers' or owners' policies. It is greater in Imuris where there is no other significant source of waged employment. State officials collaborate in the extension of working hours by failing to enforce federal labor law.

As the next chapter will show, the extension of working time is due more to the absence of effective unions that could enforce legislation than to the employment of women and children. Although workers' youth (22.8 years on average) undoubtedly makes them more amenable to changes in the labor process and predisposes them to be flexible and strong, they are not children. While Mexican labor law specifies that men and women doing the same work are to be paid the same wage, a look at table 4.2 shows that women workers, on average, earned 27,000 old pesos (U.S. $9.00) a month less than male workers. This 5 percent difference could not be empirically explained by men and women having different jobs, working in different plants, or working overtime. Because it is small, the difference may be due to error. On the other hand, differences of this kind should be followed up in future research, since they may foreshadow the future. Solís de Alba (1991) has argued that the goal of deregulating federal labor law in the eighties was salary flexibilization and has resulted in different salary levels between men and women, sectors of production, and companies. From the present study of the Nogales area, however, it cannot be concluded that profits have been sustained through hiring women at lower wages. If NAFTA results in wage increases, women might be left behind, since they are already segmented into the bottom of the occupational hierarchy.

The dual-technology thesis, that maquiladoras with low technology are being phased out in favor of those with more advanced technology and the new labor process, is not borne out by the evidence in this chapter. The skill of the labor force was not the primary concern of most managers; its cheapness made it cost ineffective to introduce the most efficient technology. This was true both in the plants in the sample that made auto accessories that were finished products, and those that made wire harnesses.

The failure to confirm the dual-technology thesis makes the notion of technological heterogeneity seem a more apt characterization of present trends in Nogales-area transport-equipment maquilas. These findings also question the argument that Mexican maquilas have passed a turning point and are on their way to modernization. Nogales managers, most having at least a decade of administrative experience in Mexican maquilas, seemed quite convinced of their technological and organizational preferences.

While some managers of automobile-engine plants in Hermosillo view flexibility as being more valuable than low wages (Shaiken and Herzenberg, 1987: 42), this is not true in the Nogales area. The situation in Nogales auto-parts maquilas does not represent the new paradigm that Shaiken and Herzenberg brought to our attention, and its managers do not envision their operations becoming like the new paradigm. They do not see their goal as "catching up" to the more modern techniques introduced at the southern end of the corridor. On the other hand, the plants studied do not fit perfectly within the old paradigm either, because of the adoption of zero inventory and SPC, and because of the growing tendency for workers to do their own quality control and maintenance. If they can be said to be flexible at all, it is a static flexibility; while they may produce more than one product, there is no keen desire to make use of relevant technologies (Cohen and Zysman, 1987: 131).

The next chapter will investigate whether workers put in extended hours because real wages have fallen so drastically. Sklair (1993: 251), for example, has argued that "economic conditions in the *frontera norte* may be forcing maquila workers to work longer hours to support themselves and their families," which he does not think will change with free trade. "It is possible that NAFTA could eventually bring in legislation to harmonize working hours in the three countries, but this is not likely to happen in the near future." If maquiladoras continue to move south through the western corridor under NAFTA, practices of extending working time can be expected to spread to more southerly locations as well.

WORKERS' REACTIONS TO WAGES
AND WORKING CONDITIONS

Proponents of NAFTA argue that the increased demand for industrial workers alone will raise wages. Why then hasn't this taken place in the border assembly plants—maquiladoras—where employment rose from 131,000 in 1981 to 505,000 in 1992? Instead, wages averaged about $1.15 an hour last year, lower than 1981 levels. (Shaiken, 1993)

The maquiladora association leader mentioned in chapter 3, who favors an "international" managerial style, related U.S. wages and working hours to maquiladoras: "Even though you give American workers a fair day's pay, they won't give you a fair day's work. They're not going to become more productive, even though working hard is an old American tradition. The unions have ruined things." The answer to Shaiken's question about why maquila wages have not increased can be found in relationships established between the *comprador* class of managers along the border, who set the length of a fair's day's work; maquila unions, which do not adequately represent workers; and the Mexican government, which determines a fair day's pay. Together, private enterprise, organized labor, and government constitute a mode of regulation in operation before NAFTA was negotiated.[1] "The government holds down wages to attract investment, labor rights are truncated and employers often conspire to set wages. As a result, rising productivity doesn't translate into better wages" (Shaiken: 1993).

Will low wages be maintained after NAFTA's implementation, putting downward pressure on wages in the rest of North America, or will some new political force emerge to modify the situation? Sklair (1993: 250) thinks it unlikely that NAFTA will have any substantial upward impact on maquila wages, because maquilas will continue to rely on their labor-cost advantage over U.S. and offshore plants. Shaiken (1994: 69) has argued that "Mexico's industrial success could serve to hold down wage growth in the United States rather than improve conditions in Mexico."

Even those commentators who predict wage increases under NAFTA do not envision them as large enough to make much difference. According to Yasuo Sasaki—who opened his own Tijuana maquila after 28 years as a Sanyo Corporation general manager—even if the predicted wage hikes occur, labor and other production costs in Mexico will still be extremely cheap, and Japanese investment in Mexico will grow in order to produce for the U.S. market (Crevoshay, 1991). The maquila association leader in Nogales predicted that under NAFTA, "Mexico will go to a 40-hour week, and that will lower unemployment. Hours per worker will go down, but costs for companies will go up because we'll have to hire more workers to get the same number of hours worked."

Political discussions about NAFTA have obscured predictions for wages and labor markets with the implication that the treaty means free trade for all sectors. Former President Salinas countered charges that free trade would bring Mexico only low-paying, unskilled jobs like those of the old maquiladoras. He said his goal for the treaty was certainly not to have Mexico specialize as a provider of cheap labor. However, Mexican labor markets have been very controlled throughout the eighties, and one of the main objects of that control has been the reduction of wages. The success of De la Madrid's and Salinas's modernization project depends on continuity. Theoretically, the new paradigm predicts higher wages as a result of more skilled work and greater productivity. However, Rosenberg (1989: 397) has argued that when flexibility is accomplished through deregulation, it takes on a "dark side" that includes lower wages as well as decreased job security and social benefits: "deregulation policies may merely lead to a shuffling of the boundaries of segmentation and perhaps a hardening of the lines of segmentation." Low wages are also characteristic of productive systems that are conceptualized as peripheral or neo-Fordist.

This chapter focuses on the forms of labor-market control pioneered in the maquilas, to help predict how free labor might be in the context of NAFTA. To examine why maquila workers put in such long hours, we look at levels of pay throughout the eighties, work satisfaction, and turnover. We ask whether a longer working day and week are sufficiently rewarding in terms of pay, skill development, and recognition, or whether long hours lead workers to seek other jobs that leave more energy for private life—a pattern shown in chapter 4 to be important economically.

How the Mexican Government Has Depressed Wages

Tremendous downward pressure on Mexican wages since 1976 has drastically reduced the real value of Mexican currency. Just how far it has dropped and, by implication, the distance it has to bounce back up is well illustrated by De los Angeles Pozas (1993: 72–73):

> [T]he buying power of the minimum wage has been reduced to nearly one-third of its 1982 level. The minimum wage is now 42.5 times its 1982 level, but consumer prices are 124.3 times their level in 1982. Basic necessities for a family of five cost . . . nearly two times the minimum wage, and this only covered essential goods—not education, clothing, recreation, etc. Therefore, just to reach 1982 conditions, wages should be increased by 193 percent. Given this figure, even firms with the highest wages are paying multiskilled workers several thousand pesos less than what the worst-paid worker received in 1982. . . . In general terms, the problem of wages is so important that some economists believe that the crisis in Taylorist and Fordist models is a crisis of the wage relation, which includes the structure of job classifications and the process of wage formation.

Even observers who predict that greater demand for labor under free trade will push wages up do not predict very large increases. In 1991, for example, Jenner cited maquila-industry projections for roughly a 50 percent increase in the following five years—from $1.50 to $2.25 an hour (Key, 1991). This is hardly enough, however, to catch up with the loss in buying power De los Angeles Pozas notes.

According to Pradilla Cobos (1993: 139), there have been three governmental sources for the downward pressure on wages, which act together as essential elements of economic *adjustment* (emphasis in the original).

1. Government policies of fiscal restraint that have imposed ceilings on wage increases, slowing the growth in wages as compared to the growth in prices of basic subsistence goods. Wage ceilings have been imposed since 1977, six months after the Mexican government signed a Letter of Agree-

ment with the International Monetary Fund in 1976. Through the Pact of
Economic Solidarity instituted in 1987, the government sets the maximum
increase for the minimum wage and for the public sector. These wage ceilings also serve as a standard for private sector wages, putting downward
pressure on them as well. With the exception of 1982, wage increases have
been inferior to the inflation rate for the last 17 years. During the administrations of Presidents de la Madrid and Salinas, from 1982 to 1994, the effect has been to set Mexican wages among the lowest in the world.[2]

2. Shrinkage in indirect wages through the reduction of government
spending on, and privatization of, infrastructure and social services for
workers. Post-revolutionary Mexico developed institutions dedicated to
carrying out some family functions, such as the subsidized tortillas program
(*tortibonos*), support for the construction of housing, health programs, education, pensions, etc. Neoconservative ideology adopted by technocratic
leaders has emphasized the necessity of reinforcing the family structure
through the promotion of the traditional model of the nuclear family (father,
mother, children). Many of the public institutions supporting the family
have now been eliminated or severely cut back.

3. Constant devaluation of Mexican currency in order to improve the
competitiveness of Mexican imports on world markets. The devaluation of
the peso has benefited maquiladoras mainly by facilitating the reduction of
wages paid to workers. The principal commodity that maquilas buy in Mexico is labor. Devaluation also benefits foreign capital in any other expendi-
tures made in Mexico. An anecdote related by the leader of the maquiladora
association provides a good illustration. One of his actions as president had
been to successfully reduce trucking rates, which had risen more in Nogales
than anywhere else along the border, according to him. His argument at
official hearings that rates had gone up disproportionately was convincing
because he reported his evidence in pesos rather than dollars. The percentage increase over time was much greater in Mexican currency than in U.S.
currency. The event received wide coverage from the Mexican press.

Government policies of wage reduction contradict the purpose for which
the minimum wage was enshrined in the constitution. Barajas Escamilla
and Rodríguez Carrillo (1989: 41) argue that "Under the present conditions
of the Mexican economy, the minimum wage has stopped being the referent
for measuring levels of well-being, fundamentally because this wage no

longer abides by that stipulated in fraction VI of Section 'A' of Article 123 of the Constitution of Mexico which holds that the wage must be sufficient and remunerative." The government has not compensated workers for devaluation by adequately raising minimum wages. Thus, the legal minimum is used to pull down income—even well-educated Mexican professionals customarily report how much they earn in terms of multiples of the minimum wage, a practice that would be inconceivable among the same class in the United States or Canada.

Foreign capital has responded to wage-reduction policies by expanding maquila operations and moving them from higher- to lower-wage areas through the process of maquilization. While the introduction of more capital-intensive operations has led to a decrease in wages as a proportion of the total value of maquila products, the cost of labor is still very relevant. Foreign capital has been able to get more skilled labor for its money in Mexico because of low wages. Carrillo (1992) studied several plants owned by the same firm, which before the boom of the eighties used to make only finished products in non-maquiladora plants in Mexico City, and paid better wages than any other. When this company moved production to northern maquilas, wages paid to workers decreased at the same time as capital-intensive technology was increased.

> On average, workers in auto parts plants at the border get 60 per cent less in wages than their colleagues in finished product plants in the center of the country. The plants studied have different wages within the same skill category. While Plant C [in the state of Mexico] was paying 1.4 dollars an hour to its workers who had jobs classified as unskilled in 1986, in Plant N [in the state of Sonora] it was paying 0.56, and in Plant F [at the border], 0.36 dollars respectively. And for jobs classified as highly skilled the differences were: 2.3, 0.84 and 0.81 dollars. The depreciation is so great that the most highly skilled maintenance mechanic at plant F earns the same as an unskilled worker in plant C in 1986. (Carrillo, 1992: 56–57)

The decrease in real wages in Mexican automotive maquilas in the eighties helps to explain their development and high level of international competitiveness. Carrillo contends that there has been a homogenization of wages in all sectors of maquila industries, regardless of the technology used.

Working Smarter, Working Longer, or Collecting Coupons?

The findings discussed above help to predict the possible outcome of a test for wage homogenization in Nogales-area transport-equipment maquilas. If we had discovered a clearly discernible dualism, we would not expect wage homogenization. Instead, we would anticipate increasing differences among wages as a more highly waged group emerged. However, Nogales-area transport-equipment maquilas have not been found to be very much a part of the second wave of maquilas, nor has a dualism of the expected variety been observed. Although a small primary sector has developed in the labor market, most managers who were interviewed believed that the cheapness of labor was one of its most important characteristics. Given these findings, it seems likely that transport-equipment workers' wages would have been homogenized in the Nogales region as well. We will explore the homogenization hypothesis, first in terms of the wages reported by workers surveyed in 1991, and then with wage data from the plants where they worked, collected from SECOFI for the years 1982 through 1990.

Transport-equipment workers in the Nogales area earned an average monthly take-home pay of 553,000 old pesos, or U.S. $184, in 1991 (see table 4.2). This included the base pay rate, benefits, and overtime pay. There was a 248,869 old peso (U.S. $83) monthly difference in what workers were paid according to the plant at which they worked, with workers at Plant J in Imuris earning the lowest at 434,773 old pesos/month (U.S. $145), and those at Plant G earning the highest at 683,642 old pesos/month (U.S. $228). Since workers at the plant with the lowest average income earned only two-thirds as much as those at the plant with the highest monthly wages, wage homogenization does not at first appear to fit the situation in Nogales and Imuris transport-equipment maquilas very well.

Three hypotheses are suggested to explain the difference in the earnings of direct workers in 1991. First, the higher pay for jobs thought to require greater skill would constitute making money by working smarter. Alternatively, if jobs evaluated as skilled are not better paid, workers may earn more money by working longer, as discussed in chapter 5. Finally, the different benefits workers are paid, often collected in coupons and redeemable for goods in kind, may account for the difference in wages. The benefits required by federal labor law, and those offered beyond this level, were discussed in the analysis of ads in chapter 3, but this chapter explores exactly how much difference those benefits make in the pay a worker receives.

Let us first look for a difference between different skill levels among direct workers to try to explain why some workers surveyed earned only two-thirds the income of others. Even though it was demonstrated in chapter 5 that four-fifths of the sample of workers held jobs that managers evaluated as low skilled, wages might vary because more skilled jobs received better pay. To find out whether this was the case, hourly wage levels for different skill categories were compared. Workers with low-skilled jobs earned 16 cents (U.S.) less an hour, on average, than workers with high-skilled jobs, which represents an increase of 25 percent, not counting benefits and overtime. When overtime and benefits were added in, the difference between the hourly pay of the most- and least-skilled jobs rose only slightly, to 22 cents per hour. In other words, someone with a high-skilled job earned 26 percent more than someone with a low-skilled job. There does not seem to be much variation in pay connected to the skill level of a job. Only nineteen workers, or 9 percent of the sample, had jobs evaluated by managers as highly skilled. Only one of the workers with a highly skilled job was from Plant G, which had the highest average wages.

Let us turn to the question of whether benefits or bonuses account for the difference in wages. Barajas Escamilla and Rodríguez Carrillo (1989), for example, found that for women electronics workers in Tijuana, the higher the gross salary, the lower the proportion coming from benefits. Workers they studied received on average 15 percent of their pay from benefits. Workers in Nogales-area transport-equipment plants were quite similar in this respect, earning 13 percent of their wages, on average, in benefits.[3] This is a fairly small proportion of the wage to come from bonuses and benefits. In comparison, professors in public universities and TELMEX company employees duplicated their real wages with "productivity bonuses" between 1989 and 1992 (Balboa and Orozco Orozco: 1994).

In order to assess the relative contribution of base, benefit, and overtime pay to total pay, we divided the sample of workers into four groups of approximately the same size. These are shown in figure 6.1, where each bar represents the wages of one quartile of the workers studied, composed of different wage segments. Workers who earn the highest wages (see the fourth quartile to the far right of figure 6.1) do so because of more base pay

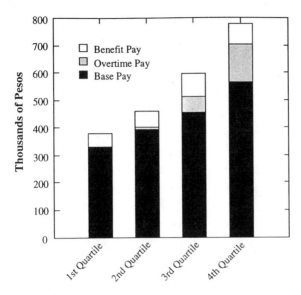

Figure 6.1   Monthly Wages from Overtime, Benefits, and Base Pay, by Monthly Wage Quartile. *Source:* Survey of direct workers in transport-equipment maquilas in Nogales and Imuris, Sonora.

and overtime pay, not because they get more benefit pay. The empty parts of the bars, which represent benefit pay, do not change much over the quartiles. The percentage of a worker's total pay that comes from benefits does not vary tremendously, ranging from 13 percent for the lowest two quartiles, rising to 14 percent for the third quartile, and dipping to just under 10 percent for the highest pay quartile. Workers who had a higher base rate of pay tended to work more overtime. Workers in the highest quartile of pay averaged 6.4 hours of overtime per week, while workers in the third, second, and first quartiles of pay averaged just 3.19, 0.64, and 0.10 hours of overtime per week, respectively.

The answer to the question posed in the subtitle, then, is that the workers studied made more money not by collecting coupons, but by earning more in basic rate of pay and by working longer. Basic rates of pay do vary somewhat by the level of skill attributed to a job, as noted above. Findings from chapter 5 also indicated that there was an element of putting in time to get the more skilled jobs, which were more likely to be filled by people who had experience on the same job at the same plant.

This conclusion holds for Nogales and Imuris transport-equipment workers in 1991. But how did the expansion of maquilas in the eighties influence wage levels? To test whether transport-equipment workers in Nogales and Imuris fit the national pattern of decline in real wages, I collected data from SECOFI on how much the ten plants in the sample had paid their employees from 1982 to 1990. Using 1982 wages as a base rate, I calculated the real worth of these wages for the other years.[4] I then calculated the wages reported in the survey of workers, in terms of 1982 values. The average monthly real wage reported per transport-equipment worker in 1991 was 324,752 old pesos, or U.S. $108.25. This 1991 real wage was more than half (59 percent) of the nominal wage at that time of U.S. $184. Thus, while workers were earning many more old pesos in 1991 than in 1982, those apparently numerous pesos would buy only 59 percent of what they used to.

In terms of buying power, real wages declined by 55 percent from 1982 to 1990; that is, direct workers earned 45 percent, or less than half, of the wages in 1990 that they had earned in 1982. The dramatic steepness of the decline in real wages for direct workers in Nogales and Imuris transport-equipment plants is represented in figure 6.2. This chart shows that all plants were not equally responsible for the drop, with the steepest at Plants F and J, where wages to direct workers were reduced by 1990 to 24 percent and 38 percent, respectively, of what they had been in 1982. Thus, at Plants F and J the percentage drop in real wages to workers was 76 percent and 62 percent, respectively. Company policy for workers in these two plants makes the effects of devaluation and state policies of wage reduction much more profound by not raising wages to compensate.

What about technicians, administrative personnel, and managers? Was the real value of their wages also reduced so dramatically? Data were also collected from SECOFI on wages paid to transport-equipment personnel above the direct-worker level in Nogales and Imuris. The results show that the state policy of wage reduction has had the greatest negative impact on direct workers, as opposed to those with better jobs. The real wages paid to each technician in the transport-equipment plants studied increased by 36 percent, on average, between 1982 and 1990. Thus, when technicians are taken into account, wage homogenization does not appear to be the case. However, the homogenization of wages between the direct worker and technician level cannot be definitely rejected with these SECOFI data,

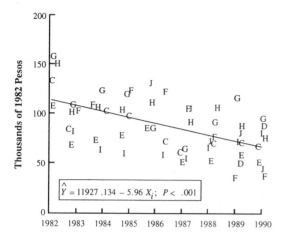

Figure 6.2   Average Annual Wages per Direct Worker in Transport-Equipment Maquilas (Plants C–J) in Nogales and Imuris, Sonora, 1982–1990. *Source:* Mexican Secretariat of Trade and Industry.

since they may reflect an increase in overtime worked by technicians rather than an increase in base pay rate. Because it is not clear from the data how technicians earned more, we cannot answer the question as to whether they worked smarter, longer, or collected coupons.

However it was earned, there is a substantial difference in what technicians earned from plant to plant. As an average, the increase of 36 percent masks differences in the real wages paid to technicians in different plants in the sample. At only two plants were real wages to technicians increased: F and J, the same ones found above to have reduced direct workers' wages the most. All the other plants reduced real wages paid per technician at rates varying from 15 percent to 54 percent. The real wages paid per administrative employee between 1982 and 1990 increased slightly, by 1 percent, with Plant G mainly responsible for this increase.[5]

Even though most technicians did not see an increase in real income (with the exception of those at Plants F and J), they still constitute a sector of the labor force that is better off than direct workers. Figure 6.3 shows that technicians' and administrators' wage gains were made at the expense of wages paid to direct workers. In 1990, direct workers' wages represented 24 percent less of all wages the ten companies in the sample paid in comparison to what they had paid in 1982. Conversely, technicians' wages as a

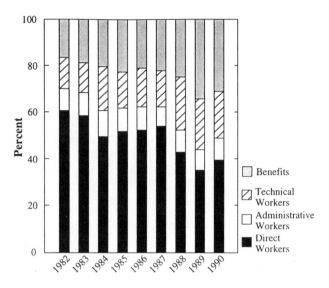

Figure 6.3   Distribution of Wages in Transport-Equipment Maquilas in Nogales and Imuris, Sonora, 1982–1990. *Source:* Mexican Secretariat of Trade and Industry.

proportion of all wages paid represented 9 percent more, administrative wages 1 percent less, and benefits 16 percent more. Benefit pay is reported in the aggregate by SECOFI, but even in the impossible case that direct workers were to earn all of the benefit pay, this would not compensate for the decrease in the proportion of all pay that went to direct workers. This finding of a growing group of technicians is consistent with findings from the analysis of ads in chapter 3, which showed that incentives like open salary and opportunities to move up had created a small primary sector of the labor market.

The decrease in the proportion of wages paid to direct workers and the simultaneous maintenance of a smaller group of workers who make higher wages contribute to social-stratification hierarchies in the communities where employees live. This analysis is based on data for wages paid only in Mexico and does not reveal the top class of employees, made up of administrators paid in the United States. Foreign-service personnel undoubtedly reinforce the middle class in the communities just north of the border where they and their families live. Mexican administrative employees and technicians can be thought of as contributing to the middle class in the communities where plants are located. Because the share of the wage pie available for the worker at the bottom was reduced during the eighties, inequality increased.

What is the approximate size of these classes? Real wages per technician in 1990 were on the average 3.9 times more than the amount paid per direct worker, and real wages per administrative worker in 1990 were 4.9 times the amount paid per direct worker. However, the number of technicians and administrative employees was very small in comparison to the number of direct workers. In 1990, there were only 18 percent as many technicians and administrative employees, together, as there were direct workers. This is only slightly smaller than the 20 percent of the labor market found in chapter 3 to represent a primary sector. Plant F, where real wages per technician had increased the most, actually decreased its number of technicians from 32 in 1989 to 11 in 1990. This is fewer technicians per direct worker than almost any other plant in the sample, since Plant F had the second highest ratio of direct workers to technicians in 1990 (see table 5.1).

In fact, the highest wages per technician in 1990 were at the same plants that had the two highest ratios of direct workers to technicians: Plants F and J. The two plants also had a lower number of technicians than other plants in the same size category. Whereas Plant J employed 9 technicians in 1990, Plant I, in the same size category and producing the same product, employed 143 technicians. Whereas Plant F employed 11 technicians in 1990, the other plants in the same size category all employed more. Plant G employed 76 technicians in 1990, and Plant H employed 20. Perhaps Plants F and J employed relatively few technicians because much of the skilled work necessary for their operation was done by direct workers or had been transferred north of the border. Chapter 5 reported that direct workers doing skilled work came disproportionately from these two plants after some production was moved to Canada.

The stratification dynamics just outlined are limited to the immediate border area. The lowest wages were paid to direct workers in Imuris. A lower average hourly wage (1,758 old pesos, or U.S. $0.59) was paid to workers at Plant J than all other plants in Nogales (2,046 old pesos, or U.S. $0.68), because those with low-skilled jobs earned less in Imuris. When the relationship between wages and location was controlled for skill level of job, low-skilled jobs in Imuris were found to pay an average hourly wage of

1,661 old pesos (U.S. $0.55), while those in Nogales paid 1,972 old pesos (U.S. $0.66). While this is above the minimum wage for both locations, the difference mirrors the fact that the legal minimum is lower in Imuris (11,000 old pesos/day, or U.S. $3.66/day) than Nogales (11,900 old pesos/day, or U.S. $3.97). As noted above, more highly paid administrative and technical personnel are shared by Plant I in Imuris and Plant F in Nogales, with most of them based in Nogales. Thus, they would not reinforce a middle-class group in Imuris. Plants with competitive strategies based mainly on low wages, a characteristic of the old paradigm, may be more likely to be drawn to interior locations because of lower wages.

Worker Benefits as Indirect Wages

If coupons, or the scrip, by which workers receive their indirect pay are not the main way of increasing direct workers' pay, why are they so often assumed to be an important component of the pay packet? There are at least two answers. Given the steep decline in the real value of Mexican currency, there is a tremendous need for any source of subsistence, whether it is paid in money or kind. Secondly, benefits are a way of making sure that workers keep up good attendance, and they can also be used to intensify work.

In their study of women workers in electronics maquilas in Tijuana, Barajas Escamilla and Rodríguez Carrillo (1989) argued that the composition of wages paid to direct workers was undergoing important modifications, with indirect wages, which were tied to productivity, gaining ground over direct wages. While they were unable to empirically demonstrate this in their study, it can be explored in Nogales and Imuris. An analysis of aggregate data on benefits paid to all maquila personnel in the ten plants sampled shows that there is a strong negative correlation ($r = -.8$) between the proportion of all wages paid to direct workers and the proportion of all wages paid for benefits.[6] There was almost no correlation between the proportion of wages paid in benefits, on the one hand, and the proportion of wages paid to technicians ($r = .073$) and administrative employees ($r = .007$). As the amount paid in benefits increases, the amount paid to direct workers decreases, a finding that supports the argument of the Tijuana study that for the working class, indirect pay is gaining ground over direct pay. Plants are moving to this type of wage flexibility in order to tie the indirect wage (in the form of benefits) to productivity, punctuality, attendance, etc., thereby intensifying the labor process.

Benefit pay also served to control the labor force and worker's reactions. All but one of the plants in the sample administered a complex set of benefits to encourage workers to be as productive as possible, and to discourage them from leaving to work elsewhere. Data from workers' benefits allows us to compare what workers received to the benefits that were advertised (see chapter 3). Plant E was the only one with no benefits; the general manager seemed unconvinced that benefits could lower turnover rates. However, the base pay rate (without overtime pay) for Plant E is higher than at any other plant. Of those companies paying benefits, workers at Plant C received the fewest, at 8,571 old pesos/week (U.S. $2.86), whereas workers at Plant H, the company paying the most, averaged 24,176 old pesos/week (U.S. $8.06).

Workers said they earned eight general types of benefits. The most frequently mentioned bonus was for attendance. Eighty-seven percent of workers reported having an attendance bonus at their plant; 84 percent said they normally received it. This bonus was usually calculated weekly, and in some companies, compounded monthly. That is, a worker might be paid an average of 13,326 old pesos/week (U.S. $4.44) if s/he had perfect attendance for two weeks, and then an extra 10,000 old pesos (U.S. $3.33) at the end of the month if no days had been missed. If one day of any two-week period was missed, however, the worker forfeited the entire bonus for the two weeks (and, of course for the month). Workers said that they would prefer that the attendance bonus be prorated by day, because if they missed one day in two weeks, they should only lose the portion of their attendance bonus represented by that day. It is clearly in their interest to have the attendance bonus integrated into the base pay rate and not administered as a bonus.

The second most frequently mentioned bonus was for subsidized meals provided in the plant cafeteria, or from 12 food stands huddled together in the middle of the industrial park. The stands looked temporary and makeshift compared to the factories that surrounded them, although they were similar in construction to much of the housing in Nogales. One couple operating a stand told me they had been doing business there for 16 years. While we could see electrical power lines running into each plant, none went to the stands, which had oil lamps for light and fuel cylinders for stoves. Almost two-thirds of all respondents reported that their plant offered on-site meals. The average value of both subsidized cafeterias and coupons for meals in food stands was 22,245 old pesos (U.S. $7.42) per week.

Most workers preferred the plant cafeterias. Some said they switched jobs to get a hot meal at work. Others liked to come outside of the plant at lunch or break time for the fresh air and view of the sky (the plant shells have no windows except in managers' offices). A manager at Plant G said that his company could not afford the total cost of a cafeteria, so it provided building materials, and the workers donated their labor to construct it. A manager at Plant C said a cafeteria was not cost effective. They gave no bonuses for food stands, but had recently built at least a lunch room in an attempt to stem turnover.

Workers receiving these benefits may have been better fed than others, but many did not think the level of the food benefit was adequate. Although there are often two meal breaks a day (breakfast and lunch), plants offering on-site meals only subsidized five meals a week. Several workers wanted all meals fully subsidized (10, if overtime was not worked on Saturday). They also complained that the meal bonus was tied to attendance. If they did not have perfect attendance for the whole week, they lost all or part of their meal bonus. This linking of the meal bonus to attendance is undoubtedly why these two factors clustered together in secondary incentives advertised for maquiladora jobs in chapter 3.

Coupons worth an average of 42,971 old pesos/week (U.S. $14.32) in groceries were available in the workplace of 64 percent of all workers. These were never paid in cash; they could only be exchanged for goods at a limited number of stores specified by the plant. In a small village like Imuris without many shopping alternatives, this often meant that the worker earning the benefit lost some of its value because of the restriction imposed on comparative shopping. One respondent from Plant J said, "I question the use of the coupons for 54,000 pesos for food in order to pressure us into not being absent. I don't think it's right that if we get sick one day we lose our right to the coupon that is used for buying the groceries for the week." The fact that, in these three different forms, food was so frequently used to encourage attendance indicates how difficult it is for workers to live on their direct pay alone. In the Nogales area, as in much of Mexico, hunger serves as one of the most immediate and powerful incentives for intensifying work.

A little more than 35 percent of workers reported that transportation bonuses were available at their plants, with an average value of 2,425 old pesos (U.S. $0.81) per week. Some plants had buses to drive workers to and from work. Some were within Nogales, and others brought workers from Imuris and Magdalena to Nogales on a daily basis. This made the already-long working day even longer. In a city where public transportation is grossly inadequate, and many of the streets remain unpaved, some form of assistance with transportation is extremely important for workers who do not earn enough to purchase cars either individually or in families.

Maquiladora managers in Nogales have convinced public-transportation authorities to reroute all buses from other city locations to the industrial park at the start and finish of shifts. Consequently, there is virtually no public transportation at these times for anyone *not* going to or coming from the maquilas. Barajas Escamilla and Rodríguez Carrillo report the same situation in Tijuana. However, transportation problems have not been solved by company buses, bonuses, and recircuiting public bus routes. Many workers still report leaving a factory because of transportation difficulties.

Other, less frequently mentioned benefits include housing, clothing, productivity, and social services (child care, on-the-job medical attention, etc.). These were available only at Plants H and I, the only ones where workers spontaneously reported satisfaction with their workplaces.

While almost all managers felt compelled to offer benefits in order to compete with other plants for labor, none felt that the benefits actually lowered turnover rates—workers still left their plants for others. Silvers and Lara Valencia (1991) show the Nogales turnover rate for 14 selected maquilas to be more than 11 percent in 1989. The leader of the maquiladora association said that if he could find an effective way of reducing turnover, he would quit his job as general manager and go out and sell it. The manager from Plant H put it this way: "There are a lot more jobs available here than people to fill them, even though the real estate people won't admit it. Let's say there's 20,000 jobs available in maquiladoras now or in the near future in Nogales. Everybody's hiring, so some managers initiate new benefits. The message is out immediately, and everyone starts new benefit programs. Even when the surplus of jobs shrinks back, you still have a high turnover rate compared to the United States."

On the other hand, most managers felt that benefits did reduce absenteeism. Two complained that their companies must make the legally required compensation payments to workers when there is not enough work available, and said that this made the Mexican labor force much less flexible than north of the border, where a company can lay off workers without having to make such payments. This is an important issue in Nogales, where former workers at Plant I took six claims before the *Junta de Conciliación y Arbitraje* (Hidalgo Blaine, 1991). The six workers, who had up to eight years of seniority, claimed the company had not paid them the severance pay they were due according to federal labor law. They had not received compensation for seniority, a benefit offered in their workplace. Many labor experts predict that indemnity payments will be greatly reduced in any future revisions of the federal labor law.

Paying workers' wages indirectly through bonuses and benefits allows companies greater flexibility because it allows greater control of the labor process. Not all of the workers who were potentially entitled to benefits actually received each benefit. The most frequent reason they cited for failing to receive an available benefit was missing work—with the benefit tied to attendance, they lost it. Another way benefits are used to control the labor process, reported by innumerable researchers, is the use of medical facilities to detect pregnancy in female job applicants. There are two major reasons pregnant women are not usually hired. First, managers reason that they would soon be gone and it is not worth the effort to train them. Second, they do not want to pay maternity benefits required by federal labor law. This refusal to hire women who are pregnant is against federal labor law in Mexico but, like so many other aspects of this law, is unenforced.

Several workers complained about favoritism in the administration of benefits, saying that they had not received their benefits when they deserved them, while other workers received them when they should not. Shaiken and Herzenberg (1987: 72) say this problem came to the attention of foreign-service personnel in the auto industry, who saw it as part of the inefficient practices of Mexican supervisors. The judgment of inefficiency holds only if one expects a standard form of payment for all employees in the same category as opposed to wage flexibility. Forms of management control, such as manipulating benefits, exert strong pressures for conformity by encouraging a client/patron relationship between the workers and supervisor. In their study of wage trends at the national level, Balboa and

Orozco Orozco (1994: 7) note that "Unfortunately, in most cases *compadrazgo, amiguismo* and *clientelismo* have prevailed instead of objective job performance."

It has been argued that workers may prefer indirect payment of wages through benefits because payment in kind is stable and cannot be whittled away by inflation or devaluation as easily as cash payments.[7] I did not find this to be the case. Instead, the distribution of benefits seemed quite flexible depending on short-term changes in the economy. When I first arrived in Nogales to carry out fieldwork in late February 1991, the automotive industry was depressed since sales were down in the United States, and the uncertainty of the war in the Persian Gulf exacerbated matters. Two workers at Plant F reported that their plant had reacted to the economic recession, which had been deepened by the war in the Persian Gulf, by "freezing" their grocery and seniority bonuses. In the case of the grocery bonus, "freezing" meant that the worker received less than previously, and in the case of the seniority bonus, it meant that regular increases in a bonus had been halted. This is an example of the effects of the U.S. recession and the war on the maquiladora industry, which more broadly included dismissals, decrease in exports, and a generalized reduction in benefits and salaries (Ortega, 1991). By the time I was finishing the fieldwork in mid-April, one of the largest plants was rehiring. I was not able to find out if the "frozen" benefits had melted, but this metaphor, together with the quotation above from the manager from Plant H, give some indication of their flexibility.

Ways to Increase Worker Satisfaction

The final question on the workers' survey asked, "If you could, what conditions would you change to increase the level of satisfaction you get from your present job?" Workers were then asked to rank the following ten aspects of their jobs in terms of whether changing them would give greater job satisfaction:

-wages
-benefits and bonuses
-opportunities for promotion inside the plant
-access to training
-acquisition of skills that will get you a better job in the future

–recognition of seniority as a basis of promotion and better pay
–conditions of health and safety within the plant
–respectful treatment
–work environment
–any other aspect of the job.

The majority (52 percent) ranked better pay first among the options that would increase their job satisfaction, and another third (32 percent) ranked benefits and bonuses second. Thus, money concerns were highest on the list of reasons for dissatisfaction with one's job for two-thirds of the sample. Next was the recognition of seniority as a basis for promotion and pay raises. Following these were skills that would get the worker a better job, health and safety, and respectful treatment. Trailing the list was "work environment." More than half (59 percent) ranked it seventh, eighth, or ninth.

The last question was placed at the end of the interview so that workers might expand on the rank ordering in their own words, and several did. The very idea of increasing satisfaction with their job was received skeptically by some. Other answers suggested that the improvements listed were not really possible. An operator who carried out the electrical test on wiring harnesses in the Imuris plant, for example, ranked respectful treatment first, better pay and bonuses last, and had this to say about the option which read "acquisition of skills that will get you a better job in the future": "I like challenges. I like to learn all I can, but not necessarily to get a promotion. I just want to be prepared if they tell me to shift to another type of operation. I want to be able to do it. It's really important to guarantee your job security here because job options are limited." Increased skill does not get workers more pay or help them move up within the plant, because they say upward mobility in the Imuris plant is not possible. The better jobs, as indicated in chapter 5, were lost. With the maquila being the only source of income in this village, workers cannot go to another plant for better pay or working conditions, and if they lose their job, they may be unemployed for a long time. In this environment, job security becomes more important than job satisfaction.

Another Imuris worker was interviewed on her 30-minute lunch break, when she chose to go home and eat to get away for a few minutes rather than stay in the plant cafeteria. Asked what changes would improve her job, the worker said she would prefer more time for lunch rather than better bonuses or benefits. In the Nogales plant owned by the same company as the Imuris plant, another worker said he was not happy with some of the decisions made by personnel, and he gave this example:

> Personnel told us we would work on Saturday. We voted on it to see if everyone agreed and we all said it was okay that we would work on Saturday. But they would not accept requests for working overtime during the week from 5 to 8 p.m. In other words, if personnel makes a decision, we should just go along and not get workers all hyped up. They don't want to hear you say that you would like to work extra time during the week so you don't have to come in on a holiday. They only want to hear you say that you will work.
>
> I'm happy that I haven't gotten bored yet. I'd like the plant to play music, because we get tired sometimes with what we're doing, sleepy. The people I work with are very happy and they sing or whistle. When we do this we're reprimanded.
>
> I don't like to be changed from one line to another because sometimes the heads of the line are inflexible and have a lousy attitude. Sometimes I feel like quitting because the head of the line has a very bad personality. We have to ask for permission to go to the bathroom, and we can only get 10 minutes in the morning and afternoon. If the head of the line is upset, she won't give us permission to go, and if we are a few minutes late, she writes up a report.

In some plants, like the commonly owned ones, there are multiple reasons for job dissatisfaction, which are difficult to capture in one list of job characteristics.

Asking workers to vote on whether they would work Saturday is a form of management-worker consultation, but the speaker obviously felt this consultation was not a genuine effort to get worker input. Hoffman and Kaplinsky (1988) have argued that the complete just-in-time labor process involves giving responsibility back to the detailed line worker, since high-quality work and the correction of errors requires the individual worker to make decisions. While chapter 5 showed that interviews with managers gave no evidence of work teams or quality circles, workers themselves were also asked a series of questions to find out how production problems and conflicts between workers and supervisors/managers were handled, and whether they agreed with the process. Workers were asked, "When some problem comes up on the production line, how is it solved?" and "When there is some difficulty or dispute between supervisors and managers, on the one hand, and workers on the other, how is it normally resolved?"

As expected from managers' disavowal of work teams and quality circles, most workers said technical and group-conflict problems were resolved in authoritarian ways. Most (77 percent) of the workers said that production problems were solved by the direct action of a supervisor, engineer, or some other administrative-level employee. Most (72 percent) also said that when a dispute arose between workers and supervisors or managers, it was normally resolved by discipline applied by the supervisor or manager. Only a fifth to a third answered that there were other alternatives for solving a production problem or disagreement between workers and their superiors, such as calling a work team in which the worker participated and discussed the best way to resolve the problem, or having representatives of the workers intervene through preestablished grievance procedures. Some other alternatives were specified. A 23-year-old male worker in Imuris said he preferred to resolve any problems outside the plant; since there were not many jobs in the area, he did not wish to lose the one he had.

When asked whether they agreed or disagreed with whatever problem-solving method was used in their plant, most agreed, albeit for different reasons. It is noteworthy, however, that these were the only questions that any workers refused to answer; a handful of workers with seniority insisted that they had never seen any production problems or disputes at their plant. This is such a sensitive issue that some workers thought it better to deny any knowledge. Thus, the level of worker agreement with problem-solving methods may also be inflated.

I interpreted the reasons given for workers' agreement and disagreement with problem-solving methods in terms of Weberian orientations to authority. Those who said they agreed for reasons that reflected a traditional orientation to authority answered: "He's the boss," "It's his job," "He's always done it." Acquiescent responses that reflected a more rational orientation to authority were, "Supervisors know more," "Workers don't understand," "The supervisor has more experience," and "The supervisor regulates other parts of the work process, like providing material and changing operators to other lines." A number said they agreed with traditional forms of exercising authority within their plant for reasons that showed they were coerced to agree, such as: "I don't want to lose my job," "Because otherwise they fire you," "Because a supervisor can discipline or fire me if I disagree," and "Because the supervisor is powerful and obeyed." These responses cannot be taken as evidence of the consensus which is supposedly part of the new labor process, but reflect the more hierarchical workplace organization of the old paradigm.

Workers organized under authoritarian control (problems solved by decision or discipline of someone above the direct-worker level) tended to disagree with it more often than those under some alternative program of solving problems. Most of the reasons given for workers' disagreement with traditional forms of authority sounded quite rational and were the same as reasons given under more decentralized forms for agreeing with it. Workers under centralized regimes said they disagreed with them, and workers under decentralized regimes agreed with them, for reasons like the following: "Operators should be taken into account more since they are the ones who are most directly related to the job," "There have been cases where I have not agreed with the solution or that I felt they had misinterpreted the problem," and "The appropriate person would be the one who is directly related to the job. The supervisor is not efficient." Others under traditional structures said they disagreed because they did not like supervisors coercing them. While decentralized decision-making and problem-solving are certainly not the norm in Nogales and Imuris transport-equipment maquilas, those who do work with less centralized structures are in more agreement with them than those who work in more centralized structures. Workers expressed a desire for more movement in this direction.

Unions' Failure to Represent Nogales-Area Maquila Workers

They promised us a rose garden. They gave us a desert. (Phil Keeling, United Auto Workers president at Mazda's Flat Rock plant, 1990. Quoted in Berggren, 1993: 164)

U.S. labor unions have been the greatest threat to maquilas since the beginning of the BIP, according to Martínez (1978: 135). They believe U.S. workers lose jobs every time a maquiladora opens in Mexico. As early as 1972, they promoted legislation to remove the tax advantages enjoyed by

U.S. companies producing abroad. Had this legislation passed, maquilas would have had to pay duty not only on the value added in Mexico, but on the full value of goods re-imported to the United States.

Although this legislation lost support and did not pass Congress, U.S. unions' opposition to maquiladoras was re-ignited with the proposal to fast-track NAFTA in 1990, and again during its negotiation in 1992 and 1993. Marchand (1994b) identifies four different positions in the debates taking place in Washington during NAFTA's negotiation: strongly opposed, moderately opposed, moderately in favor, and ardently in favor. Those who were moderately in favor tended to emphasize that NAFTA would result in a "win-win" situation—a liberal economic perspective. This is the "rose garden" scenario referred to in the quotation above. Applied to maquiladoras, this argument is similar to the unfounded hope that the maquilas would be one-half of the "twin plants" that would bring good jobs to the U.S. side of the border. Herzenberg (1993) is an example of a moderate supporter of NAFTA who argued that in the auto industry, it could lead to highly skilled and well-paid jobs for workers in all three countries. Marchand says that those who ardently favored NAFTA thought of it as a zero-sum game the United States would win, believing that a production-sharing strategy would mostly benefit U.S. companies and, by implication, the United States as a whole. This second position would see the rose garden growing on only the U.S. side of the border.

It has been argued that unions must lead the way in implementing the flexible, highly skilled production of the new paradigm, and that they have a special role in establishing cooperative coalitions between workers and employers (Kern and Sabel, 1992; Hoffman and Kaplinsky, 1988: 54). Quite the opposite has happened in Mexico. As the reference to "union problems" in Hermosillo from the Plant I manager quoted in chapter 5 hinted, one form of union representation has been recognized at the plant in the southern part of this corridor, where flexible methods are used. In the aftermath of violent conflict in 1990 at the Ford Hermosillo plant, in which one worker died, the workers pursued a strategy of passive resistance in their attempts to bring wages more into line with productivity and to democratize their union. Red armbands have replaced strikes, demonstrations, boycotts, and other direct confrontations among the new type of worker recruited by the company after 1990: older men from rural backgrounds with family commitments. It is difficult to imagine even this passive resistance moving northward to Nogales-area maquilas, since the union in Hermosillo is concerned only with local protectionism and the achievement of short-term demands (Sandoval Godoy and Wong Gonzalez, 1994).

Without the effective representation of labor, flexible production is implemented in a one-sided way, in the interest of capital. This has been characterized by Lipietz (1995: 45) as "a cosmetic and ideological Japanization, a shoddy Japanization." He concurs with Mexican researchers who say forms of work organization in the Ford Hermosillo plant which some call "Japanese" are really a scheme for eliminating the classical corporate unionism of the large Mexican industries and imposing flexibility. He goes further than the Mexican researchers, however, and also argues that the organization of work in the Ford plant at Hermosillo represents a sophisticated Taylorization in which workers are isolated a dozen meters from each other. He observed a vertical structure of work organization that leads workers to compete with each other for perfection instead of cooperating.

In the Nogales area, where peripheral or neo-Fordism of the old paradigm is more prevalent than the flexible production of the new paradigm, the perception is that there are no unions, not even to look after local interests in a passive way. On my first meeting with the manager from Plant D, he volunteered his opinion (before I could get to the question of labor relations) that "the unique thing about Nogales in comparison to Tijuana or Juárez is that it has no unions. When businesses come here from somewhere else, they think they are in heaven. The only unions here are ones which the company pays the dues for, and the workers don't even know they belong." The contradiction in this statement between the absence of unions and unions paid for by the company can be understood by a look at the history of labor relations in Nogales maquilas. In fact, there is a union structure in place that prevents workers from exercising their rights under the law. It is known as yellow unionism, or unionism that protects companies.

Very little research has been done on unionization in Nogales. Middlebrook (1991) argues generally that the move northward by the auto industry within Mexico was undertaken so that labor relations could be redefined in the newer facilities to lower labor costs and limit unions' influence. A spontaneous movement of workers arose in Nogales in 1980 to protest the violation of their rights under the law (lack of recognition of elected workers' representatives), increases in production quotas, and work rules within the factory.[8] Eight hundred and forty workers struck when their protests were not satisfactorily dealt with, the CTM became involved, and the factory was reopened. A short time later, fourteen of the most important maquilas in Nogales signed a collective contract with the *Sindicato Industrial Progresista de Trabajadores*, a state-level branch of the CTM in Hermosillo, without consultation with the workers locally in Nogales.

Lara (1990: 231) shows how the signing of this contract and recognition of the union by the authorities fulfilled two functions: first, to act as an instrument of protection for plants against any attempt at independent unionization, and second, to guarantee the freedom to dispose of and disregard the worker whenever management needed to. In an analysis of the collective agreement, Lara finds a total absence of the spirit of federal labor law, with its roots in social justice and a concern for balance between workers and management. One of the transport-equipment plants in the present study is among those listed as having signed the CTM contract analyzed by Lara. The shelter company is also listed as having its plants unionized under this contract; two of the plants in our sample are serviced by the shelter, and are covered under this contract.

In view of the weakness of union structures throughout the western industrial corridor, it may be more useful to look for comparisons latitudinally, in other maquila centers along the U.S.-Mexico border.[9] In fact, the most effectively unionized maquila workers are not in the Sonoran, Mojave, or Chihuahuan Deserts, but in the Gulf of Mexico corridor, particularly in the city of Matamoros. Williams and Passé-Smith (1992) say the more effective unionization of Gulf-corridor maquilas is related to social and political factors as opposed to geographical ones. Unlike the state of Tamaulipas, which has the highest rates of unionization, Sonora and Chihuahua contain strong agro-industrial capitalists who have challenged labor's power. In Sonora, an agreement to ban the unionization of Nogales maquilas is backed by the state government. In contrast, the governor of Tamaulipas has little power outside the capital and could not enforce such an accord if he could negotiate it.

An effective union presence in Matamoros and other Gulf maquila centers has meant that management has had less of a free rein to shape the labor force there than in Nogales, since the union acts as an active hiring agent. Matamoros workers put in fewer hours and receive higher pay than almost all other workers in maquila industries: 40 hours work per week with pay for 56. As Williams and Passé-Smith (1992: 103–4) note of the leader of many of the Tamaulipan unions, "Agapito González . . . runs a union that contributes to good working conditions, the shortest work week in the industry, and relatively high pay."

Nogales and Matamoros might be seen as two ends of a continuum of union strength. At the Matamoros end there is mutual accommodation of unions, industry, and the state. At the Nogales end, the maquila association of managers is dominant. Toward which end of such a continuum are maquilas more likely to move under NAFTA? Williams and Passé-Smith (1992: 37) do not see Matamoros as a model that will be emulated by other centers, but "the last bastion of *sindicato* political power." The influence of labor within the PRI has declined; since the Tamaulipan unions are associated with that party, their influence is deteriorating. True to this prediction, in January 1992, one week after eight plants unionized by Agapito González went out on strike, he was arrested for tax evasion—allegedly committed in 1988—and flown to Mexico City. The accommodation between labor, capital, and the state had ended.

It would seem that without an independent union movement apart from the CTM and the official party, unionization trends in the maquila industry will swing toward the Nogales end of the continuum. New forms of worker organization might introduce other dimensions to the continuum. A possible source of dynamism in maquila workers' response has been ties of communication and solidarity that arose during the negotiation of NAFTA, and the addition of the side deal on labor. As noted in chapter 5, the labor side deal has begun to be tested with complaints brought forward to the U.S. National Administrative Office (NAO) against General Electric, Honeywell, and Sony for firing Mexican workers who were attempting to organize. It is noteworthy that one of the issues over which there was conflict was the imposition of a six-day workweek, which Nogales workers have had for some time. The unions won the complaint against Sony, and the fact that Mexico's labor laws were not being observed was officially recognized. Future research will have to evaluate how effective the NAO is in strengthening Mexican workers' rights under the law. Some critics have predicted that complaints of this kind cannot proceed very far since basic worker rights are not covered by NAFTA.[10]

Bringing complaints to the NAO in the United States is a very indirect way of defending Mexican labor. Mexican workers need to be able to resist violations of labor law within their own country, at their workplaces.

Otherwise, the danger of increasing downward harmonization to the low standards of workers' wages in Mexico is more likely.

Turnover

Workers have little say in how plant decisions are made. If they strongly disagree with how production is supervised or conflicts are resolved, one of few options is to look for work elsewhere, if it is available. Ramírez (1988: 113) has drawn a clear link between the failure of unions to defend workers' rights and turnover, arguing that high rates of worker movement between plants will not be reduced until free and open unionism prevails. Contreras, on the other hand, says that

> evidence indicates that maquiladora employment constitutes a temporary option in the labor trajectory of the life of workers. . . . Only in the case of the reduced nucleus of highly qualified workers does there appear to be a segment forming oriented to the maquila as a labor career. This subjective experience of the maquiladora labor force as temporary and transitory constitutes one of its most important characteristics, a characteristic which could be called "social flexibility," and which implies a strong disposition to change jobs, both within the maquiladora sector and even leaving the labor market. In these conditions, the possibility of articulating collective strategies appears very limited, beyond the restrictions deliberately imposed by the companies and by the labor policies of the government. All this suggests the existence of two differentiated areas in the structuring of workers' strategies. First, mobility strategies governed by the dynamic of regional economies, structured under the logic of regional actors in the labor market. . . . Secondly, strategies of mobility and negotiation in the work place, stimulated by the competition outside of labor markets, and by the requirements for quality and stability associated with new managerial strategies and new processes of work. Here, we are talking about individual strategies and collective strategies which allow for a beginning system of regulation in the work place. (1990: 7)

Contreras's use of the concept of social flexibility is noteworthy because it is one of the few times that the term "flexibility" is defined from the point of view of the worker. For the majority of workers who are not considered

highly skilled, there appears to be a transfer of the strategy of using migration and job change to improve one's situation. Companies have moved
production from central Mexico, the United States, and Canada to maquila
centers in Mexico's northern industrial belt to avoid unions, high wages,
and rigid labor markets. Workers adopt parallel strategies when they migrate between locations and change plants to enhance their rewards. As
shown in chapter 4, most workers had migrated from within the western
corridor. A substantial number had moved within Sonora more than once
and, before moving to the Nogales area, had done maquiladora work elsewhere in Sonora. Migration from the south to the north through a regional
labor market often takes place in stages. While wages are higher and the
supply of jobs larger at the border, the cost of living is also higher, so that it
takes some time to become settled.

There is also evidence of social flexibility in the work history of
Nogales-area transport-equipment workers. Half of Nogales and Imuris
transport-equipment workers said they had previous maquila experience;
they had worked in from one to seven plants, with an average of almost
two. The average seniority at the worker's present place of work was 24
months. Seniority at the last maquila workplace was on average 16 months,
with 12 months in the next most recent one. Workers with previous experience had worked at their current job an average of 8 months less than those
with no previous experience. When companies flexibilize the labor force by
not recognizing seniority, workers develop a comparable disaffection in
their company loyalty.

Workers gave three kinds of reasons for leaving maquilas before their
present job: economic (better wages, bonuses), personal (family, return to
school), and work-related (inadequate working conditions, problem with
supervisor or manager, fired, plant closure). More than half of those with
previous maquila experience had left their last one or two maquilas for better pay; about a quarter had left for personal reasons. Although men and
women were equally likely to have previous maquila experience, the reasons given for leaving previous jobs revealed a slight gender difference,
with men more likely than women to have left for better pay, and women
more likely than men to have left for personal reasons.

The personnel manager in Plant I said that her department had done
some research on the causes of turnover; while they had hypothesized that
gender would be a related factor, with women leaving more often, they did

not find this to be true. Instead, they found that those who quit were likely to have migrated recently, to be from distant locations where they had done agricultural work, and to have paid high rent. Her findings were based on exit interviews conducted with workers when they quit.

I looked for empirical relationships between previous maquila experience and migration and other background variables in the data from the 1991 sample of workers and did not find much confirmation of her findings. Nogales-area transport-equipment workers did not say they had quit a maquila job to return to a previous location. Lupe, whose story introduced chapter 4, was the only worker who had done this, and she would have preferred to take a leave of absence rather than quit. The inability to support the personnel manager's hypothesis about recently arrived agricultural migrants being more likely to quit may be because workers who are interviewed by the company feel pressured to respond in a way they think is expected or socially acceptable. Family obligation is a socially acceptable reason for a worker to leave his or her job, although it may not be the real reason. On the other hand, the family does compete with private enterprise as a source of authority. The maquiladora association leader did not have much faith in exit interviews as a key to the secret of turnover at his electronics plant, and he said that "workers only tell you what they want you to hear, like that they have to go back south to help their family. Then you see them a week later working for Plant X down the road, which doesn't have the subsidized cafeteria that we do, or our attendance bonuses, but they do have a nice nursery. Plant Y also has a nursery."

There is a little support in the survey of Nogales-area transport-equipment workers for the hypothesis that turnover is influenced by benefits. Those who had previous maquiladora experience were more likely than those who did not have previous experience to report receiving bonuses that helped pay for rent and transportation. Workers with previous experience were also more likely to receive social bonuses like child care, life insurance, and medical attention on the job, but only seven men and seven women received any of these. In fact, previous maquila employment was not related at all to total earnings. While workers cannot use turnover to get higher wages in a community where wages are so similar, they may change jobs to at least help reproduce their labor power by getting them to and from work, getting them medical attention, and helping with shelter and child care.

There was evidence that other characteristics of the plant besides the kind of indirect pay offered in benefits influence whether or not workers were likely to have previous maquila experience, with the two largest plants having labor forces that were the most unlike each other with regard to turnover. At Plant J in Imuris, workers without any previous maquila experience were most highly represented, with 72 percent of workers having no previous maquila experience. This is undoubtedly due, in large part, to the fact that Plant J is the only maquila in Imuris, so that the only way a worker can switch plants for a better job is to commute to Nogales or another location. At Plant I, however, workers with previous maquila experience were most highly represented, with 65 percent of workers having previous maquila experience. Workers from Plant I reported earning some of the highest wages from benefits compared to other plants in the sample. On the other hand, none of the Imuris workers reported receiving housing, child care, or medical attention bonuses, which workers with previous maquila experience were more likely to have than workers with no previous maquila experience. Some complained that they had to go to Magdalena to get the health care benefits they were due by law, because there was no IMSS office in Imuris. To the extent that Imuris workers are captives of an interior labor market, they cannot put pressure on plants to improve benefits by quitting.

Conclusion

This chapter shows how transport-equipment workers in Nogales and Imuris experienced the decline in real wages throughout Mexico during the 1980s. The hypothesis that wages have been homogenized was only weakly supported. Workers at the plant with the lowest pay earned two-thirds of what workers earned at the plant with the highest pay. Workers who earned more did so by working longer hours and by living in Nogales, where their base pay was higher than in Imuris (paralleling differences in the minimum wage). Benefits and bonuses did not contribute greatly to the variation in workers' wages but were used by management to control attendance. Those who earn more also do so because the skill level of their job is recognized to a small degree in their pay, but this is not the major cause of higher wages.

Stratification among different employee groups in Nogales-area transport-equipment maquilas increased during the 1980s. Direct workers received a smaller proportion of what the ten plants paid out in wages as the decade proceeded, and technicians received a higher proportion. Real wages paid per technician increased by more than a third from 1982 to 1990, whereas direct workers earned less than half of the real wages in 1990 that they had earned in 1982. The more privileged group, technicians and administrative employees, made up 18 percent of all Mexicans employed in Nogales-area transport-equipment plants in 1990.

Neither the old nor the new paradigm predicts lower wages for direct workers. However, the process of maquilization has the lowering of real wages as a central dimension. Maquilization interacts with both the old paradigm and the new to create neo-Fordism in the former, and shoddy Japanization in the latter. Similarly, Taddei Bringas (1992) concluded that the 15 Japanese-owned maquilas she studied in Tijuana implemented only one side of lean production, having omitted the active involvement of the worker and higher wages. While the increasing inequality between groups of transport-equipment workers observed in this chapter might be seen as predictable by the dual-technology thesis of modernization theory, the temporary nature of the inequality predicted by this theory is difficult to accept given how low real wages have fallen.

A study of General Motors maquilas avoids the bifurcated conclusion inherent in the dual-technology thesis. Researchers observed some technological change (automation in very specific areas) and implementation of flexible systems of organization (statistical process control, work teams, and involvement of workers in increasing efficiency) that did make them an example of a new stage in Mexican maquilas. Rather than suggesting two or three waves, one of which would eventually replace the other(s), the researchers pointed toward "one of the new contradictions which the restructuration of labor in Mexico brings: a reskilling of the worker and his higher productivity, together with a devaluation of his work as the basis of international competition" (Arteaga G., Carrillo, and Micheli T., 1989: 4).

Nogales-area workers were very aware of this contradiction and expressed most dissatisfaction with the low level of their wages. They also wanted recognition of seniority and more opportunities to learn skills. Some did not consider job satisfaction as a realistic possibility. Living in a community with few other opportunities for paid employment, and working in a plant that had already shipped production back north across the border, their focus was job maintenance. The findings in this chapter that authoritarian methods of problem solving predominate reinforce managers' reports in chapter 4 that work teams and quality circles of the new paradigm are not used. The hierarchical structure of work organization is part of the old paradigm rather than the new. However, recent research on examples of the new paradigm's application at the Ford plant in Hermosillo indicates that it is also closer to the old paradigm than was earlier supposed.

The yellow, or protective, quality of unions in the Nogales area means that transport-equipment workers who are dissatisfied with wages, working conditions, or lack of decision-making power have few alternatives except to quit their jobs and find work at other maquilas with better conditions. High turnover may be workers' response to workplaces with low wages that do not reward them adequately, in that loyalty to one company is rejected in favor of the worker's self-interest. Half of the transport-equipment workers were found to have previous maquila experience in one to two plants. They had also built up a substantial amount of experience given their youth, with average seniority at the present workplace being two years, average seniority at the last maquila being 16 months, and 12 months at the maquila before that. Many had accumulated some of this previous experience in other Sonora locations besides Nogales or Imuris, so that they had navigated their way through the regional economy of the western corridor.

Managers interviewed in the Nogales area said they had received no government subsidies. They meant that they had not received such things as tax breaks and free property for locating in Mexico. However, keeping wages low is a way of getting Mexican workers to subsidize the companies profiting from maquilas. While Baker (1991; 1992) has made the argument that Mexican labor is not cheap, what he is referring to is the social cost of infrastructure, which is estimated to be from one-third to one-half the market value of a product, and attributable to neither management nor workers.

If the Mexican government were willing and able to change its policy of wage reduction and allow wages to rise, my prediction is that this would not be a general increase across the board but would follow the internal structure of the labor force discovered in this study. In Nogales-area transport-equipment maquilas, it would probably mean that the 20 percent of the direct labor force with jobs defined as skilled would get increases, and also the 18 percent of the total labor force who are technicians and administrators. However, the overwhelming majority with jobs classified as unskilled, the segment in which women are most likely to work, would probably not get wage increases. The utility of even making such a prediction is questionable given that, despite the introduction of more complex forms of production, the trend for wages has been reduction. The purpose of downgrading mechanical and quality-control jobs, found in chapter 4, must have been to reduce the amount paid out in wages. To predict that they would be paid more because their jobs are considered skilled even though they are direct workers does not make much sense. Workers have no collective bargaining power to pressure for an increase in wages, but react individually to job dissatisfaction by quitting.

Modernization theory predicts a temporary increase in inequality between a new industrial sector and an old agricultural sector, and in chapter 1 it was shown how this usage has been adopted to apply to the old and new maquilas. However, it is questionable whether this best characterizes Mexican maquilas in the eighties, since they were not the first industry developed within the country. As Lipietz (1995: 44) indicates, Mexico is one of the old industrialized countries of the third world, which have known an earlier form of industrialization: a regime of import substitution and semi-Fordist salary relations regulated by corporatism. The semi-Fordist character of its industry (that is, not having enough of the characteristics of the new paradigm to really fit, like first-world wages) meant that it was already flexible by international standards, so that what is happening now is a reflexibilization. The lowering of real wages throughout Mexico must be understood as part of the economic opening of the De La Madrid and Salinas administrations.

Chapter 1 indicated that maquiladoras paid about half the wages of Mexican industries even before the economic opening. One example of the pressure that traditional Mexican industry is now under is Ciudad Sahagún, in the state of Hidalgo, just north of Mexico City, which was created in the early 1950s as a model of regional development during import-substitution industrialization. It has good infrastructure by Mexican standards and has been the home of heavy industry, which built up its own supply of skilled workers from migrants in the surrounding areas. In the 1980s, many of the state-owned companies there were privatized, and in 1993 NAFTA provided them with stiff foreign competition. Mexican industry has not fared well against international competitors because it has lacked a gradual transition to allow it to emerge in a strengthened form from its previous protected position. The result is high unemployment for workers there, and pressure on their wages.

According to Hidalgo State Development Director Manuel Núñez, maquiladora plants are hard to attract to Hidalgo. "The problem with Ciudad Sahagún is that the kind of industry we have there pays a relatively high wage, and it would be hard to get them to settle for less," Núñez explains. Maquiladora plants, while they pay two to three times the Mexican minimum wage of under 3.50 dollars a day, just can't match steelworkers' wages—even Mexican steelworkers' wages. As Detroit learned, it's hard to go from making autos to flipping hamburgers; it's even harder in a city like Sahagún where there are no McDonald's. . . . Yet after 40 years, the legacy of Mexican industrialization policy can be reduced to just one single accomplishment in Ciudad Sahagún: it lured a majority of Mexicans permanently from the land, creating an urban industrial workforce. Now the question is what Mexico will do with that workforce. (Stevenson, 1995: 14)

The Mexican auto-parts industry is also having a very difficult time competing with auto-part maquilas. Ninety-four percent of all auto parts have been imported to Mexico since 1989 (Granados, 1994: 48, 50). SECOFI is reported to have ignored the obligation of assemblers in Mexico to use a certain proportion of domestically produced parts, which was established under the 1989 Decree for the Development and Modernization of the Auto Industry. According to Oscar Véjar de la Barrera, head of the National Autoparts Industry (INA), the domestic auto-parts producers could have doubled their production between 1990 and 1995 if the decree had been carried out. Domestic auto-parts producers have not successfully exported to the same extent as the joint ventures or foreign maquilas. They have called for a correction in the application of the decree, and for the auto industry in general, and support in helping to make them competitive. Without such corrections and assistance, maquiladoras will eventually absorb all auto-part production in Mexico. The 150 firms that make up the INA have lost approximately 30,000 jobs in the last 18 months, so that they presently employ 175,072 people. They are highly critical of the present foreign control of their auto industry, and they say that it makes Mexico into a maquiladora country. According to Végar, "the 164 maquiladoras set up in México paid on average, between 1989 and 1990, 1,240 new pesos monthly per employee, with sales of 3,800 million dollars and a value added of 23 percent or 800 million dollars. In contrast, the domestic autoparts industries paid 2,966 new pesos to their employees, who generated sales of 6,500 million dollars and with a value added of 4,550 million as a country. . . . Although with NAFTA the maquiladoras will be able to buy more inputs in México, they presently only buy 2 percent, a figure that has stayed the same in the last 10 years" (Duran, 1994: 55).

HETEROGENEOUS MAQUILA DEVELOPMENT AND CORRIDOR INTEGRATION IN CRISIS

Modern-day Sonora is located mid-way between the land it once was, a region of crops, patios and corrals, and what it strived to become: an industrial and tourist area filled with small houses cramped in the summer heat. Its mission is to serve as a border. (Heller, 1993: 28)

The maquiladoras in modern-day Sonora also seem to be midway between what they used to be in the early days of the BIP, and the promise of what they might be. The results of this study indicate that Nogales-area transport-equipment plants do not fit either alternative of the dual-technology thesis. This final chapter integrates the findings presented earlier and elaborates on their implications for the major questions addressed in the book. It also examines the immediate effects of the 1994 crisis in Mexico, to better understand the future maquiladora development in the border that it is Sonora's mission to be.

Maquiladoras never fit the old paradigm of Fordism as it developed in more industrialized countries because they did not have equally high wages, strong unions, or job security for workers. They were closer to third-world adaptations of the old paradigm, known as neo-Fordism, or peripheral Fordism, because they had very similar workplace organization without the same benefits for workers. The findings of this study indicate that Nogales-area transport-equipment maquilas have changed somewhat with the incorporation of statistical process control, just-in-time production techniques, and the collapsing of skilled jobs into unskilled jobs in the maintenance and quality-control areas. These are characteristic of the new paradigm, which is often called lean or flexible manufacturing. Moreover, unlike the old maquilas, Nogales-area transport-equipment plants have highly visible Mexican managers and technicians. This is true despite the fact that the cultural style with which such work is carried out is still a contentious issue, and U.S. managers occupy the top positions in the maquila association.

Although the above characteristics indicate that Nogales transport-equipment maquilas are not the same as the old maquila of the sixties and seventies, they are still similar. Plants D, E, F, G, I, and J did simple assembly, although Plant D was planning to expand into some manufacturing. It cannot be said, then, that simple assembly is disappearing among maquila industries, as some proponents of the dual-technology thesis have argued.

Neither has a second wave of maquilas emerged in the image of the new paradigm, implementing capital-intensive production methods, among Nogales-area transport-equipment maquilas. The new labor process with work teams, quality-control circles, and rotation of multiskilled workers has not been implemented. Most workers have jobs that are considered low skilled, although the measurement of skill based on managers' labeling underestimates workers' skills. Companies can and do take production away from maquila plants when defect rates are too high, and they relocate it north of the border. In the company that did this in the Nogales area, the jobs that disappeared were the most skilled ones, shortening the job ladder for Mexican workers. Some of the work formerly done by technicians has been or will be classified downward in most plants and carried out by direct workers. This also contributes to an underestimation of the skills workers use on the job. Workers are not involved consensually in the administration of work. Instead, hierarchical structures within the plant resolve conflict in authoritarian ways. Worker empowerment is absent.

Both the old and the new paradigm predict a strong presence of women workers in the maquila labor force. Chaney (1979: 65), on the other hand, argued that maquiladoras along the Mexican border were an exception to the usual maintenance of separate spheres for men and women in Latin America, and that women's participation in the maquiladora labor force was likely to be a temporary phenomenon. Women workers in the Nogales area have decreased their participation rates. They were 61 percent of the labor force in Nogales and Imuris transport-equipment plants in 1982, and only 40 percent in 1990. We conclude, however, that they will continue to be a permanent part of the maquila labor force. This study has shown that they are preferred by industry for some jobs, and that their income is not merely supplementary to their households but essential for meeting basic needs.

Previous literature debated whether women would benefit or be exploited by maquila work. The conclusion was that their position in the labor market had not been enhanced (Tiano, 1987). We find that the restructuring of the eighties has segmented them into less-skilled jobs at the bottom of the occupational hierarchy in Nogales-area transport-equipment maquilas. Labor-market segmentation, which has been found to be one of the major causes of gender discrimination in the labor forces of more advanced industrial societies, can now be observed in Mexican maquilas as well. The question of whether women would benefit from maquila employment has been answered to a large extent in the negative.

Women workers may not necessarily experience their work in maquilas as oppressive. They may prefer maquila work to isolated and unpaid work within the home. However, this does not negate the fact that women workers have lost many of the potential opportunities maquila work might have brought them, such as the best jobs. We found that women transport-equipment workers, in comparison to men, were more likely to have unskilled jobs. They were sometimes heads of the line or supervisors, but never technicians. The only other positions in which women were observed were secretary and personnel manager. In a study of the electronics and apparel sector in nearby Mexicali, Tiano (1994: 112) did find some mobility of women workers from the less to the more desirable sectors of the maquila industry. This mobility falls short of that recommended in the early eighties by Valdés-Villalva, who advised the government to implement educational policies that would allow women workers to have their workplace experience recognized as apprenticeships in engineering, repair, maintenance, and process and machinery innovation. Then, if women workers left their jobs, as they have often done at very young ages, the state should find a way of systematizing the practical knowledge they had gained and make the related theoretical education available (COMO, 1984).

Nogales-area transport-equipment maquilas acted as magnets in the eighties, drawing workers from within the western corridor. People came for employment reasons, and most had entered the labor force with their first maquila job. They showed little propensity to move to the United States. A substantial proportion lived in very poor housing, which is not congruent with the new paradigm's highly skilled and well remunerated workers.

Workers' earnings were not found to vary much, with most of them earning about the same amount. Those who had better housing lived in larger households and had more people contributing income. The small variation detected in earnings did not come from bonuses and benefits, as the new paradigm predicts. More highly paid workers put in more hours and were sometimes classified as having medium- or high-skilled jobs.

We can see five different moments, or turning points, in the maquilization process. In the early days of the BIP, maquilization was a simple diffusion of maquila-type production through growth in the number of plants and people employed. The second moment was in the 1980s, when auto plants adopted the social aspects of maquiladora production outside of the legally defined maquila sector, thereby increasing its presence informally. At the same time, the new auto maquilas incorporated more advanced technology and flexible work methods, creating a different kind of maquila from that produced in the first moment. Non-maquila Mexican industry began to fail in this period because of the opening of the economy, thereby increasing the proportion of industry that is like the maquiladora. The third moment of maquilization was the 1989 government decree that allowed the creation of maquilas in other sectors, like agro-industry, mining, fishing, and forestry, and allowed Mexican industries to do maquila production when they were not using their full capacity for domestic production. In the third moment, the legal distinction between the maquila and non-maquiladora sectors of the Mexican economy began to be erased. The fourth moment of maquilization occurred with the 1994 crisis, and its effects will be discussed more fully below. The fifth will occur in the next millennium, when maquilas no longer exist as a separate legal category, although the phenomena they represent will be more widespread in Mexico than ever.

The data for this study were collected two years after the 1989 decree in the auto sector, which has been a leader in maquila evolution. The literature suggests that many aspects of the new paradigm have or are being adopted in all areas of the auto industry in Mexico. The findings of this study indicate that what has happened in Nogales-area transport-equipment maquilas is maquilization without automation or flexibilization. The plants studied have not been drawn in to the second moment of maquilization. The transformations represented by the second wave have only been partially adopted in most subsectors of the Mexican auto industry. In a study of three plants that assemble cars and produce motors (one of which was the Ford plant in Hermosillo), Micheli (1994: 235) found a hybrid application of the new paradigm.

Nogales transport-equipment maquilas represent maquilization even though they have not adopted the changes of the second moment because they are growing while the domestically owned auto-parts industry, which is not maquilized, is failing. Although the historic isolation of Nogales has sometimes led to the assumption that it lags behind other places, we do not think this explains why transport-equipment maquilas have not refashioned themselves in the image of the new paradigm. Instead, it appears that the managers and owners have chosen not to go in the direction of lean production.

Maquiladora managers and owners of the Nogales plants in this study prefer to continue along the path of maquiladora development that they have followed for the last quarter of a century. The direction in which they have been heading, neo-Fordism or peripheral Fordism, is more like that of nonunion manufacturing in the United States (Milkman, 1991) than mass or lean production. Mexico provides a context for industry in which unions have been prevented from protecting workers' rights, in comparison with either the United States or Canada. Nevertheless, as the findings presented in this study indicate, the creation of a new labor force that meets managers' requirements can still be problematic, and adjustments are required along the way.

Other research indicates that Nogales-area transport-equipment maquilas are not alone in their location between the old and new paradigm. In a study of 19 electronics plants in Nogales, Magdalena, and Hermosillo, Lara (1992) also found great heterogeneity.[1] Plants introduced new automatic technology, just-in-time production, and total quality control, but also maintained Fordist or Taylorist practices. The great difference between the theoretical Japanese model and its application in these companies was due to managers' lack of training. The traditional industrial culture between managers and workers is still dominant and has produced a skepticism toward anything new, and an incapacity to completely reconvert factories.

In the Gulf corridor from 1980 to 1988, Flores (1993: 108) found great dynamism in manufacturing production and employment. However, in the state of Coahuila in particular, his evidence indicates that this was probably not the kind of industry expected by the new paradigm. As in most other states, Mexican industry in Coahuila contracted during this period. Increases in employment were due to the fact that devaluations made it more profitable for maquilas to substitute labor-intensive production for capital-intensive production. The simultaneous depression in real wages led to a labor force eager for jobs. This was true not only at the border but as far south as Atlapexco in Hidalgo, where very few sources of income were available to begin with, and the population was enthusiastic about the possibility of maquila employment.[2]

To say that Nogales-area transport-equipment plants are between the old and new paradigms is not to imply that they are stuck in the middle, or marginal. Berggren (1993: 185) has argued against the inevitability of the new paradigm, saying that " 'Lean production' is certainly not the ultimate station of industrial development." The results of this study and others reinforce the critique that modernization theory erroneously assumes that there is a unidimensional path of development with everyone marching along to the same end point.

The Advance of Desert Capitalism

The kind of maquilas these are—neither old or new—has implications for regional development, which are illustrated throughout the book. First, it is clear that they do not constitute by themselves, nor are they part of, an industrial district predicted by the new paradigm. Even though seven of the ten plants studied produce similar products, they do not use local suppliers, nor do they supply local clients in an integrated way. A look back at the third column in table 2.1, headed "Mexican Materials," indicates how much was spent by each plant to buy supplies in Mexico in 1990. All plants for which data were available, except D and H, spent absolutely nothing in Mexico on supplies. When I showed table 2.1 to the general manager at Plant D and asked him what he had bought for U.S. $11,800 in Mexico (which made him the greatest buyer of Mexican materials), he denied spending this much within Mexico in 1990 and said cleaning supplies and some wood to build platforms had been the only purchases. The manager of Plant H said his plant had spent U.S. $300 for cardboard for packing. He said he would purchase more Mexican products if possible; however, transportation from Nogales to other Mexican locations was not good enough to get Mexican products to his plant efficiently. Other managers echoed the belief that Mexican suppliers could not provide enough of the products they needed, at a high enough quality, on an adequate schedule.

The inadequacy of transportation for backward linkages (e.g., raw materials, components, services) would impede the development of a strong regional economy in the western corridor. Most Mexican railroads, for example, run north and south, and were first built at the turn of the century. They were nationalized during the depression and are presently overburdened at best. Rail traffic picked up dramatically on January 1, 1994, when NAFTA came into effect, carrying grain, autos, and forest products. Kraul (1994) says that "the railroads also stand to benefit from what many expect will be a shifting of manufacturing from the maquiladoras concentrated along the border to Mexico's north-central industrial belt, which is closer to population centers and has a less transient work force. The longer hauls would be more suited to rail transit." New railroad investment was announced in several border locations in 1994. In the western corridor, Arizona and Sonora worked together to improve rail links between Nogales and Guaymas. The privatization of Mexico's railroads that resulted from the 1994 crisis will undoubtedly bolster these trends.

For some Nogales transport-equipment maquilas, however, improved transportation within Mexico might not increase Mexican purchases, because they are prevented from sourcing in Mexico by their clients or parent firms. At Plant G, the major buyer specified where supplies had to be bought, and they had stipulated no Mexican suppliers. Suppliers to Plant I have to be approved by the final assembly firm of which it is a subsidiary. The most important criteria for choosing suppliers are delivery time and the quality of the product and technology; geographic proximity of the supplier is not considered very important.

The absence of industrial districts has been noted in other sectors of the maquila industry and other Sonora locations. Lara (1992) also found that the 19 electronics maquilas she studied in Nogales, Magdalena, and Hermosillo have difficulties applying the just-in-time production model because of their distance from suppliers. While some advances have been made with the installation of warehouses in Nogales, Arizona, geography still leads to severe limitations in their attempts to maintain zero inventory.

A 1988 study of the 17 transport-equipment maquilas in Tijuana provides an interesting Pacific-corridor comparison regarding the use of Mexican materials. The assumption has sometimes been made that Mexican-owned maquilas and joint ventures buy more in Mexico than foreign-owned maquilas. Nine of the Tijuana transport-equipment maquilas were owned by Mexicans; four were joint ventures. All 13 of these maquilas were in the micro and small size categories, in keeping with the fact that Tijuana maquilas tend to be smaller than those in Nogales. However, Mexican raw materials were used in only 2 of the 7 micro plants, and 4 of the 8 small-size plants. Although more Mexican materials were used in the small- than the micro-size plants, the small-size plants still used more foreign materials than those from Mexico. Fuentes Flores and Barajas Escamilla (1989) explain the low level of Mexican materials by saying that, in general, Mexican-owned plants and joint ventures are really maquila subcontractors, which supply the industrial shop, labor, and administration. The foreign company for which they are subcontracting supplies all capital, machinery, parts, components, and supervision. Even if Nogales transport-equipment maquilas were not all foreign owned, they still might buy no more of their materials in Mexico because of the character of the industry.

Although the Nogales plants do not constitute an industrial district, they contribute to regional development through their growing size and numbers, thereby employing more Mexicans. We have conceptualized this as maquilization and the diffusion of modernization theory. Increasing growth means there will be more competition for resources at the border, and pressure to move south. The comparison of the Imuris and Nogales plants provides one example.

There are several ecological differences between the two locations that create separate working environments. Imuris's population is less than a tenth of Nogales's. Imuris is perceived as a more rural, hinterland area, whereas Nogales is thought of as "civilization" in comparison. Imuris is a "one-company town" in that Plant J was the only maquila of note, the main employer, and had transformed the economy of the village.

Some of the infrastructural problems that are endemic at the border are worse in Imuris. Electric-power outages, for example, are more common in Imuris than Nogales, and when they occur, companies often end up paying overtime to meet the terms of their contracts (O'Brien, 1990a). There is also a second customs station between Nogales and Imuris where vehicles must stop for inspection, delaying the delivery of materials imported from the United States, and the return of the completed products to the buyer.

Findings indicated that workers in Imuris were far less likely than those in Nogales to have been recent migrants from outside Sonora, or to have had any previous experience working in maquiladoras. Wages paid in Imuris were lower, on average, than wages paid in Nogales. While a lower minimum wage in Imuris is an effect of state policy, the company was also responsible for the wage difference. In the analysis of maquiladora advertisements, it was found that while "wages above the minimum" were often offered as an incentive for jobs in Nogales, it was never offered for any jobs advertised outside of Nogales in Imuris, Magdalena, or Agua Prieta. Also, none of the workers surveyed at the Imuris plant received transportation or rent bonuses. These were the two bonuses workers with previous maquiladora experience were found to receive more often than those without experience, indicating that workers may change jobs to get them. Since there is only one maquila in Imuris, workers cannot change plants in order to improve the indirect pay they receive through bonuses. They cannot play one plant off against another through turnover to serve their own interests unless they move.

While the cost of living may be lower in Imuris than Nogales, workers are not able to comparison shop as much in Imuris, and they would not have as easy access to U.S. shops, where prices are lower than in Mexico. Other important services in Nogales, like the IMSS office which provides medical care, are not available in Imuris. An IMSS office is located in the middle of the industrial park in Nogales, whereas workers in Imuris complained that they had to travel all the way to the Magdalena IMSS office to get the health services for which they were insured under law. Not having time or transportation to go to Magdalena often meant they went without these services.

Despite these differences associated with location, there are several similarities between Plants F and J, which derive from the fact that they are owned by the same company. They were shown to have adopted a competitive strategy whereby they extended the working week (overtime) and manipulated holidays more often than other plants. This caused dissatisfaction among workers, who in Nogales could consider working elsewhere more easily than in Imuris. In fact, several of the Imuris workers had previously worked for the same company in Nogales and had been persuaded to move south with the company to provide it with some experienced workers. One worker who had moved with the company felt that she had lost in the process, because the company had not lived up to its promises. After ranking "benefits and bonuses" as the number one thing that could be changed to improve her job, she said: "I used to work in Nogales for the same company, and they sent me a letter offering me Nogales wages and good benefits if I would move to their Imuris plant, but I'm very dissatisfied with the way things have worked out in this maquila. I disagree with the way administrators apply discipline. The person handing out discipline plays favorites and is not the right person for the job. I'm thinking of quitting very soon."

In both locations, the commonly owned plants reduced the number of technicians in comparison to direct workers, and had direct workers doing work more often done by technicians in other plants. Workers in the commonly owned plants were also more likely to report that they had held more than one job where they worked, giving evidence of rotation across jobs. However, they did not believe there had been any improvement for them after having had more than one kind of job at their workplace.

Other research conducted in nearby Agua Prieta in two maquiladoras manufacturing electronic and automotive materials indicates that repressive administrative policies do not improve production in the long run. Miller (1992) reported that the wage savings of an Agua Prieta company were being eroded by problems in product quality, on-time delivery, and employee turnover, until the company totally turned around its style of managing workers. After changing the plant culture from a "reactionary-type of management" to a culture of continuous "improvement-driven management," product quality was enhanced, and worker turnover greatly reduced.

The reactionary-type management is part of the old paradigm, and the improvement-driven management part of the new one. If a company wanted to maintain the management styles of the old paradigm, it would probably do so with fewer problems in an interior location like Imuris. Workers in such locations have fewer alternatives and less possibility of resisting. Maquilas that move south in order to continue such management styles do not bring the most modern kinds of facilities, but the old paradigm.

In general, the managers of Nogales transport-equipment plants were committed to staying right at the border. The general manager of Plant H said he did not believe it was worth it to "chase cheap labor." His company had considered moving south to solve high turnover problems. Instead, they had decided to remain in Nogales and offer some of the best benefits and bonuses in order to control turnover and absenteeism. The interior can provide opportunities for the maintenance or increase of profits, especially in areas with infrastructure and an established labor force, as in Guadalajara and Monterrey. As Wilson (1992) has shown, however, companies can move south to use fresh labor without necessarily taking advantage of Mexican suppliers and provisioners.

Koido (1992: 414) pointed out in his study of wiring-harness production in Chihuahua (in the central corridor) that there is an ongoing tension between companies' desires to reduce the cost of labor and yet stay close to U.S. markets. Chinese labor, for example, is still cheaper than Mexican labor, but many companies do not wish to "chase" cheap labor that far—geographically or culturally. While many companies owning maquilas may threaten to leave Mexico for cheaper labor if the business climate is not to their liking, NAFTA provides an economic and legal structure that will probably contain them in North America and contribute to the maquilization of all the industrial corridors along the U.S.-Mexico border. As discussed earlier, when production is removed from Mexico, it is likely to go north of the border.

Nevertheless, the industrial corridors differ from each other and are in competition. Some leaders of the central corridor, which has El Paso/Juárez as its focus, want to control all the other corridors as well. El Paso architect-designer Lorenzo Aguilar said, "In Sinaloa, Monterrey, Sonora, Nuevo León, Coahuila, Chihuahua, we see ourselves here in El Paso as being the area of influence. . . . We serve as a link between the corridors to Arizona, California. We're the major intersection for vehicular transportation" (Ivey, 1994). They see the Gulf of Mexico corridor as their main competition for dominance.

The potential of any corridor to harness the business confidence that resulted from NAFTA will depend on its political will and ability to creatively solve problems. In order to avoid being casualties of free trade, the city governments of both Nogaleses announced an attempt early in 1993 to change their economic base from curio shops and maquiladoras to retail stores and cleaner industries. Abraham Zaid, a businessman from Nogales, Sonora, said in support of the proposal, "The maquilas take and don't give anything back. A moratorium must be put on maquilas in Nogales. These foreign-owned factories should be located in cities in the interior of Mexico, where the jobs are needed and services can be provided. The maquilas should pay into a general fund to help with public works and repairs."[3] The maquilas do pay 10 percent of their payroll in taxes that are supposed to address infrastructural needs, but in the past this money has always gone to Mexico City, so that electricity, sewage-treatment facilities, roads, and other public services are grossly inadequate. Also supporting economic diversification, Alicia Romero González, the secretary general of the Council of Women in Nogales, Sonora, complained about the insufficient number of retail stores and said the government must stimulate more shopping opportunities. "There are no Sears or other similar department store chains in Nogales, such as exist in Hermosillo."[4]

While capital is not about to exhaust labor resources, continued social and economic development throughout this region will be stymied without political cooperation and investment in infrastructure. Transportation, communications, and especially water supply and treatment remain high on the agenda of what needs immediate attention. As Ingram, Milich, and Varady (1994: 9) note in a recent environmental study of Ambos Nogales, "Human use of the Santa Cruz River and its Nogales wash tributary was destined by climate to be complex even without considering the political map." The economic interdependence of Ambos Nogales puts a premium on cooperation and agreement to come up with new institutional arrangements that are long overdue. Institutions for managing new infrastructure must have broad jurisdiction and be responsible to the public by acting before problems reach a crisis stage.

The Immediate Effects of NAFTA and the 1994–95 Crisis

In October 1994, ten months after NAFTA was implemented, experts on the auto industry were still predicting an increase in the kind of production observed in Nogales. David Cole, director of the Office of Auto Transport at the University of Michigan, was asked in an interview with the Mexican business magazine *Expansión*: "General Motors has invested in enormous maquila operations in Mexico through its Automotive Component Group which produces exclusively for the U.S. market. Will the auto maquilas continue to expand?" He answered that "with or without NAFTA, labor intensive products would have gone to Mexico. A good example of a typical maquila product is the electrical wiring for cars. In fact, automotive components which need low labor costs already have gone to Mexico" (Werner,

1994: 67). It is important to note that this conclusion still holds six years after Hoffman and Kaplinsky (1988: 108) were predicting that "the move towards centralized control and multiplex wiring in automobiles is likely to
eradicate the need for this labor-intensive product." Booz-Allen and Hamilton and Infotec's (1987: 44) study of the auto-parts industry even set a date
when labor-intensive parts like harnesses and radios would become obsolete: 1993.

Many of the Nogales managers were not looking forward to the increased growth that they predicted NAFTA would bring. They saw it as a
political scheme for which adequate groundwork had not been done, so that
implementation would be haphazard at best. They proved to be correct. Implementing the new rules of origin under NAFTA has been very complicated and has slowed down, rather than enhanced, delivery of goods across
the border. Nevertheless, Arizona exports to Mexico for 1994 were expected to increase by 10 percent over previous years (Carlile, 1995).

Nogales transport-equipment managers were also unhappy about the
international attention NAFTA debates focused on maquiladoras, and it
made them defensive about environmental concerns and working conditions. They had, in many cases, spent years learning how to run their operations on the border, developing their own "best practices" that had little
to do with what was fashionable in other industrial circles. NAFTA was
sometimes seen as a threat to the delicate balance they had established.
More investment would mean more competition for labor and more stress
on the already-inadequate infrastructure.

As practitioners immersed in the field of industrial relations, the Nogales
maquila managers may also have been aware that "[p]aradoxically, the very
success of the program carried the seeds of its potential demise" (George,
1990: 231–232). More maquila plants with a greater proportion of skilled
personnel, and more Mexican businesses to service maquilas, have been
predicted to create "an untenable pressure on the supply of labor to the
industry," which will eventually cause saturation and an increase of wages.

It also seemed that managers had little control over some other aspects
of doing business in Mexico. The maquiladora association had improved
their control in some areas, but in other areas, control might still elude
them, causing negative political repercussions. While they did not refer
directly to illegal traffic crossing the border, they were, of course, aware of
parallel, informal economies. This became an issue as NAFTA negotiations

unfolded, when it was argued that improved infrastructure such as transportation routes would facilitate the drug trade, which has been especially active in Sinaloa, just south of Sonora. It was argued that plans were afoot by drug traffickers to use maquiladoras as "front" operations, which would really serve as transshipment points for drugs grown in Sinaloa, the historic source of North America's salad greens in the winter (Puig, 1993). While no concrete evidence was collected on this topic, it came up so many times informally that it would be naive to dismiss it. The black market, or informal economy, increased throughout the country during Salinas's presidency, with lower purchasing power and increased unemployment making it more likely that Mexican investors and workers might enter more risky forms of making a living than secure ventures with increasingly dwindling returns (Vigueras, 1995).

This study found that the Nogales industrial labor market followed the pattern of growth nationally. There was a plateau in growth between 1980 and 1983, great expansion between 1983 and 1987, and a slowdown at the end of the decade. Management has also made very distinct adjustments to the reality of employing a newly constituted labor force by implementing such policies as new regulations of holiday schedules, and recruitment campaigns in January.

Despite managers' repeated and often-quoted complaints about the difficulties caused by labor shortages, real wages continued to decrease throughout the decade. This brings into question the very concept of shortage as it is used to describe maquiladora labor markets. Researchers, as well as the public at large, become habituated to the idea that there really is a maquila labor shortage, when that is no longer the case in many places like Nogales. The fact that wages were not forced up indicates that, in fact, the supply of labor met the demand. This labor market is working very well for managers and capital in the sense that they have been able to employ adequate labor without increasing their wage costs. I concur with Sklair (1993: 179) when he says that "there is no real labor shortage in Juárez, or Tijuana, or anywhere else along the *frontera norte,* but an artificial shortage has been unintentionally created by the maquila industry being reluctant to pay decent wages, caring little about excessive labor turnover, and its gradually changing attitudes to the employment of men."

Workers, on the other hand, have not been able to make this labor market work for them as well, since they confront it as individuals, given the absence of effective labor unions. Rather than being able to negotiate collectively, workers must rely on the possibility of pooling incomes in the household, and on individual strategies for seeking better working conditions by leaving one company for another. This study found that moving from plant to plant did not increase wages, although it may be part of a larger household strategy to get the best combination of benefits for the whole family. If markets only work consistently for some of the players involved in them, then they cannot be considered to be free markets. What can be discerned in newspaper reports of a labor market in crisis because of insufficient labor, then, are the voices of those who command this system: managers and owners of maquilas. Representatives of the state are complicit by their silence, and their lack of enforcement of legislation like that on holidays for workers, or making workers do extra time to "pay for" their holidays.

It is unlikely that continued growth of maquiladoras under NAFTA, and their movement southward, will take place at the booming rate of the eighties, even though plenty of labor still exists in Mexico. As Scott Grant of the Dallas–Fort Worth International Trade Resource Center said of free trade, "People are looking for levers of advantage, but I don't think there are any. Dallas is not going to replace the Port of Houston. Somebody else is not going to replace Dallas as the center of the communications industry. If you do a good job, you can build on your skills" (Young, 1991). It takes time to build the kind of infrastructure Sonora and Arizona need to support more maquilas, "time that can't be swallowed up by building a committee," as Al Ochoa of the Tucson Economic Development Department has said (Pérez, 1991).

Maquiladora employment was still falling in 1993 because of the slowness in the U.S. economy. It has been argued that the boom of the eighties will not be repeated under NAFTA because it was based on the drop in real wages that Mexican workers cannot sustain repeatedly. Ever since 1977, Mexican families have had to send more members off to work. The number of minimum-wage salaries needed to buy a basic basket of goods for a family of five was 1.8 in 1981 and 2.7 in 1988, and had jumped to 5.4 in June of 1993 (Hughes and Watling, 1993). It has been suggested that while maquila growth is not limited by a lack of workers, it cannot continue to increase based on the assumption that wages will drop further. As Pradilla Cobos (1993: 148) has argued, the Mexican labor force has neither the capacity nor the will to cope with a constant decrease in their subsistence levels.

Nevertheless, the economic crisis that began with Zedillo's presidency at the end of 1994 lowered the cost of Mexican labor for foreign investors through devaluation once again. Wage increases that had previously been approved by the government were wiped out, so that wages fell further behind, and workers' real buying power dropped even more profoundly. Maquiladoras responded immediately by multiplying and increasing production. Almost half of Mexico's trade surplus for the first quarter of 1995 (the first surplus which had occurred since 1988) came from maquiladora exports.[5]

This devaluation is predicted to reverse the slow growth in maquila employment, production, and plants that has occurred since 1988, although an explosion of the magnitude similar to that of the mid-1980s is not expected (Nagel, 1995). This will undoubtedly intensify the maquilization of the western industrial corridor and increase migration northward within Mexico and to the United States. Don Michie, vice president of Nafta Ventures Inc., an El Paso firm that consults on the maquiladora industry and joint-venture manufacturing said, "I think you're going to see a boom in maquiladora activity. There are some very significant cost factors which will come into effect, particularly for labor intensive activity on goods which are assembled, as opposed to manufactured. Those operators are going to get a two-[year] to three-year reprieve from rising costs in the popular border manufacturing region, where the labor supply has been tight in recent years" (Nagel, 1995).

Varela Ramírez, the president of the Nuevo León Association of Maquilas, estimated that the devaluation of the peso against the dollar made maquila investments more attractive since it actually reduced operating costs by about 15 percent.[6] The boom will probably not be in direct investment (which is more necessary for the new maquila than the old), since parent companies may very well hesitate to construct new plants in such an uncertain economy. It will be more likely to boost shelter operations, which protect the foreign owner from losses. Michie said that "the immediate benefit will accrue to those who are able to minimize the investment risk while still providing the cost advantages in terms of labor" (Nagel, 1995).

Even in the industrially developed city of Monterrey in Nuevo León, famous for its advanced level of manufacturing, business leaders predicted that the weakened peso would not bring direct foreign investment but instead would swell the numbers of maquilas, which are not as preferable. John Barrett, executive director of the local American Chamber of Commerce said, "Companies [are] waiting for a little more stability in Mexico's economy. We're not about to see a huge net inflow of U.S. firms. There are, however, going to be more maquiladoras here." More advanced forms of production fell into decline with the devaluation, deeply disappointing local entrepreneurs. As Dombey (1995b: 16) observed, "That this proud, ambitious state now yearns after transitory investment in the maquiladora industry is something of a comedown."

Devaluation of Mexican currency works in favor of the companies owning or subcontracting to maquiladoras for several reasons. Because they are subsidiaries of major U.S., European, or Far Eastern firms, they conduct their business in dollars, with the exception of paying workers' wages and benefits. Since such a tiny fraction of the components used by maquilas originates in Mexico, they do not suffer from the same inflationary pressures that face other Mexican companies. This makes maquilas almost immune from the effects of Zedillo's austerity plan, which promotes high interest rates in an attempt to hold down inflation. As Carlos de Orduña, former president of the National Council of Maquiladoras said,

> the devaluation won't affect us negatively. Almost everything we use is a temporary import, and everything is done in U.S. currency. Maybe it will help us in that we'll be getting more pesos for our money to cover costs in Mexico. The maquiladora industry actually saw its biggest growth during past devaluations in the 1980s, when the peso's repeated loss of value and an upward inflationary spiral gave offshore manufacturers who held dollars tremendous labor-cost advantages. (Nagel, 1995)

Predictions that the number of maquiladoras would increase because of the crisis were supported immediately. In January 1995, Canadian and Japanese investors together started more than 300 maquilas along the northern border, and the Mexican Social Security Institute reported that 6,000 new workers were signed on during January. Senzek (1995: 12) estimated that the number of new maquila workers might reach 100,000 before the end of the year, and characterized the maquiladoras as "life-savers." In April, Decio de María Serrano, SECOFI deputy trade minister, said his department had approved two to three new maquiladoras a day, and that this was an indicator of how maquilas were likely to grow during the rest of 1995 and 1996.[7] Most of the newly approved maquiladoras in the first quarter were located on the northern border, but a significant number also opened inside the country.

The 1994 crisis reinforced and extended tendencies of maquilization. For example, in the first days of the crisis, several Mexican-owned textile and candy companies in Aguascalientes were converted into the maquiladoras of foreign companies in order to keep them operating instead of closing. The director of one of the plants explained to journalists that "in these times of crisis, it is better that companies teach themselves how to be maquilas."[8] The second moment of maquilization that appeared in the eighties meant the qualitative change of plants that were already owned by foreign capital and had been installed to served the domestic Mexican market. In the crisis of 1994, it appears to be happening to Mexican-owned companies as well.

While those with dollars get more for their money, pesos buy much less and are in shorter supply. Increased interest rates raised the already-high cost of borrowing money for Mexican individuals and businesses. Higher interest rates have been especially hard on agricultural producers throughout Mexico, many of whom were barely surviving before the devaluation of the peso. The Sonoran state Regional Cattle Producers Union, for example, warned that increasing interest rates would make it more difficult for agricultural producers to pay back their loans.[9] If ranchers and their employees default on their loans or are not able to get new credit, they may well turn to southwardly moving maquiladoras as an economic alternative.

The trade in consumer goods suffered on both sides of the border, but in different ways. This is not only because the peso buys fewer goods denominated in dollars, but also because inflation was much higher in Mexico's northern cities than in the rest of the country.[10] Retail sales fell off on the U.S. side. In mid-January 1995, Fred Johnson, executive director of the Nogales, Arizona, Chamber of Commerce said, "Business is down substantially this week. You can park just about anyplace in town. It's not very encouraging. City merchants are having plenty of problems marketing their business across the border" (Mader, 1995).

Maquila workers, who were shown in chapter 3 to do most of their shopping on the U.S. side of the border, have turned their attention to domestically produced items even though supplies are inadequate and quality inferior. The decrease in the amount Mexicans are buying in the United States is more severe than in past devaluations. Their decreased buying power will undoubtedly slow maquilas with sales and marketing plans for 2001, and may make them try to tie prices for their products to the dollar. In anticipation of this, Joe López, president of the El Paso Hispanic Chamber of Commerce, said that "the expected positive effects of the North American Free Trade Agreement have hit a road block and the recovery will be a long time coming."[11]

The weakness of the Mexican labor movement makes Mexican workers even more vulnerable in times of crisis than they usually are. Fidel Velázquez, the leader of the CTM, announced in mid-January 1995 that each Mexican worker should contribute one day's pay to the nation to help pay the debt. "It will be an act of solidarity with the rich and with the country," he said.[12] Many workers were very offended by this proposal at a time when their basic costs were rising, and other labor leader were pointing to inadequacies in Zedillo's new economic strategy rather than asking workers to bail out the country (Dombey, 1995a).

Workers in northern maquilas were among the most militant in responding to the devaluation. This may be because they do not have a strong union presence to control them, and they are able to see firsthand how their employers benefit from the devaluation. While labor unions in the central part of Mexico were afraid to strike during the crisis and were focusing on job security, workers in the maquila sector were winning strikes for higher pay (Dombey, 1995c, 1995d; Weddell, 1995).

In the first quarter of 1995, the number of legal strikes in Mexico decreased by 17 percent in comparison to the same period for 1994.[13] However, Juárez maquila workers went out on six wildcat strikes in comparison to one in previous years. Workers in the maquila sector had no need to fear the closure of plants should they strike, since they could observe maquila investment increasing. The fear of plant closure was what prevented their fellow workers in non-maquila plants in the central part of Mexico from going out. Moreover, Zedillo's action plan of March 9, 1995, cleared the way for workers and management to reach individual pay settlements in different industries, since the *Pacto,* whose effect on wages was discussed in chapter 5, was no longer in force.

All Juárez strikes were settled quickly, with the workers gaining pay increases and more benefits. Workers did not follow their CTM unions but instead formed dissident coalitions that won the recognition to negotiate for the workers. State-level leaders of the CTM intervened in one case and acceded to the provision in the agreement between management and strikers that called for the dismissal of the union representative and a new union election. After the settlement of these wildcat strikes, more Juárez maquilas are reaching agreements with their workers before conflicts turn into work stoppages. Ford, which has traditionally helped set the standard for pay hikes and wage disputes in the country's manufacturing industry, agreed to a 25 percent increase in its new maquilas in Cuautitlán, Chihuahua, and Hermosillo, hours before a formal strike deadline on March 31, 1995 (Dombey, 1995e: 3).

The issues over which Juárez workers struck went beyond wage increases and union democratization. Workers in one plant successfully wildcatted in response to their company's attempt to cut one week of paid vacation per year. We have seen how Nogales and Imuris workers have been paying for their holidays since 1990.

It is doubtful, however, whether the growth of maquilas resulting from the devaluation will be great enough to absorb the increased flow of migrants northwards. The severe recession that resulted from the devaluation sharply increased the rate of illegal immigration of Mexicans to the United States at the beginning of 1995. While this occurred in many border locations, the increase has been highest in the western industrial corridor. In January 1995, more than 19,000 undocumented immigrants were arrested in Tucson, Arizona, twice as many as during the first month of 1994. This number of undocumented migrants is almost as high as the total number of direct workers employed in all Nogales-area maquilas in 1990. It is clear that such a large number could not be absorbed into the maquila labor force even with growth in maquilas in 1995. Chapter 3 showed that January was the month with the greatest number of ads for maquila jobs, and the highest estimate for absenteeism in January was 50 percent. Even if an undocumented migrant had taken every job left by an absent worker after the Christmas break, there would still have been 10,000 without jobs.

The number of illegal migrants arrested also increased in El Paso, Texas, but by only 25 percent. The slight drop in arrests in the San Diego–San Ysidro area was attributed in part to the passage of Proposition 187 in California. This led President Clinton to order tougher enforcement measures along the border, with special attention to the Nogales-Tucson district, where 62 new Border Patrol agents were assigned.[14]

This increase in migration during the renewed economic crisis speaks to some of the questions raised about migration in chapter 4. Nogales has not traditionally been one of the most frequent crossing places for immigrants from Mexico to the United States. Findings from our 1991 survey reinforced previous research that showed that almost all Mexicans have traditionally migrated to Nogales, Sonora, for employment on the Mexican side of the border. We were not able to conclude on the basis of the data presented in chapter 4 whether maquila wages might provide Mexicans with the needed resources for migration, since the poorest Mexicans have not been the most likely to migrate in the past, or whether maquila wages would root them more firmly on their own side of the border, giving them less reason to go north. The drop in real wages experienced at the end of 1994, and the ensuing increase in migrants to the United States, shows that lack of funds is not something that by itself will keep poor Mexicans at home. It remains to be seen whether increased enforcement by the Border Patrol will truncate this new route northward through the western industrial corridor.

The implications of the 1994 crisis for the dual-technology thesis do not indicate a more thorough adoption of the new paradigm. It is clear that growth has been spurred, but with a preference for plant development through shelters rather than direct investment. It is also feared that NAFTA created a window of opportunity that Mexicans will not be able to pass through due to government cuts resulting from the crisis. In 1993, J. Bermúdez, one of the fathers of the maquila program, said that in order to establish a high-technology industry in Juárez, a labor force that was much better educated technically would have to be prepared within three to five years. Without such a labor force, the opportunity could pass by (Dwyer, 1994). The crisis threatens educational spending right at the time when it is needed most, according to Bermúdez's thinking.

Regardless of attempts to enhance regional integration of the western industrial corridor, the border still divides realities and creates contradictory perceptions. Throughout the eighties, a crisis in the labor supply for maquiladora managers provided an opportunity for workers to improve their situations by moving from plant to plant. In 1994, the crisis of the Mexican economy, which lowered the buying power of Mexican workers and increased their interest rates, provided opportunities for foreign investors to buy up Mexican companies cheaply and turn them into maquiladoras, or start entirely new ones. The contradictory realities for transnational corporations and their labor force were so clearly perceived by workers that they went out on a flurry of wildcat strikes to demand a fairer share. This will not be one, complete industrial corridor until all the inhabitants understand the same thing by "crisis," and when they share goals in a more complete way. This is a cultural argument that rests on a consensus in perception. It is undergirded, however, by the necessity for structural changes that will have to take place for the western corridor to be truly continuous in the minds and hearts of its inhabitants: structural changes that have to do with equity and more implementation of distributive justice.

Introduction

1. *The Compact Edition of the Oxford English Dictionary*, s.v. "desert."
2. In March 1993, 465,400 of the 539,800 workers, or 86.2 percent of all workers employed by Mexican maquilas, worked in the northern border states. Of the 100,500 technicians and administrative personnel who worked in all Mexican maquilas, 89,000 (88.6 percent) worked in the northern border states. Reported in INEGI, Avance de Información Económica, *Industria Maquiladora de Exportación*, Aguascalientes, Ags., (June 1993): 7.
3. Castillo Peraza, the president of the *Partido Acción Nacional* (PAN)—which is the only opposition party recognized as having won state elections—argued in May 1993 that with or without NAFTA, Mexicans were already living with the consequences of the opening and globalization of their economy (Galarza, 1993: 18). He pointed to the fact that for over a decade, Mexican government policy had facilitated foreign investment in three areas: the stock exchange, privatized state companies (such as telecommunications), and maquiladoras. While the stock market and privatized state industry have been of interest to foreign capital only in the last few years, maquiladoras have been growing for more than a quarter of a century.

Chapter 1

1. The value added to maquiladora products comes from wages paid to employees and the operating expenses of maquila plants in Mexico, with less than 2 percent from materials purchased in Mexico.
2. The importance of severance pay lies in the fact that in Mexico, workers cannot be laid off, but must be terminated if the employer does not have adequate work for them to do. Unemployment insurance does not exist in Mexico.
3. Unfortunately, government protocols established in preparation for NAFTA often reflected the official view rather than the more realistic picture of how industries actually operate in Mexico. As stated in the introduction to an otherwise excellent publication by Labour Canada (1991) comparing labor legislation in the three countries, "With respect to Mexico, although it is a federal republic made up of 31 States throughout the country, labour law comes exclusively within federal jurisdiction and applies throughout the country, including the export processing zones (EPZs)" (n.p.). The only possible qualification of this legal fact is another statement in the introduction that "This report . . . does not examine the degree to which these laws are applied in the three countries" (n.p.).

4. Benería and Roldán (1987: 32) report that in Mexico City, the term "maquila" does not mean export processing, but production for the domestic market which is subcontracted and often done by women at home. This is not the meaning of "maquila" in the present study.

5. This area consists of Aguascalientes plus the six Mexican states that border the United States.

6. The North American content requirement for passenger vehicles, light trucks, engines, and transmissions is 62.5 percent.

7. Industrial reconversion had been one of the major pillars adopted by ex-President de la Madrid in 1986 to achieve long-term structural reform in response to falling oil prices. Its goal was the increased efficiency of Mexican industry through technological innovation that would lower the cost of wages and increase production, introduction of organizational work forms that would promote cooperation and consensus, territorial relocation of capital and workers, and so forth. As de la Garza Toledo (1990: 155) has indicated, the reconversion of small and medium-sized Mexican industry in the private sector consists in converting them into maquiladoras of the big industries, taking advantage of their low wages, tax breaks, and legal benefits to workers.

8. This oligarchy is made up of those who bought the banks when President Salinas privatized them.

9. Shaiken and Browne (1991: 35) cite the definition of quality circles developed by the Japanese Union of Scientists and Engineers:

> The QC circle is a small group within the same workshop that voluntarily carries out quality-control activity. The small group continuously conducts control and improvement of the workshop as one part in the chain of companywide quality-control activity. In this fashion, utilizing quality control techniques, the small groups carry out self-development and mutual development. . . .
>
> Unlike quality circles, which are a parallel organizational form, work teams are part of the production process itself. They generally consist of eight to ten workers from one area of production, each of whom is cross-trained to perform any of the tasks assigned to that area. Members sometimes choose the team leader, although leaders may also be appointed by management. . . . In its most far-reaching form, the teams make decisions regarding job assignments, training opportunities, quality, productivity improvement, and personal matters such as discipline for absenteeism. (39)

10. Jenson (1989: 144–45) explains that the development of a more-flexible labor force also means rising rates of feminization because female and male workers are employed in different ways. Women (most often married) are more likely to take part-time work because of their responsibility for work in the home. Also, women workers often have more-flexible labor contracts in which they are less protected because they are not as well organized by unions. Standing (1987: 1077) shows how

the 1980s saw a spread of the types of work, labor relations, income, and insecurity associated with women's work, "resulting not only in a notable rise in female labor force participation, but in a fall in men's employment, as well as a transformation—or feminization—of many jobs traditionally held by men."

Chapter 2

1. See "World Finds a Bargain Basement for Labor," *Arizona Republic,* July 31, 1987; and L. Brooks, "Produce Firms in Nogales Ask For Federal Aid," *Arizona Daily Star,* July 7, 1992.

2. These are the monthly averages calculated from total firms present from January to November 1990, in INEGI, *Avance de información económica, industria maquiladora de exportación,* Aguascalientes, Ags. (Mar. 1991): 30.

3. Calculated from data in *Indicadores económicos,* Mexico: Banco de Mexico, 1991.

4. Oct. 24, 1990.

5. Personal communication with Sergio Sandoval at the first part of the conference on Cars and Continentalism, University of Toronto, June 1994.

6. As a frame of reference for selecting companies, the author used the definition of the auto-part industry composed by Fuentes Flores and Barajas Escamilla (1989: 37) from several government sources in Mexico: "The widest definition of the auto parts industry includes 11 classifications of activities which are 1) fabrication and assembly of bodies and trailers for cars and trucks; 2) fabrication of motors and their parts for cars and trucks; 3) fabrication of the transmission system for cars and trucks; 4) fabrication of the suspension system for cars and trucks; 5) fabrication of parts and accessories for the brake system of cars and trucks; 6) fabrication of parts and accessories for cars and trucks; 7) fabrication and repair of fabric upholstery for cars; 8) fabrication of plastic upholstery; 9) fabrication of parts and accessories for the auto electric system; 10) fabrication of batteries and electrical cells and, 11) fabrication and assembly of cars and trucks." Two of the companies in the sample make products listed in the above definition for vehicles other than cars or trucks. They were included in the sample because their production processes are essentially similar to production of the same products for cars and trucks.

7. These areas are called *Areas Geoestadísticas Básicas* (AGEB) and contain about 2,500 people. Strata were defined on the basis of the services (water, electricity, sewerage) available in an area, and the external appearance of dwellings (number of windows, cars, TV antennas). Because growth in northern urban centers like Nogales has never been regulated by any kind of urban planning, such areas are heterogeneous, and the strata cannot be considered pure.

8. INEGI defines "direct workers" as the number of men and women whose work is related directly to the productive process of the maquila, in assembly, inspection, maintenance, repair, etc. "Indirect workers" are all other employees who do not fit this definition.

9. As M. Appel Molot points out in her introduction to *Driving Continentally* (1993: 1), "one out of every ten jobs in Canada and the United States is dependent on the automotive industry." This dynamism has motivated other maquila research recently. For example, González-Aréchiga (1989a: 5) focused his team of investigators on Tijuana auto-parts and electronics maquilas because these two subsectors had the most innovation in technology, products, and administrative strategies. They also had the majority of value added and personnel for all maquilas. He expected, for these reasons, to find the emerging new maquila in these two subsectors.

10. While the term "Midwest" is only used to connote areas in the United States, the author assumes that the area of Canada to which Womack is referring is Ontario.

Chapter 3

1. Defined in P. Kumar and M. L. Coates, eds., *Glossary of Common Industrial Relations Terms* (Industrial Relations Centre, Queen's University), 1989, 26.

2. See Banco de Mexico, *Indicadores Económicos* (Nov. 1991).

3. During the period of data collection, the *Wall Street Journal* was running a series of articles on maquiladoras as part of the nascent debate on NAFTA. Several of these articles were very critical of how the maquila labor force was constituted. An example is Matt Moffett, "Working Children: Underage Laborers Fill Mexican Factories, Stir U.S. Trade Debate—Vicente Guerrero, 12, quits school for footwear plant; Dad: 'We eat better now,' " *Wall Street Journal,* Apr. 1, 1991, 32–33.

4. Personal communication with Francisco Lara Valencia, coordinator of El Colegio de la Frontera Norte, Nogales, Sonora, Mar. 4, 1991.

5. *La Voz del Norte,* Nov. 9, 1989.

6. Unfortunately, newspapers for January and February 1990 were not available.

7. On occasion, the ads used vague quantifiers for the number of positions involved. In those cases, an estimate of the number of positions was calculated by averaging the number of positions in other ads for the same job.

8. The standard deviation for the day an ad appears in January was higher than for other months, with February, September, and October having fewer ads in the second half of the month.

9. Poulantzas (1975) equates the working class with productive laborers who do not have mental expertise and do not exercise power in the workplace. Given this definition, only about 3 percent of all positions classified as unskilled productive personnel would not be considered in the working class: cleaners, concierge, etc., who do not do productive labor in the Marxist sense.

10. The hierarchical agglomerative method of cluster analysis with the single-linkage form (Sneath and Sokal, 1973) was performed with the Systat computer program. After a few preliminary trials, it was decided to exclude the variables measuring attitude, marital status, and rootedness from the analysis, since they showed very little similarity to any of the other prerequisites and clustered only at the very

last stage when they were forced by the method to do so. The maintenance of these three variables in the analysis would not alter the three-cluster solution eventually chosen, but would make its presentation less clear visually in the figures. The similarity measure employed was Jaccard's coefficient, since the absence of prerequisites was not meaningful in this study, as explained in "Prerequisites for Employment" in chapter 3. In order to test for the validity of the cluster-analysis solution, random subsamples were selected, and the cluster analysis and multidimensional scaling were run again. The same results appeared for the subsamples as for the whole sample.

11. One company had added a connecting chapel to its plant, which was obviously meant to be a statement in industrial architecture since it was positioned to be visible from the main highway passing by the industrial park.

12. Incentives that did not appear often enough to provide enough cases to include in the cluster analysis were (1) social, religious, and sports events, (2) permanent contract, (3) life insurance, (4) personal loans, and (5) benefits according to law. All of these appeared in five or fewer ads. The method of cluster analysis used here was the hierarchical agglomerative one with average linkage. Unfortunately, there were not enough incentives to validate them by randomly dividing them in half and performing the cluster analysis again, as was done with the cluster analysis for prerequisites.

Chapter 4

1. All interviews were conducted anonymously so that the respondent's real name is unknown.

2. In late 1992, the Mexican government lopped off three zeros from the end of their currency, so that what used to be 3,000 pesos became 3 new pesos, or 3,000 old pesos. Wages are reported in old pesos because that was the currency in use when the data were collected. The exchange rate at the time of data collection was used for calculating equivalents in U.S. currency. The transition from the old to the new peso is gradual. For example, at the time of writing the final draft of this book, four years after data collection, postage stamps for 5,000 pesos (really old pesos) were still in circulation, presumably because the government had already printed them before moving to new pesos and wanted to use them up.

Many Mexicans still count their pesos in thousands, the old way, in what seems to be an acknowledgment of what they have lost through the devaluation process. I found the old usage of maintaining three zeros and calling the currency simply "pesos," without the suffix "old," especially prevalent at the end of 1994 when the crisis began. As Mexicans watched the new peso deflate, the word *mil* (thousand) could be heard added back on to the increasingly large number of new pesos that the U.S. dollar was worth.

3. The household was operationally defined as the group of people that pooled costs for food. Respondents were asked how many of the people who lived with

them in the same dwelling shared grocery expenses, in order to take into account that there may have been more than one household in a dwelling.

4. In terms of questionnaire design, respondents were asked if they were the head of their households, and if they responded that they were not, they were then asked their relationship to the head of the household. Thus, it cannot be ascertained whether those who responded that they were the head of the household were in fact kin to the other members of their household. Those who lived in single-person households were not asked how they were related to other households.

5. All of the 14 women workers who reported their relationship to the head of the household as spouse lived in households where there were both male and female wage earners. Twelve of them lived in households where there was only one other male wage earner. If heading a household is understood in terms of economic contributions, these women may very well have shared the headship of their households, since there was not much difference between what they earned and the average income that others in their household earned. The ratio of wives' income to the average income of other wage earners in their household was .91, whereas the ratio of male heads of households to the average income of other wage earners in their households was 1.1.

6. This difference is at least partly due to the different methodologies utilized in the two studies. Heyman used the household as the unit of analysis and did not include any single-person households. This study considered the individual direct worker as the unit of analysis and did not include supervisors and other indirect workers in the sample.

7. Single parenthood was operationalized as respondents who had children and were either single, widowed, separated, or divorced. Barajas Escamilla and Rodríguez Carrillo (1989) found the same (about 11 percent) proportion of single parents in their sample of women maquiladora workers in Tijuana.

8. Thus, migrants seem to be contained by regional definitions consistent with industrial corridors, as set out by Barajas Escamilla, and discussed in chapter 1.

9. Interviewers in this study were instructed to record the respondent's belief about home ownership, even though some people living in *Infonavit* housing might say they did not own their housing when they actually did, and squatters might say they owned their housing when they actually did not.

Chapter 5

1. Plants having greater flexibility (27 percent of the sample) were those in which direct workers were found to be involved in more than 30 percent, on average, of eight activities related to flexible work organization. Plants classified as having less flexibility (73 percent of the sample) where those with 30 percent or less of their direct workers involved in these same eight activities: a) maintenance of equipment and machinery; b) diagnosing and solving production problems; c) control or inspection of quality; d) quality circles or groups; e) work teams, work

groups, or production groups; f) multiskilling; g) rotation of skills and operations; h) involvement in work.

2. INEGI defines technicians as people whose work is related directly to the production process or with assembly and who are not considered direct workers, for example operation supervisors, quality control, etc. (including men and women). Foreigners are only included if their salaries are paid in Mexico by the maquiladora (INEGI, Cuestionario mensual para la estadística de maquiladoras de exportación, Forma 604.1).

3. Restructuring was defined simply as new technology and flexible work organization. INEGI defines direct workers as the number of men and women whose work is related directly to the productive process of the maquila in assembly, inspection, maintenance, repair, etc. Indirect workers are all other employees who do not fit this definition (ibid.).

4. During the interview, I did not probe the manager on the contradiction underlying his comment. If his plant were to achieve zero defects, then it might not matter how much inventory was on hand.

5. When there was a discrepancy with regard to the skill level that managers attributed to a particular job, the skill level attributed by the majority of managers was used for all workers holding that job, unless the activities carried out by the worker were different from those of the majority of workers with that job title.

6. This is an overestimation, since workers who reported receiving less than a day's training were coded as receiving one day's training so as not to have to deal with fractions of days.

7. Personal communication, Feb. 26, 1991.

8. *SourceMex* 5 (42), Nov. 2, 1994.

Chapter 6

1. Brenner and Glick (1991: 48) define the mode of regulation as an expression of institutional structures governing intra- and inter-firm relations, the relations among capitals, and the relationship between capital and labor. The network of institutions that composes the mode of regulation governs the accumulation process by establishing a) the nature of the capital-wage labor nexus and b) the type of intercapitalist competition, as well as c) the character of monetary and credit relationships, d) the manner of adhesion of the firms of the national economy to the international economy, and e) the forms of the state's intervention into the economy.

2. In January 1993, then-president Salinas used government statistics to argue that although wages had fallen in the eighties, they had begun to recover since 1989. His version of wage reality was contradicted immediately by several commentators, including the head of the CTM, Fidel Velázquez, who argued that government statistics showing an increase in wages and a drop in unemployment were fictitious attempts to hide the alarming social cost of the economic opening (Hinojosa, 1993). Balboa and Orozco Orozco (1994) have shown how statistics were deliberately

manipulated by government authorities. For example, data only refer to less than half of the workers in the manufacturing and commercial sectors, those making the highest wages, and should not be generalized. Also, administrative employees and laborers were collapsed into one category in the calculation of averages, so that income distribution is not visible.

With the devaluation at the beginning of the Zedillo presidency, denial of the Salinas regime's statements became even more widespread. In mid-January 1995, Ramos (1995) said in an editorial in *El Financiero International,* "Until recently, official propaganda led many Mexicans to believe that they had made it, and that it was only a matter of months before First-World lifestyles became the norm. But the devaluation proved to be a very rude wake-up call. Suddenly the dream is over. . . . During the last administration, officials were adamant that the good times had already begun. One need only recall such mad assertions as then-Finance Secretary Pedro Aspe's insistence in an early-1993 speech to an audience of academics that reports of growing unemployment and declining purchasing power were 'brilliant myths.' "

3. Since Barajas Escamilla and Rodríguez Carrillo did not report any wages coming from overtime, it is assumed here that working overtime was not a significant factor in their workers' gross pay, and that the base pay rate must have been a bigger component of higher salaries than lower salaries.

4. Wage data collected from SECOFI were aggregated into the following categories: wages paid to direct workers, technicians, administrative employees, and benefits. The benefits category includes benefits paid to all of the three categories of employees. Real wages were calculated with the following formula:

$$\frac{\text{actual reported wage in a given year}}{\text{consumer price index for that year} / 100}$$

CPI data are from *Indicadores económicos, Banco de México.* Note, however, that Heyman (1991: 177) says that the problem with using these official data to calculate real wages "is that there is reason to suspect that for political reasons these figures underestimate the real increases in the cost of living."

5. Administrative employees are those referred to in chapter 3 as skilled administrative and skilled control personnel.

6. SECOFI does not break down the amount paid in benefits by type of job.

7. This argument was made to me by Kevin Middlebrook at a seminar I gave at the Center for U.S.-Mexican Studies, University of California at San Diego, on June 12, 1991.

8. The company against which these complaints were made is not part of the sample in this study, but it is one that had a presence in Imuris, albeit a very small and insignificant one, in 1991.

9. The exception to low levels of unionization in the western corridor is Agua Prieta, in which 45 percent of maquila workers are unionized.

10. Union complaints test NAFTA's labour side deal, *CCPA Monitor* 1 (1) (May 1994): 14. Dombey (1995f: 1) cites Arturo Alcalde, a labor lawyer and official of one of the organizations that filed the complaint, as believing that the ruling would not be very effective because it was largely restricted to minimum wage, health and safety regulations, and child labor, which are not the major concerns of the formal industrial sector.

Chapter 7

1. One of the 19 is also in the sample of transport-equipment plants used for this study.

2. Personal communication from Frans Schryer, who discovered this in the fieldwork for *Ethnicity and Class Conflict in Rural Mexico* (Princeton: Princeton University Press, 1990).

3. "Economic Development: Retail Outlets on the Way," *Tucson Citizen,* Apr. 5, 1993.

4. Ibid.

5. *SourceMex* 6 (18), May 3, 1995.

6. "Nuevo Leon Gets New Maquiladoras," *El Financiero International,* Feb. 13–19, 1995, 5.

7. *La Jornada,* Apr. 14, 1995, as cited in "Government Approves 250 New Maquiladoras," *El Financiero International,* Apr. 24–30, 1995: 5.

8. "Cambian Empresas Textiles a Maquiladoras, en Aguascalientes," *República,* Dec. 18, 1994, 1.

9. *SourceMex,* 6 (2), Jan. 11, 1995.

10. *SourceMex,* 6 (11), Mar. 15, 1995.

11. "Mexicans Buying Less North of the Border," *El Financiero International,* Mar. 13–19, 1995, 5.

12. "Continflas Lives (Inside Fidel Velázquez's Body)," *El Financiero International,* Feb. 13–19, 1995, 2

13. "Strikes Down in First Quarter," *El Financiero International,* Apr. 17–23, 1995, 8.

14. "Devaluation of Peso Resulting in Increase of Undocumented Immigrants to the U.S.," *SourceMex* 6 (9), Mar. 1, 1995.

BIBLIOGRAPHY

Allahar, A. 1989. *Sociology and the Periphery: Theories and Issues.* Toronto: Garamond.

Allen, C. 1990. Trade Unions, Worker Participation, and Flexibility. *Comparative Politics* 22: 253–272.

Angulo P., C. 1990. Foreign Investment and the Maquiladora Export Industry. *Inversión extranjera directa: Direct Foreign Investment,* 139–143. México: Banamex.

Appel Molot, M. (ed.). 1993. *Driving Continentally: National Policies and the North American Auto Industry.* Ottawa: Carleton University Press.

Arteaga G., A., J. Carrillo, and J. Micheli T. 1989. *Transformaciones tecnológicas y relaciones laborales en la industria automotriz.* México: Fundación Friedrich Ebert.

Ayala, E. 1991. El patrón de las exportaciones de México a los Estados Unidos. *Estrategia* 2: 2–4.

Baker, G. 1992. Ellwyn R. Stodard's Rejoinder and Critical Commentary of "Mexican Labor is Not Cheap." *Río Bravo* 1 (2): 126–132.

———. 1991. Mexican Labor is Not Cheap. *Río Bravo* 1 (1): 7–26.

Balboa, F., and M. Orozco Orozco. 1994. Wage Policy in Mexico. Paper presented at the International Conference on Economic Integration and Public Policy: NAFTA, the European Union and Beyond, York University, Toronto.

Barajas Escamilla, R. 1989a. Complejos industriales en el sur de Estados Unidos y su relación con la distribución espacial y el crecimiento de los centros maquiladores en el norte de México. In B. González-Aréchiga and R. Barajas Escamilla (compiladores), *Las maquiladoras: Ajuste estructural y desarrollo regional.* Tijuana: Fundación Friedrich Ebert.

———. 1989b. Estructura y composición de la industria maquiladora en México y Tijuana. In B. González-Aréchiga et al., *La industria maquiladora mexicana en los sectores electrónico y de autopartes,* 13–16. México: Fundación Friedrich Ebert.

———. 1992. Reestructuración industrial: subcontratación internacional, cambio tecnológico y flexibilidad en la maquiladora. *Estudios Fronterizos* 23: 33–54.

Barajas Escamilla, R., and C. Rodríguez Carrillo. 1989. *Mujer y trabajo en la industria maquiladora de exportación en Tijuana, Baja California.* Tijuana. Mimeographed.

Benería, L., and M. Roldán. 1987. *The Crossroads of Class and Gender.* Chicago: University of Chicago Press.

Berggren, C. 1993. Lean Production—The End Of History? *Work, Employment, and Society* 7 (2): 163–188.

Booz-Allen and Hamilton and Infotec. 1987. *Industria de autopartes.* México: Bancomex.

Borquez R., V. 1989. Incompetente el inspector del trabajo ante las amenazas a los empleados de maquiladoras. *Diario del Yaqui* (April 29).

Brannon, J., and G. Lucker. 1989. The Impact of Mexico's Economic Crisis on the Demographic Composition of the Maquiladora Labor Force. *Journal of Borderland Studies* 4 (1): 39–70.

Brenner, R., and M. Glick. 1991. The Regulation Approach: Theory and History. *New Left Review* 188: 45–119.

Brown, F., and L. Domíngez. 1989. Nuevas tecnologías en la industria maquiladora de exportación. *Comercio Exterior* 39 (3): 215–223.

Brown, K. 1992. *Understanding Industrial Organisations.* London: Routledge.

Bustamante, J. 1979. Condiciones estructurales e ideologias de la emigración mexicana indocumentada a Estados Unidos. *El Economista Mexicano* 13 (2): 29–38.

Camberos Castro, M., and R. Barojas. 1988. El problema de la vivienda en la frontera (Nogales, Sonora). *Estudios Demográficos y Urbanos* 3 (3): 563-573.

Carlile, W. 1992. Arizona Roads Raise Doubts. *Arizona Republic,* May 28, 1.

———. 1995. State exports up 10 percent in '94. *Arizona Republic,* January 8, 1.

Carrillo, J. 1988. Calificación y trabajo en la industria automotriz. *Estudios Demográficos y Urbanos* 3 (3): 453–477.

———. 1989a. Calidad con consenso en las maquiladoras: ¿Asociación factible? *Frontera Norte* 1 (2): 105–132.

———. 1989b. Transformaciones en la industria maquiladora de exportación. In B. González-Aréchiga and R. Barajas Escamilla (compiladores), *Las maquiladoras: Ajuste estructural y desarrollo regional,* 37–54. Tijuana: Fundación Friedrich Ebert.

———. 1990a. Maquilización de la industria automotriz en México: de la industria terminal a la industria de ensamble. In J. Carrillo (compilador), *La Nueva Era de la Industria Automotriz en México,* 67–114. Tijuana: El Colegio de la Frontera Norte.

———. 1990b. Legislación laboral y flexibilidad en la industria maquiladora. In F. Mora and V. Reynoso (coordinadores), *Modernización y legislación laboral en el noroeste de México,* 155–194. Hermosillo: El Colegio de Sonora.

———. 1991a. *Reporte de Investigacion. Mercados de Trabajo en las Actividades Maquiladoras.* Secretaría del Trabajo y Previsión Social y El Colegio de la Frontera Norte. Mimeographed.

———. 1991b. Las maquiladoras en el TLC. Integración complementaria o competencia desigual. *Trabajo* 5–6: 53–61.

———. 1992. *Mujeres en la industria automotriz en México.* Tijuana: El Colegio de la Frontera Norte.

Carrillo, J., and O. Contreras. 1992. Calificación y restructuración industrial: examen de la industria maquiladora. *Frontera Norte* 4 (8): 49–78.

Carrillo, J., O. Contreras, N. Fuentes, R. González, J. Montenegro, J. Santibáñez R., and G. Valdés-Villalva. 1991. *Mercados de trabajo en la industria maquiladora de exportación: Síntesis del reporte de investigación.* México: Secretaría del Trabajo y Previsión Social.

Carrillo, J., and M. Ramírez. 1990. Maquiladoras en la frontera norte: opinión sobre los sindicatos. *Frontera Norte* 2 (4): 121–152.

————. 1992. Modernización tecnológica y cambios organizacionales en la industria maquiladora. *Estudios Fronterizos* 23: 55–76.

Chande, R. 1990. Origen, objectivos, y métodos de la encuesta socioeconómica anual de la frontera: 1987–1988–1989. *Frontera Norte* 2 (4): 183–225.

Chaney, E. 1979. *Supermadre: Women in Politics in Latin America.* Austin: University of Texas Press.

Cohen, S., and J. Zysman. 1987. *Manufacturing Matters: The Myth of the Post-Industrial Economy.* New York: Basic Books.

COMO (Centro de Orientación de la Mujer Obrera, A.C.). 1984. *Primer taller de analisis sobre aprendizaje en la producción y transferencia de tecnología en la industria de maquila de exportación.* Juárez: Centro de Estudios Fronterizos del Norte de México.

Contreras, O. 1990. Flexibilidad laboral en la industria maquiladora. *El Correo Fronterizo* 5 (4): 6–7.

Cornelius, W., and P. Martin. 1991. Effects of a Free Trade Agreement on Mexican Rural Migration to the United States: Alternative Scenarios. Paper presented at the Executive Policy Seminar on Agriculture in a North American Free Trade Agreement, Center for U.S.-Mexican Studies, University of California, San Diego, May 24–25.

Crevoshay, F. 1991. Japanese Investment and NAFTA. *San Diego Business Journal* 12 (December 16): 4A.

DeForest, M. 1994. Thinking of a plant in Mexico? *Academy of Management Executive* 8 (1): 33–40.

De la Garza Toledo, E. 1990. México: ¿Desindustrialización o reconversión? In J. Blanco y G. Guevara Niebla (coordinadores), *Universidad nacional y economía,* 121–162. México: UNAM, Centro de Investigaciones Interdisciplinarias en Humanidades.

De la Garza, E., and M. Leyva. 1993. Restructuración productiva y crisis del sincidalismo en México. In P. Castro (coordinador), *Las políticas salinistas: balance a mitad de sexenio (1988–1991),* 71–90. México: Universidad Autónoma Metropolitana (UNAM).

De los Angeles Crummett, M. 1985. *Class, Household Structure, and Migration: A Case Study From Rural México.* Working paper 92, Women in International Development, Michigan State University, East Lansing, MI.

De los Angeles Pozas, M. 1993. *Industrial Restructuring in Mexico: Corporate Adaptation, Technológical Innovation, and Changing Patterns of Industrial Relations in Monterrey.* San Diego: Monograph Series, 38, Center for U.S.-Mexican Studies, University of California.

Denman, C. 1990. Tiempos modernos: trabajar y morir. In F. Mora y V. Reynoso (eds.), *Modernización y legislación laboral en el noroeste de México.* Hermosillo: El Colegio de Sonora.

Deters, B. 1991. Tucson Ready to Pop: Signs of Life Survive Tough Period. *Arizona Republic,* September 21, 1.

Dombey, D. 1995a. New Lease on Life. *El Financiero International* (January 16–22): 14.

———. 1995b. Monterrey Plop. *El Financiero International* (February 13–19): 16–17.

———. 1995c. Confederation of Woes: What has the CTM Done for You Lately? Not Much, Say Union Dissidents. *El Financiero International* (March 13–19): 15.

———. 1995d. Labor Low: Organized Labor Poses Little Threat for Zedillo's Economic Plans. *El Financiero International* (March 13–19): 13.

———. 1995e. Ford Grants 25 Percent Pay Hikes. *El Financiero International* (April 10–16): 3.

———. 1995f. Nafta Off-Shoot Censors Sony. *El Financiero International* (April 17–23): 1.

Domínguez Y., J. 1994. La economía mexicana: ¿Hacia la maquilación? *Investigación Económica* 54 (209): 203–248.

Dower, R. 1992. U.S., México Pledge to Clean Up Shared Border. *San Diego Business Journal* (July 12): 1.

Duran, J. A. 1994. Autopartes: Es hora de aliarse. *Expansión* (October 12): 52–57.

Dwyer, A. 1994. *On the Line: Life on the U.S.-Mexican Border.* London: Latin American Bureau.

The Economist. 1993. If You Can't, Yucatan Can. (May 22): 49–50.

Edwards, J. 1991. Free-Trade Pact May Pose Unique Lending Opportunity. *Arizona Business Gazetter,* March 22, 17–18.

Fajnzylber, F. 1990. *Unavoidable Industrial Restructuring in Latin America.* Durham: Duke University Press.

Fernandez, C. 1993. Wake Up, Wake Up: Japanese Official Says NAFTA Will Obstruct Asian Investment. *El Financiero International* (November 1–7): 12.

Fernández Kelly, P. 1983a. *For We Are Sold, I and My People: Women and Industry in Mexico's Frontier.* Albany: State University of New York Press.

———. 1983b. Mexican Border Industrialization, Female Labor Force Participation, and Migration. In J. Nash and P. Fernández Kelly (eds.), *Women, Men, and the International Division of Labor,* 205–223. Albany: State University of New York Press.

————. 1987. Technology and Employment Along the U.S.-Mexican Border. In C. Thorup (ed.), *The United States and Mexico: Face to Face with New Technology*, 149–166. New Brunswick: Transaction.

Figueroa, M. 1989a. Absentismo en la maquila de Nogales. *El Imparcial* (January 4).

————. 1989b. Vacaciones 16 dias obreros de maquilas. *El Imparcial* (December 5).

Flores, A. 1993. Componentes del crecimiento económico de la industria manufacturera de la región fronteriza del noreste de México. In A. Flores (coordinador), *TLC: Impactos en la frontera norte*. México: UNAM.

Flores Cartas, R. 1992. Se desalentará la inversión en las maquiladoras. *El Financiero* (February 28).

Fröbel, F., J. Heinrichs, and O. Kreye. 1980. *The New International Division of Labor: Structural Unemployment in Industrialized Countries and Industrialization in Developing Countries*. New York: Cambridge.

Fuentes Flores, N., and R. Barajas Escamilla. 1989. Características y cambios en la industria maquiladora: el caso de la rama de auto partes en Tijuana. In B. González Aréchiga et al. *La industria maquiladora mexicana en los sectores electrónico y de autopartes*, 37–48. Tijuana: Fundación Friedrich Ebert.

Fukuyama, F. 1989. The End of History? *The National Interest* 16: 3–18.

Galarza, G. 1993. Es inadmisible que el nerviosismo oficial por el TLC ocasione graves tropiezos políticos: Castillo Peraza. *Proceso* 862 (May 10): 17–19.

Gambrill, M. 1981. *Maquiladoras*. México: Centro de Estudios Economicos y Sociales del Tercer Mundo.

————. 1989. Sindicalismo en las maquiladoras de Tijuana: Regresión en las prestaciones sociales. In J. Carrillo (compilador), *Reestructuración Industrial. Maquiladoras en la Frontera México-Estados Unidos*, 183–220. Tijuana: Colegio de la Frontera Norte de México.

————. 1992. El impacto del tratado de libre comercio sobre la industria maquiladora. In B. Driscoll de Alvarado and M. Gambrill (eds.), *El tratado de libre comercio, entre el viejo y el nuevo orden*, 35–59. México: UNAM.

————. 1994a. Maquiladoras and North American Integration. Paper presented at the Latin American Studies Association conference in Atlanta, Georgia, March 10–12.

————. 1994b. NAFTA and the Mexican Maquiladora Industry. Paper presented at the Internatioanal Conference on Economic Integration and Public Policy: NAFTA, the EU, and Beyond, at York University, Toronto, May 27–29.

George, E. 1990. What Does the Future Hold for the Maquiladora Industry? In K. Fatemi (ed.), *The Maquiladora Industry: Economic Solution or Problem?* 219–234. New York: Praeger.

Gereffi, G. 1992. Mexico's Maquiladora Industries and North American Integration. In S. Randall, H. Konrad, and S. Silverman (eds.), *North America Without*

Borders? Integrating Canada, the United States, and Mexico, 138–151. Calgary: University of Calgary.

————. 1994. Contending Perspectives on Regional Integration: Development Strategies and Commodity Chains in Latin America and East Asia. Paper presented at the conference of the Latin American Studies Association, Atlanta, Georgia, March 10–12.

Gertler, M. 1988. The Limits to Flexibility: Comments on the Post-Fordist Vision of Production and Its Geography. *Transactions, Institute of British Geographers, N.S.* 13 (4): 419–432.

Godínez Plascencia, J. 1990. El cambio tecnológico en la industria maquiladora de exportación en México: Un enforque metodológico. *Estudios Fronterizos* 23: 9–32.

González-Aréchiga, B. 1989a. Introduction to González-Aréchiga et al. (eds.) *La industria maquiladora mexicana en los sectores electrónico y de autopartes,* 5–6. México: La Fundación Friedrich Ebert.

————. 1989b. Fuentes de crecimiento y el cambio en la composición laboral de la maquiladora. In González Aréchiga et al. (eds.), *La industria maquiladora mexicana en los sectores electrónico y de autopartes,* 16–25. México: La Fundación Friedrich Ebert.

González-Aréchiga, B., R. Barajas Escamilla, N. Fuentes, and J. Ramírez, (eds.). 1989. *La industria maquiladora mexicana en los sectores electrónico y de autopartes.* México: La Fundación Friedrich Ebert.

González Aréchiga, B., and J. Ramírez. 1989. Perspectivas estructurales de la industria maquiladora. *Comercio Exterior* 39 (10): 874–886.

González Pérez, L. 1994. Maquiladoras, principal fuente de ingresos para México: SECOFI. *El Financiero* (August 12): 16.

González Ramírez, R. 1990. Evaluación de la encuesta socioeconómica anual de la frontera, 1987. *Frontera Norte* 2 (4): 183–214.

Granados, O. 1994. Acelerador a fondo. *Expansión* (October 12): 47–50.

Griffith, W. 1991. Free Trade and the Caribbean. *Hemisphere* 3 (3): 6–7.

Hanson, G. 1992. Localización industrial, especialización vertical y libre comercio entre México y Estados Unidos. In *Ajuste estructural, mercados laborales y TLC,* 309–336. México: El Colegio de México.

Heller, L. 1993. *The State of Sonora.* México: Grupo Azabache.

Herr, J. 1992. Selling to Japan: Savvy Ariz. Firms Finding Way into Rewarding Market. *Arizona Daily Star,* March 9.

Herzenberg, S. 1993. Continental Integration and the Future of the North American Auto Sector. In M. Appel Molot (ed.), *Driving Continentally.* Ottawa: Carleton University Press.

Heyman, J. McC. 1991. *Life and Labor on The Border.* Tucson: University of Arizona Press.

Hidalgo Blaine, P. 1991. Demandan a una maquila de Nogales. *El Imparcial* (March 27): 3D.

Hinojosa, J. 1993. Tripulación en la estadística. *Proceso* 848 (February 1): 34–38.

Hoffman, K., and R. Kaplinsky. 1988. *Driving Force.* Boulder: Westview.

Holstein, W. 1990. Mexico: A New Economic Era. *Business Week* (November 12): 104–110.

Howes, C., and A. Markusen. 1993. Trade, Industry, and Economic Development. In H. Noponen, J. Graham and A. Markusen (eds.), *Trading Industries, Trading Regions, International Trade, American Industry, and Regional Economic Development,* 1–44. New York: Guilford Press.

Hughes, S., and J. Watling. 1993. The Economic Equation. *El Financiero Internacional* (November 1–7): 10–11.

Husson, M. 1991. Maquiladorización de la industria mexicana. *El Cotidiano* 41: 3–13.

Ingram, H., L. Milich, and R. G. Varady. 1994. Managing Transboundary Resources: Lessons from Ambos Nogales. *Environment* 36 (4): 6–38.

Ivey, E. 1994. Southern Corridor: Putting the Puzzle Together. *New Mexico Business Journal* 18 (7): 47.

Jarman, M. 1992. Mexican "Shelter Operators" Show the Way. *Arizona Business Gazette* (January 17): 13.

Jenson, J. 1989. The talents of women, the skills of men: Flexible specialization and women. In S. Wood (ed.), *The Transformation of Work?* 141–154. London: Unwin Hyman.

Jones, A. 1987. Maquiladoras Need Workers, Houses. *Tucson (Arizona) Citizen,* June 2.

Kaplinsky, R. 1994. From Mass Production to Flexible Specialization: A Case Study of Microeconomic Change in a Semi-industrialized Economy. *World Development* 22 (3): 337–353.

Kelley, M. 1989. Alternative forms of work organization under programable automation. In S. Wood (ed.), *The Transformation of Work?* 235–246. London: Unwin Hyman.

Kenney, M., and R. Florida. 1994. Japanese Maquiladoras: Production Organization and Global Commodity Chains. *World Development* 22 (1): 27–44.

Kern, H., and C. Sabel. 1992. Trade Unions and Decentralized Production: A Sketch of Strategic Problems in the German Labour Movement. In M. Regini (ed.), *The Future of Labour Movements,* 217–249. London: Sage.

Koido, A. 1992. *Between Two Forces of Restructuring: U.S.-Japanese Competition and the Transformation of Mexico's Maquiladora Industry.* Ph.D. dissertation. Johns Hopkins University.

Kopinak, K. 1993. Maquiladorization of the Mexican Economy. In R. Ginspun and M. Cameron (eds.), *The Political Economy of a North American Free Trade Area,* 141–162. New York: St. Martin's.

Kraul, C. 1994. Making Tracks for the Border: U.S. Railroads' Business with Mexico Booms. *Los Angeles Times,* July 6.

La Voz del Norte. 1989. Renuncian a causa del frio el 12% de los empleados de las maquiladoras. November 9.

Labour Canada. 1991. Comparison of Labour Legislation of General Application in Canada, the United States and Mexico. Ottawa: Labour Canada.

Lara, B. 1990. Tecnología flexible y flexibilidad en el trabajo: nuevo reto para los trabajadores. en F. Mora y V. Reynosa (coordinadores), *Modernización y legislación laboral en el noroeste de México,* 221–243. Hermosillo: El Colegio de Sonora y Fundación Friedrich Ebert.

————. 1992. Cambio tecnológico y heterogeneidad productiva en las maquilas electricas-eclectrónicas de Sonora (1980–1989). *Estudios Sociales* 3 (6): 123–162.

Lara Valencia, F. 1990. Maquila y fuerza de trabajo en Nogales: Elementos para una reevaluación. Mimeographed.

————. 1991. Empleo y migracion en la zona fronteriza de Sonora. Paper presented at the sixteenth Symposium of History and Anthropology of Sonora. Mimeographed.

————. 1992. El gasto trasfronterizo de los empleados de la industria maquiladora: Patrones e implicaciones para Sonora y Arizona. In *Industria maquiladora y mercados laborales* 2: 139–162.

Lazaroff, L. 1992. Desert Capitalism: Agribusiness, Maquiladoras, and a Gold Rush Spur Economic Development in Sonora-Sinaloa. *Business Mexico* 2 (9): 24–27.

————. 1993. Maquilas No More. *El Financiero International* (December 13–19): 10.

————. 1994. Free Trade Blues. *El Financiero International* (April 11–17): 16.

Lipietz, A. 1995. De Toyota-City a la Ford-Hermosillo: La japonización de pacotilla. *Cotidiano* 67: 39–47.

Lovera, S. 1993. Importan maquiladoras 98.2% de sus insumos. *La Jornada* (October 25): 1, 40.

Lovera, S., and Chousal, Y. 1993. Razones y sinrazones de CIMAC y la población. *Fem* 17 (128): 8–10.

MacFarlane, L., K. Kopinak, and P. Dewdney. 1971. The Women's Equal Opportunities Act. *The Pedestal* (January): 9.

Mader, R. 1995. Border Retailers Report Drop in Sales. *El Financiero International* (January 16–22): 11.

Marchand, M. 1994a. Gender and the Regionalism in Latin America: Inclusion/exclusion. *Third World Quarterly* 15(1): 63–76.

————. 1994b. Selling NAFTA: Gendered Metaphors and Silenced Gender Implications. Paper presented at the international conference Global Politics: Setting Agendas for the Year 2000, Nottingham Trent University, Nottingham, U.K., March 28–April 1.

Marón Manzur, M. 1992. Tendencias recientes de la industria maquiladora. *El Financiero* (April 1): 31a.

Martínez, O. 1978. *Border Boom Town. Ciudad Juárez since 1948.* Austin: University of Texas Press.

Martínez Morales, G. 1993. Libre comercio, maquiladoras, y desarrollo regional (La industria maquiladora en la región noreste ante el TTC). In A. D. Flores (coordinador), *TLC: Impactos en la frontera norte,* 53–72. México: Facultad de Economía, UNAM.

Marx, K. 1887. *Capital.* Moscow: Progress.

McKitrick, R. 1989. *The Economy and Labour Markets Reference Tables.* Kingston, Ontario: Industrial Relations Centre of Queen's University.

Medina, J. 1989. El problema de rotación de los obreros en las maquiladoras de Agua Prieta. *El Imparcial* (November 14).

Micheli, J. 1994. *Nueva manufactura, globalización, y producción de automóbiles en México.* México: UNAM.

Middlebrook, K. 1991. The Politics of Industrial Restructuring: Transnational Firms' Search For Flexible Production in the Mexican Automobile Industry. *Comparative Politics* 23 (3): 275–297.

Milkman, R. 1987. *Gender at Work: The Dynamics of Job Segregation by Sex During World War II.* Chicago: University of Illinois Press.

———. 1991. *Japan's California Factories: Labor Relations and Economic Globalization.* Los Angeles: University of California, Institute for Industrial Relations.

Miller, W. 1992. Textbook Turnaround. *Industry Week* 241 (8): 11–14.

Millman, J. 1991. There's Your Solution. *Forbes* 147 (1): 72–76.

Nagel, J. 1995. More for the Money. Lower Costs and Dollar Financing Should Boost Border Industry Exports. *El Financiero International* (January 16–22): 1, 10.

Nielsen, F. 1994. Income Inequality and Industrial Development: Dualism Revisited. *American Sociological Review* 59 (October): 654–677.

O'Brien, P. 1990a. Young Workers Flock to Maquiladora Plants. *The Business Journal—Phoenix and the Valley of the Sun* 10 (July 23): 1.

———. 1990b. Should State Do More to Promote Maquilas? *The Business Journal—Phoenix and the Valley of the Sun* 10 (July 30): 1.

Olivares, R. 1989a. Crisis de mano de obra en Nogales. *La Voz del Norte* (March 15).

———. 1989b. Deficit de mano de obra en la frontera, retrasos y perdidas en producción sufren las empresas ante la falta de dos mil trabajadores. *La Voz del Norte* (March 17).

———. 1990. Deficit de mano de obra en maquiladoras. *La Voz del Norte* (January 9).

Orantes Gálvez, L. 1987. *La industria maquiladora y su impact sobre la fuerza de trabajo (el caso Nogales, 1960–1986).* Tésis que para obtener el Título de Lic. en Sociología. Universidad de Sonora, Hermosillo.

Orozco Orozco, M. 1991. Los estragos salariales de la política neoliberal. *La Jornada* (November 1).

Ortega, F. 1991. Sonora: Bajan exportaciones y turismo y hay despidos. *Proceso* 745 (February 11): 17–18.

Ortega Pizarro, F. 1992. En la industria automotriz, reticencia de los empresarios mexicanos: Estados Unidos quiere todas las ventajas. *Proceso* (809): 20–23.

Ortiz González, L. E. 1992. Caída en sus ventas, Cementos Portland, Producción y personal en Sonora. *El Financiero* (March 11): 11.

Pavlakovic[h], V. and Kim, H. 1990. Out-Shopping by Maquila Employees: Implications for Arizona's Border Communities. *Arizona Review* (spring): 9–16.

Pérez, J. 1991. Economic Crossroad: Border Town Worries About Free Trade Burden. *Phoenix Gazette,* November 29, 1.

Piore, M., and C. Sabel. 1984. *The Second Industrial Divide. Possibilities for Prosperity.* New York: Basic Books.

Ponce, A. C. 1989. Deficit de 1,500 obreros en Agua Prieta. *La Voz del Norte* (January 12).

Poulantzas, N. 1975. *Classes in Contemporary Capitalism.* London: New Left Books.

Pradilla Cobos, E. 1993. *Territorios en crisis: México 1970–1992.* México: Universidad Autónoma Metropolitana, Unidad Xochimilco.

Puig, C. 1993. Para aprovechar el TLC, narcos de Ciudad Juárez y Torreón preparan maquiladoras, bodegas, y terrenos fronterizos. *Proceso* 864 (May 24): 7–9.

Ramírez, J. 1988. La nueva industria sonorense: el caso de las maquilas de exportación. In J. Ramírez (coordinador), *La nueva industrialización en Sonora: El caso de los sectores de alta tecnología,* 17–132. Hermosillo: El Colegio de Sonora.

Ramírez, J. C., and N. Fuentes Flores. 1989. La nueva era de las plantas electrónicas y automotrices. In B. González Aréchiga (coordinador), *La industria maquiladora mexicana en los sectores electronico y de autopartes,* 6–12. México: Fundación Friedrich Ebert. OEKO-México.

Ramos, A. 1995. Picking Up the Tab. *El Financiero International* (January 16–22): 6.

Rodríguez Gómez, J. 1992. Los dos Méxicos: La pobreza de muchos; el privilegio de pocos. *El Financiero* (July 20).

Romo, D., y M. Osuna. 1989. En serios problemas la maquiladora de Nogales para contratar personal. *El Imparcial-*Hermosillo (May 3).

Rosenberg, S. 1989. From Segmentation to Flexibility. *Labour and Society* 14 (4): 363–407.

Rosenblum, K. 1991. Carpet Firm Seeking Trade South of Border. *Arizona Republic.* November 23: 1.

Rozenberg, D. 1994. Frutos del corredor mexicano. *Expansión* (October 12): 37–44.

Rubery, J. 1987. Flexibility of Labor Costs in Non-Union Firms. In R. Tarling (ed.), *Flexibility in Labor Markets*. London: Academic Press.

Sánchez, R. 1990. Condiciones de vida de los trabajadores de la maquiladora en Tijuana y Nogales. *Frontera Norte* 2 (4): 153–182.

Sandoval Godoy, S., and P. Wong Gonzalez. 1994. Labor Relations and Trade Union Action in Hermosillo's Ford Plant, 1986–1994: A Pending Agenda In the Face of the North American Integration. Paper presented at the conference on Cars and Continentalism, Toronto, May 1994.

Sareigo Rodríguez, J. 1990. Trabajo y maquiladoras en Chihuahua. *El Cotidiano* 33 (January–February): 15–25.

Sarmiento, S. 1994. My Enemy, My Friend. *El Financiero International* (July 11–17): 7.

Scheinman, M. 1990a. Report on the Present Status of Maquiladoras. In K. Fatemi (ed.), *The Maquiladora Industry: Economic Solution or Problem?* 19–35. New York: Praeger.

———. 1990b. Maquiladoras in the Automobile Industry. In K. Fatemi (ed.), *The Maquiladora Industry Economic Solution or Problem?* 117–134. New York: Praeger.

Schoepfle, G. 1990. *U.S.-Mexico Free Trade Agreement: The Maquilazation of México?* Washington, D.C.: Bureau of International Labor Affairs.

Seligson, M. A., and E. J. Williams. 1981. *Maquiladoras and Migration: Workers in the Mexico-United States Border Industialization Program*. Austin, Tex.: Mexico-United States Research Program.

Senzek, A. 1995. Sink or Swim for Mexican Business. *El Financiero International* (April 3–9): 12.

Shaiken, H. 1990. *Mexico in the Global Economy: High Technology and Work Organization In Export Industries*. San Diego: Monograph Series, 33, Center for U.S.–Mexican Studies, University of California, San Diego.

———. 1993. Two Myths About Mexico. *New York Times,* August 22.

———. 1994. Advanced Manufacturing and Mexico: A New International Division of Labor? *Latin American Research Review* 29 (2): 39–72.

Shaiken, H., and H. Browne. 1991. Japanese Work Organization in Mexico. In G. Székely (ed.), *Manufacturing Across Borders And Oceans,* 25–50. Monograph Series 36, Center for U.S.-Mexican Studies, University of California, San Diego.

Shaiken, H., and S. Herzenberg. 1987. *Automation and Global Production*. San Diego: Center for U.S.-Mexican Studies.

Schiffman, S., M. Reynolds, and F. Young. 1981. *Introduction to Multidimensional Scaling: Theory, Methods, And Applications*. New York: Academic Press.

Silvers, A., and F. Lara Valencia. 1990. Labor Absorption and Turnover in the Maquila Industry at the Sonora-Arizona Border. In D. Dimon and R. Lenberg (eds.), *Opening Markets In the Americas—Free Trade 1990 BALACS Proceedings.*

————. 1991. High Turnover and Low Wages in the Maquiladoras: A Consequence of Market or Non-market Processes? Working Paper 91-08, Drachman Institute for Land and Regional Development Studies, Tucson, Arizona.

Silvers, A., and V. Pavlakovich. 1994. Maquila Industry Impacts on the Spatial Redistribution of Employment. *Journal of Borderland Studies* 9 (2): 47–64.

Silvers, A., and C. Rookley. 1993. *Trade Flows and the CANAMEX Corridor: Impacts of Growth and Transportation Policy.* Report from the Office of Community Public Service, University of Arizona, August 16.

Sinclair, M. 1991. Women, Work, and Skill: Economic Theories and Feminist Perspectives. In N. Redclift and M. Sinclair (eds.), *Working Women: International Perspectives on Labor and Gender Ideology,* 1–24. London: Routledge.

Sires, T. M. 1990. Sonora. *Twin Plant News* (August): 41–49.

Sklair, L. 1989. *Assembling For Development.* Boston: Unwin Hyman.

————. 1992. The Maquilas in Mexico: a Global Perspective. *Bulletin of Latin American Research* 11 (1): 91–107.

————. 1993. *Assembling For Development.* 2d ed. La Jolla, Calif.: Center for U.S.-Mexican Studies, University of California, San Diego.

Sneath, P., and Sokal, R. 1973. *Numerical Taxonomy.* San Francisco: W. H. Freeman.

Solís de Alba, A. 1991. Política laboral, productividad y mujeres trabajadoras. *Fem* 15 (105): 4–8.

Solórzano-Torres, R. 1987. Female Mexican Immigrants in San Diego County. In V. Ruiz and S. Tiano (eds.), *Women on the U.S.-Mexico Border: Responses to Change,* 41–60. Boston: Allen and Unwin.

Standing, G. 1989. Global Feminization through Flexible Labor. *World Development* 17 (7): 1077–1095.

Staudt, K. 1986. Economic Change and Ideological Lag in Households of Maquila Workers in Ciudad Juárez. In G. Young (ed.), *The Social Ecology and Economic Development of Ciudad Juárez.* Boulder: Westview.

Stevenson, M. 1995. A Failing Development Miracle. *El Financiero International* (February 13–19): 14–15.

Strang, B. 1970. *A History of English.* London: Methuen.

Taddei Bringas, C. 1992. Las maquiladoras japonesas: ¿Modelo de las "maquiladoras posfordistas"?: Un analisis empirico. *Estudios Sociales* 3 (6): 99–122.

Taddei Bringas, C., and S. Sandoval Godoy. 1993. Límites en la implementación del modelo japonés de organización del trabajo: Los casos de la Ford y las maquiladoras japonesas. In A. Covarrubias and V. Solís (eds.), *Sindicalismo, relaciones laborales, y libre comercio,* 125–134. Hermosillo: El Colegio de Sonora.

Talarico, L. 1990. Sonora: Opportunity for an Arizona Business. *Twin Plant News* (August): 61.

Tarling, R. 1987. Preface to *Flexibility in Labor Markets.* London: Academic Press.

Teichman, J. 1995. *Privatization and Political Transition in Mexico.* Pittsburgh: University of Pittsburgh Press.

Thompson, E. P. 1965. *The Making of the English Working Class.* London: Victor Gollancz Ltd.

Thompson, P. 1983. *The Nature of Work.* London: Macmillan.

———. 1984. The Labour Process and Deskilling. In K. Thomson (ed.), *Work, Employment, and Unemployment.* Philadelphia: Open University Press.

Thorup, C. 1993. Redefining Governance in North America: Citizen Diplomacy and Cross-Border Coalitions. *Enfoque* (spring): 1, 12–13.

Tiano, S. 1987. Women's Work and Unemployment in Northern Mexico. In V. L. Ruiz and S. Tiano (eds.), *Women on the U.S.-Mexico Border,* 17–40. Boston: Allen and Unwin.

———. 1994. *Patriarchy on the Line: Labor, Gender, and Ideology in the Mexican Maquila Industry.* Philadelphia: Temple University Press.

Tilly, L., and J. Scott. 1978. *Women, Work, and Family.* New York: Holt, Rinehart, and Winston.

Tolan, S. 1990. The Border Boom: Hope and Heartbreak. *New York Times Magazine* (July 1).

Valle Baeza, A. 1992. De salarios y asalariados en México, EUA, y Canadá. *El Financiero* (April 27): 38a.

Velasco, E. 1993. Industrial Restructuring in Mexico During the 1980s. In R. Grinspun and M. Cameron (eds.), *The Political Economy of North American Free Trade,* 163–177. New York: St. Martin's.

Vigueras, C. 1995. Informal Reality: Devaluation Pushes Up Prices on Contraband. *El Financiero International* (January 16–22): 11.

Wagner, D. 1991. Hurting: Border Stores Say War Keeps Tourists Away. *Phoenix Gazette,* February 22, 1.

Waits, M. 1992. Arizona and Free Trade: Catching Up. *Arizona Republic,* August 23, 1.

Walby, S. 1988. Segregation in employment in social and economic theory. In S. Walby (ed.), *Gender Segregation and Work,* 14–28. Philadelphia: Open University Press.

Walmsley, A. 1992. Turning the Tide. *The Globe and Mail Report on Business Magazine* (June): 20–31.

Waring, M. 1988. *If Women Counted: A New Feminist Economics.* New York: HarperCollins.

Warner, J. 1990. The Sociological Impact of the Maquiladoras. In K. Fatemi (ed.), *The Maquiladora Industry: Economic Solution or Problem?* 183–198. New York: Praeger.

Weddell, J. 1995. When Juárez Strikes, Indiana Listens. *El Financiero International* (March 13–19) 14.

Welti, C. 1993. Políticas públicas de población: U tema en debate permanente. *Fem* 17 (128): 16–18.

Werner, J. 1994. David Cole. Una vision desde Michigan. *Expansión* (October 12): 66–69.

Western, K. 1991. Arizona Forseen as Hub for Pacific Rim if U.S., Mexico Back Free Trade. *Arizona Republic,* May 18, 1.

———. 1992. State Trails in Mexican Initiatives. *Arizona Republic,* July 22, 1.

Williams, E., and J. Passé-Smith. 1992. *The Unionization of the Maquiladora Industry: The Tamaulipan Case in National Context.* San Diego: Institute for Regional Studies of the Californias, San Diego State University.

Wilson, P. 1990. The New Maquiladoras: Flexible Production in Low–Wage Regions. In K. Fatemi (ed.), *The Maquiladora Industry Economic Solution or Problem?* New York: Praeger: 135–158.

———. 1992. *Exports and Local Development: Mexico's New Maquiladoras.* Austin: University of Texas Press.

Womack, J., D. Jones, and D. Roos. 1990. *The Machine That Changed the World.* New York: Rawson.

Wood, S. 1989. The Transformation of Work? In S. Wood (ed.), *The Transformation Of Work?* 1–43. London: Unwin Hyman.

Young, C. 1991. Not Our Business: Phoenix, State Slow to See Mexico's Value. *Phoenix Gazette,* October 15, 1.

Young, G., and S. Christopherson. 1986. Household Structure and Activity in Ciudad Juárez. In G. Young (ed.), *The Social Ecology And Economic Development Of Ciudad Juárez.* Boulder: Westview.

ABOUT THE AUTHOR

Kathryn Kopinak studied history and sociology at the University of Western Ontario and York University in Canada. She is currently teaching political sociology and social stratification at King's College, University of Western Ontario, and she is an Associate Fellow at the Center for Research on Latin America and the Caribbean at York University. Her previous publications focus on gender differences in Canadian political ideology, and the impact of religious belief on Mexican women's efforts to organize for change. Her current research interests include the study of regional realignment and gender differences in the effects of economic restructuring.